CONTEMPORARY
FREUD

Turning Points & Critical Issues

CONTEMPORARY FREUD
Turning Points and Critical Issues

Series Founded by Robert Wallerstein

On Freud's "Analysis Terminable and Interminable"
Edited by Joseph Sandler

Freud's "On Narcissism: An Introduction"
Edited by Joseph Sandler, Ethel Spector Person, and Peter Fonagy

ON FREUD'S

"Observations on

Transference-Love"

EDITED BY ETHEL SPECTOR PERSON

AIBAN HAGELIN

PETER FONAGY

FOR THE INTERNATIONAL

PSYCHOANALYTICAL ASSOCIATION

Yale University Press

New Haven & London

Grateful acknowledgment is made to Sigmund Freud Copyrights; The Institute of
Psycho-Analysis, London; The Hogarth Press; and Basic Books for permission to reprint
"Further Recommendations in the Technique of Psycho-Analysis: Observations on
Transference-Love" as published in *The Standard Edition of the Complete Psychological
Works of Sigmund Freud,* vol. 12, trans. and ed. James Strachey; and in *The Collected
Papers of Sigmund Freud,* vol. 2, authorized translation under the supervision of Joan
Riviere, published by Basic Books, Inc., by arrangement with The Hogarth Press Ltd.
and the Institute of Psycho-Analysis, London. Reprinted by permission of Basic Books,
a division of HarperCollins Publishers, Inc.

Designed by Jill Breitbarth
Set in Times Roman and Optima types by
The Composing Room of Michigan, Inc.,
Grand Rapids, Michigan.
Printed in the United States of America by
Vail-Ballon Press, Binghamton, New York

Library of Congress Cataloging-in-Publication Data
On Freud's "Observations on transference-love" / edited by Ethel
Spector Person, Aiban Hagelin, Peter Fonagy
p. cm. — (Contemporary Freud turning points & critical
issues)
Includes bibliographical references and index.
ISBN 0-300-05437-8. — ISBN 0-300-05525-0 (pbk.)
1. Freud, Sigmund, 1856–1939. Bemerkungen über die
Übertragungsliebe. 2. Transference (Psychology) I. Person, Ethel
Spector. II. Hagelin, Aiban. III. Fonagy, Peter, 1952–
IV. Series: Contemporary Freud.
RC489.T73O5 1993
616.89'17—dc20
92-41560
CIP

A catalogue record for this book is available from the British Library.

The paper in this book meets the guidelines for permanence and durability of the
Committee on Production Guidelines for Book Longevity of the Council on
Library Resources.

10 9 8 7 6 5 4 3 2 1

Contents

Preface
ETHEL SPECTOR PERSON, / vii
AIBAN HAGELIN, AND PETER FONAGY

Introduction
ETHEL SPECTOR PERSON / 1

PART ONE OBSERVATIONS ON TRANSFERENCE-LOVE
(1915)
SIGMUND FREUD / 15

PART TWO DISCUSSION OF "OBSERVATIONS ON·
TRANSFERENCE-LOVE"

A Rereading of Freud's "Observations on Transference-Love"
FRIEDRICH-WILHELM EICKHOFF / 33

On Transference Love: Revisiting Freud
ROBERT S. WALLERSTEIN / 57

Five Readings of Freud's "Observations on Transference-Love"
ROY SCHAFER / 75

Footnote to a Footnote to "Observations on Transference-Love"
MAX HERNÁNDEZ / 96

On Transference Love: Some Current Observations
BETTY JOSEPH / 102

One-Person and Two-Person Perspectives: Freud's
"Observations on Transference-Love"
MERTON MAX GILL / 114

The Oedipal Tragedy in the Psychoanalytic Process: Transference Love
FIDIAS CESIO / 130

A Cry of Fire: Some Considerations on Transference Love
JORGE CANESTRI / 146

Amae and Transference Love
TAKEO DOI / 165

Acting versus Remembering in Transference Love and Infantile Love
DANIEL N. STERN / 172

Contributors / 187

Index / 189

Preface

This is the third volume of the series "Contemporary Freud: Turning Points and Critical Issues," following *On Freud's "Analysis Terminable and Interminable"* and *Freud's "On Narcissism: An Introduction."* The series, first conceptualized by Robert Wallerstein during his presidency of the International Psychoanalytical Association, was designed to improve intellectual communication among centers of psychoanalysis in different parts of the world.

Each volume opens with one of Freud's classic papers, followed by contributions from distinguished psychoanalytic teachers and theoreticians of diverse theoretical positions and geographic locations. In addition to reviewing the literature he or she deems pertinent, each participant has been asked to extract the essay's important and enduring contributions, to clarify ambiguities, to establish some line of continuity between the original paper and current issues and concerns, and to express the reviewer's own views as if he or she were actually teaching the paper. These texts have already proved useful as teaching adjuncts around the world. It has also been our hope that each reader will be drawn into a personal dialogue with each of the contributors.

The choice of Freud's paper and of the modern contributors to each volume is made by the IPA Committee on Publications, based on recommendations from a large advisory committee and in consultation with IPA president Joseph Sandler. The current Committee on Publications, consisting of Ethel Person, chairperson; Aiban Hagelin; and Peter Fonagy; is indeed grateful for the input of the Advisory Board. The contributors, in turn, have been generous and extremely successful in their participation in this project. As in the former volumes, we believe that the excellent results are self-evident.

Special thanks go to Valerie Tufnell, administrative director of the IPA, and Janice Ahmed, IPA publications administrator, for their organizational skills and perseverance in coordinating an international venture such as this. In addition, we want to give special thanks to Dr. Person's administrative assistant, Jessica Bayne, who has been painstaking in tracking deadlines and manuscripts. Gladys Topkis and her associates at Yale University Press are superb, diligent, and tactful editors. Their editorial input has been of the highest quality, and their patience and care in bringing this volume into existence must be lauded.

ETHEL SPECTOR PERSON
AIBAN HAGELIN
PETER FONAGY

Introduction

ETHEL SPECTOR PERSON

Today, with psychoanalysis so well established and knowledge (as well as folklore) about it so widespread, many people believe that patients are "supposed to" fall in love with their analysts. But although it is common enough for patients to fall in love with their doctors, the reasons why they do so are not intuitively obvious.

Freud was the first to describe transference love, to theorize about its precursors in our developmental lives and its meaning in the psychoanalytic process, and to make a connection between transference love and real-life love. But an understanding of the erotic transference did not spring full-blown, even to Freud. The first story of transference love to come to his attention concerned the therapy of his mentor and collaborator Josef Breuer with Anna O., and it was told to him by Breuer. Although their conversations about Anna O. took place in 1882, Freud only gradually appreciated their full significance, embodying his insights in the 1915 paper "Observations on Transference-Love."

The "talking cure," an early antecedent of psychoanalysis, developed more or less by accident in the course of Anna O.'s therapy. Anna O., a woman with many hysterical symptoms, initiated the process of a kind of free

1

association, in which her speaking of the origins of each symptom magically caused it to disappear, a process she called chimney sweeping. The dramatic events surrounding the termination of her therapy were such that they lead circuitously to the conceptualization of transference, specifically the erotic transference and its hazards to both patient and doctor.

In one rendering of the end of that treatment, it was said to be Breuer who terminated the therapy, in another it was the patient (see Sulloway, 1979, for the alternative accounts). In the more widely known version, Breuer, who had become increasingly fascinated with Anna O.'s treatment, is thought to have ignored his wife and consequently evoked her jealousy. Belatedly recognizing her discomfort, Breuer abruptly terminated Anna O.'s treatment. Shortly thereafter, he was called back to find his patient in the midst of an hysterical childbirth. He calmed her down and, the next day, took his wife on a second honeymoon. Freud recounted this story in a letter to his own wife, Martha. According to Jones (1953, 225), Martha "identified herself with Breuer's wife and hoped the same thing would not ever happen to her, whereupon Freud reproved her vanity in supposing that other women would fall in love with her husband; 'for that to happen one has to be a Breuer.' " In other words, Freud denied the possibility that one of *his* patients might fall in love with him, while Martha seemed to understand intuitively the universal nature of the problem. Only later did Freud come to see Anna O.'s reaction to her doctor as more the rule than the exception. In the second account, it was the patient herself who pressed for termination of the treatment. But both accounts agree on the crucial fact that the end of treatment, however initiated, eventuated in the patient's phantom pregnancy, with the explicit statement on her part, "Now Dr. B.'s child is coming!" (Sulloway, 77).

Nonetheless, at the time, the phantom pregnancy did not appear to be the salient feature of the case to either Breuer or Freud. Sulloway reports that in 1932 Freud wrote to Stefan Zweig claiming to have forgotten all about Anna O.'s phantom pregnancy and to have remembered it only several decades later when he was writing his "History of the Psycho-analytic Movement" (Sulloway, 1979, 80). Thomas Szasz (1963) calls attention to the discomfort that transference love may cause the therapist and suggests that it may have been inevitable that the theoretical observations on transference love were originally made by someone other than the object of that love. But simply being Breuer's fellow physician appears to have brought Freud too close to transference love for comfort, contributing to his lapse in recollecting the specific content of the traumatic end of Anna O.'s therapy. It took Freud some time to appreciate what Martha intuited immediately: that the very situation of therapy might facilitate the emergence of erotic feelings on the part of the patient, and, as it turned out, on the part of the therapist as well. Freud's insight into the phenomenon of transference love was facilitated by his growing acquaintance with reports of erotic feelings engendered in the therapy situation, problems he heard about from a few analysts and sometimes from their patients as well, including at least one or two accounts of enacted patient-doctor affairs, and by his awareness of his own erotic feelings toward a patient (occurrences documented by several of our contributors). Only with subsequent exposure to the phenomenon of transference love was Freud able to reinterpret the case of Anna O. His slowness in recognizing the widespread potential for transference love may be some measure of the power and threat which it exercised then and which it continues to exercise today.

By 1915, when Freud's insights into the phenomenon took shape in "Observations on Transference-Love," the last of the six brief papers on technique he published between 1911 and 1915, he had formulated a theory about transference and the relationship between the erotic transference and the state of being "in love." Claiming to be addressing his remarks to beginners, Freud chose as an example of a serious difficulty in the management of the transference a very circumscribed situation: one in which a female patient declares that she has fallen in love with her male analyst. Freud summarizes the three possible outcomes of such a situation: a permanent legal union, the disruption of the therapy, or an illicit love relationship. However, as Freud points out, there is still another possibility—a specifically psychoanalytic one. The analyst must recognize that it is the analytic situation, not his person, that has stimulated the patient to fall in love with him; that is, that transference love is essentially impersonal. The analyst must insist to his patient that her experience of falling in love with him is "an inescapable fate," one that must be analyzed; otherwise the treatment must come to an end.

The outbreak of transference love is a resistance, occurring at a time when the patient is facing the painful lifting of a repressed memory. Freud in 1915 believed that the erotic transference was primarily an impediment to therapy and advised the therapist to demonstrate to the patient that she has fallen in love with him only as a means of avoiding the painful discoveries about to be made. As an admonition to the therapist, Freud emphasized not only the "universally accepted standards of morality" but, more important from his point of view, that abstinence on the part of the analyst arises out of a commitment to "truthfulness." The patient's craving for love can be neither suppressed nor gratified. Rather, the analyst must treat transference love as something unreal, "as a situation which has to be gone through in the treatment and traced back to its unconscious origins and which must assist in bringing all that is most deeply hidden in the patient's erotic life into her consciousness and therefore under her control."

Freud was well aware that the transference looked different to the patient and the doctor. What the analyst calls transference the patient often experiences as genuine feelings of love. Freud struggled with what he saw as the continuities—not just the discontinuities—between transference love and real love. His observations in the consulting room enabled him to see that the object of both transference and romantic love is a reedition of the original objects of childhood. According to Freud, all love is a re-finding, repeating infantile reactions; but transference love, he claimed, for reasons not altogether clear, was dominated by the straitjacket of repetition to an even greater extent than was romantic love.

Freud's insights into the overlap between transference love and "real" love were important to an understanding of love, but they also opened a different kind of question, albeit a somewhat tangential one, about the nature of reality. The first reference to reality in the paper seems somehow off the point: it deals with Freud's conflict in wanting to present accurate patient data, yet "constantly coming up against the obligation to professional discretion . . . [but] so far as psycho-analytic publications are a part of real life, too, we have here an insoluble contradiction" (159). I take this comment, which appears almost as an aside, as a foreshadowing of a larger problem, that of delineating overlapping, contradictory, or different realities and how this makes the appraisal or definition of a singular reality difficult if not impossible. For example, Freud raises a question about the "real" nature of transference love: "It is as though some piece of make-believe had been stopped by the sudden irruption of reality" (162). Having advised the therapist to instruct the patient that transference love is merely transferential, he returns to the question of truth and reality vis-à-vis transference love, asking: "Can we truly say that the state of being in love which becomes manifest in analytic treatment is not a real one? I think we have told the patient the truth, but not the whole truth regardless of the consequences" (168). In this very subtle and searching observation, Freud opens up the question of the nature of reality, the question of what is illusory and what real, and of what constitutes the difference. This is a theme that reverberates throughout the comments of several contributors to this volume.

Over the years since Freud first described transference love, the psychoanalytic view of transference gradually has expanded. Far from being viewed as an impediment, the development of the transference and its analysis are now viewed as the very heart of the psychoanalytic process. Transference analysis appears to have replaced dream analysis as the "royal road" to the unconscious. Nonetheless, despite its limitations, Freud's paper not only describes and interprets some ongoing verities within the psychoanalytic situation but opens up many issues relevant to current theoretical questions and technical problems and thus is a starting point from which to explore the nature of transference and post-Freudian contributions to the study of countertransference: it discusses the special psychology of women who exhibit extreme forms of transference love; it addresses a series of technical precepts, some of which have stood the test of time while others have been modified; and it is an early contribution to the psychology of love. Implicit in the paper is an assumption of gender difference (or what some believe to be a gender distinction), insofar as the paper deals exclusively with situations in which women patients fall in love with male analysts. Indirectly, this paper anticipates discussion of the role of gender in the psychoanalytic situation. And finally, the paper explicitly places the love of truthfulness at the heart of the psychoanalytic enterprise while at the same time raising questions about the nature of virtuality (what we might now call virtual reality) as compared with reality.[1]

The contributors' discussions of these various topics have more than fulfilled the editors' hopes. Not only do they convey different theoretical perspectives; they also choose different emphases, ranging from countertransference to the developmental perspective, from paradigm shifts within the compass of Freud's work to the nature of romantic love. Each of our contributors assumes a particular strategy in approaching Freud's essay: for example, citing the contemporary clinical questions that prompted Freud's inquiry; teasing out those questions, previously either unasked or unanswered, that Freud was addressing; or placing the theme of transference love, and transference and countertransference in general, in the context of today's psychoanalytic theories.

Friedrich-Wilhelm Eickhoff observes that Freud's paper on transference love, though brief, "occupies an outstanding place in the debate on the curative significance of the interpretation of psychical conflicts versus direct emotional experience." In a scholarly tour de force, Eickhoff locates the

---

1. There are also intimations in Freud's paper that love cannot be fully understood as an aim-inhibited sublimation of the sexual instinct; hence the paper points the way to an enlarged concept of motivation.

transference love paper within the context of Freud's evolving thinking on transference and transference love, referring to, among other works, the case of Anna O., Freud's correspondence, the paper "Delusions and Dreams in Jensen's 'Gradiva,'" the Dora case, and the paper "Remembering, Repeating and Working Through." He calls attention to Heine's little-known poem "The Roving Rats" as the probable source of Freud's remark that those women who display extreme transference love are accessible only to "the logic of soup, with dumplings for arguments."

In a scholarly and fascinating appendix, Eickhoff cites important cases of enacted or close-to-enacted patient-therapist love affairs known to Freud (referring not only to the well-known case of Jung and Sabina Spielrein but also to a recently reported treatment by Ferenczi of a woman who later became his stepdaughter), which made writing the transference love paper necessary, if not urgent. He presents an insightful account of the major tenets of Freud's paper, discussing neutrality and abstinence, the differences between interpretation and gratification and appeasement, Freud's commitment to truth, and the difference between love transference and transference love (which some have referred to as the difference between the eroticized transference and the erotic transference).

Perhaps Eickhoff's most interesting contribution in his subtle discussion of Freud's description of transference as "an intermediate region between illness and real life through which the transition from one to the other is made" ("Remembering, Repeating and Working Through"). He traces the influence and evolution of this concept in the work of Loewald (the intermediate region as "an illusion, a game, whose specific impact depends on its being experienced simultaneously as reality and as a creation of the imagination"); of Winnicott (a "third sphere, that of the game, which covers creative life and the whole of human cultural experience"); of the art historian Ernst Gombrich (the "intermediate region between truth and deception . . . in which we consciously and freely surrender ourselves to illusion"); and of Kohut ("the analytic situation is not real, in the usual sense of the word . . . [but it] has a specific reality, which resembles, to a certain extent the reality of the artistic experience"). These considerations lead Eickhoff to a succinct paraphrase of Freud's advice to analysts: "The analyst's duty not to return the offered affection is based on considerations of analytic technique—namely, the need to treat the situation as 'something unreal,' to understand and interpret the transference in its virtuality."

Robert Wallerstein's contribution, a model of clarity, draws on both the transference love paper and Freud's earlier paper "The Dynamics of Transference" (1912) to demonstrate that Freud held two somewhat contradictory attitudes toward transference. On the one hand, he seemed to imply that very intense transference reactions were an artifact of the psychoanalytic treatment situation; on the other, he viewed transference as ubiquitous, shaping all behaviors and relationships in everyday life. This dichotomous view, Wallerstein suggests, was characteristic of Freud's penchant for dualisms that alternate with, and sometimes give way to, a more sophisticated perception of the continuum between normal and abnormal behavior. (Freud's tendency to dichotomize is evident in his distinction between the negative transference and the erotic transference on the one hand and the "unobjectionable" positive transference on the other—a dichotomy that has not held up well over time.) Our concept of transference has been sufficiently refined so that analysis of the so-called unobjectionable positive transference is considered part and parcel of analysis, as revealing of underlying dynamics as any other form of transference.

Nonetheless, Wallerstein recognizes enduring and major insights in the transference love paper: (1) Freud's identification of the high incidence of erotic feelings evoked in the treatment setting and the technical and moral dangers they pose; (2) his elucidation of a small class of patients for whom erotic love is mobilized as resistance and proves incapable of resolution; and (3) his establishment of technical prescriptions for handling such transferences—the "rule of abstinence" and neutrality on the part of the analyst. Wallerstein points out that all these insights into transference love were written in the context of topographical theory. The subsequent development of structural theory has allowed a more complex understanding of these phenomena and, consequently, refinements of technical prescriptions. For example, neutrality—which in topographical theory was viewed as virtually synonymous with abstinence—now relates to the imperative that the analyst remain equidistant from manifestations of the patient's ego, id, and superego; while abstinence retains its meaning of refusing to gratify the patient's libidinal and aggressive drives. Of particular usefulness is Wallerstein's review of the ways in which different theorists have explained the predispositions to developing extreme erotic transferences (now referred to as eroticized transferences) and the reasons these transferences may prove intractable. Among other formulations, he discusses Rappaport's emphasis on "the preoedipal and dependent attachment hunger of these patients."

Roy Schafer, remarking on the breadth of scope of Freud's paper despite its brevity, discusses it from five perspectives that delineate the essay's major contributions and, at the same time, "its limitations and its controversial aspects." A key part of Freud's strength, he writes, is his gift for "the demolition of conventional boundaries" of thinking by emphasizing "differences of degree rather than of kind." In the essay under review, Schafer points out that from a narrow perspective Freud demonstrated the continuity between transference love and real love and, in a broader perspective, the continuity between the analytic relationship and real-life relationships. However, Freud's recognition of the continuity between transference love and "real-life" love did not lead him to presage contemporary formulations (such as Loewald's) that open up the possibility of new modes of experience of the self and of others, and therefore of "new" love within the aegis of the analysis. Apparently, what prevented Freud from following his insights to their logical conclusion was the fact that ego psychology had yet to be developed, an approach that allows us to hold to the concepts of determinism and continuity and still theorize a place for the new and the autonomous.

In his second perspective, Schafer turns to the management of the erotic transference. Erotic transference substitutes action for remembering but at the same time is a window to the unconscious. Here, too, Freud's understanding was limited insofar as he was still grounded in topographic theory, thus his overemphasis on making the unconscious conscious as the sole curative factor.

Musing on why Freud focused on transference love more as a resistance than as a form of communication, Schafer turns to his third perspective, countertransference. He suggests that while Freud's insights were groundbreaking, they nonetheless remained rudimentary in that he was writing prior to any understanding of the usefulness of countertransference to interpretive work. Schafer wittily proposes that Freud had a countertransference to countertransference, expressed as his belief in the possibility of the analyst's reacting in a totally rational fashion—a kind of myth of control and mastery.

Part of Freud's countertransference was authoritarian in still another way. In his fourth perspective, Schafer suggests that Freud held to a patriarchal bias, which gave men the dominant role; this kept him from giving balanced coverage to other forms of transference love (the various gender permutations).

Finally, in his fifth perspective, Schafer turns to an abiding interest of his own, discussing Freud's essay from the point of view of "positivism, perspectivism, and narration." Here he deconstructs the major differences one would anticipate between a Kleinian and a Freudian interpretation of transference love, contrasting them in order to suggest that a hermeneutic view "provides knowledge that is not available to the traditional positivistic approach." What Schafer introduces alongside material reality and psychical reality is narrative truth.

Max Hernández chooses to focus on what Freud's paper tells us about love, transference, female sexuality, and conventional morality. Freud makes it clear that "love, like everything else in the psychic realm, is subject to the compulsion to repeat." Hernández believes that knowledge of the psychic nature of love helps protect against the tendency to countertransference. He observes the paradox that while in real life neuroses interfere with the capacity for love, in the treatment situation it is love that interferes with the capacity for insight. When transference love arises, passion intervenes. In a further paradox, "love is the motor of the analytic cure as well as the main obstacle to it."

Hernández, too, treats of the situation in which transference love appears to be "a piece of reality impinging on the illusory condition of the process." The subject who experiences transference love undergoes a kind of change; "the subject, the analysand who speaks, and the subject of which 'she' speaks seem to have become one." Hernández aptly describes this as a situation in which the analytic space is narrowed. But he does not view this problem as one in which a new reality appears. Instead, he sees that another subject occupies the center of the scene, namely, the analyst to whom the patient addresses her wishes. For Hernández, the conundrum of considering transference as both illusory and real suggests that the analyst must conduct the analysis along a middle course: "between the Scylla of detached hermeneuticism and the Charybdis of analytic 'realism'." This way one recreates the intermediate region between illness and real life of which Freud had spoken in his paper "Remembering, Repeating and Working Through." When this is successfully accomplished, the analyst restores to the patient the space between her self and her discourse. Regarding Freud's gender pattern—male analyst, female patient—Hernández makes the insightful point that this paradigm contains echoes of the biblical Fall and Eve's temptation of Adam.

Betty Joseph, while affirming the importance of Freud's seminal insights into transference love, suggests two important ways in which they must be extended. First, she emphasizes broadening the concept of transference love to include transference of object relationships in general, the habitual attitudes and behavior the patient brings into the relationship with the analyst. In a significant insight, she insists that "what is transferred is not just figures from the past, from the patient's actual history, but complex internal fantasy figures that have been built up from earliest infancy, constructed from the interaction between real experiences and the infant's fantasies and impulses toward them." Her perspective is important in countering any lingering reductionist position that transference is no more than a repetition of an earlier response to a real situation.

In her second major contribution, Joseph emphasizes that transference love cannot be understood in terms of libido only; we must also take account of the destructive drive. But, as Joseph points out, when Freud wrote about transference love he was still five years away from formalizing his understanding of aggression and destructiveness. Joseph's case vignette is an outstanding example of the role played by aggression in a transference epitomized by sadomasochistic loving.

In his contribution, Merton Gill enlarges the dialogue about transference and transference love in still another way. He sees in Freud's paper a dialectical tension between two perspectives—a one-person and a two-person psychology. As Gill puts it: "If the analysand is seen as a closed system of forces and counterforces, the perspective is one-person. If the analytic situation is seen as a relationship between two people, the perspective is two-person and the analyst is a participant in that situation." Although, as Gill sees it, Freud goes back and forth between these two points of view, his emphasis on the stimulus to transference love resides largely either in the patient's dynamics or in the analytic situation, not in the person of the analyst. But Gill is unwilling to leave the analyst out of it. He quotes Racker to the effect that the analyst, by putting his name on the door, is already an accomplice to what transpires in the analysis. Gill's point is that an adequate analytic stance must continually take account of both the one-person and the two-person perspective, with one or the other appearing in the foreground at any given moment.

Fidias Cesio goes even further than Gill in implicating the analyst in the genesis of the patient's transference love. He suggests that "its direct emergence in a reasonably well-conducted analysis is exceptional"; in his own experience he encountered only one case of transference love, and that at the very beginning of his work. He makes the point that in the case of Anna O., transference mushroomed because the physician (Breuer) was unable to analyze it—not too surprising since the analytic method had yet to be developed. Some analysts may feel that Cesio goes too far in the direction of implicating countertransference in *every* case of transference love, since many analysts, beginning with Freud, believe that some patients, by virtue of their pathology, will almost inevitably form an eroticized transference, irrespective of who the analyst is. No one, however, can fail to be impressed by the rigorous way in which Cesio investigates how the therapist's unconscious may lead him to collude with the patient and thus invoke a full-blown erotic transference. As Cesio puts it, "The 'spirits of the dead' that the psychoanalyst invokes become manifested in the oedipal, incestuous, tragic, transference love, and, when not adequately heard and interpreted, end up destroying the treatment." When the analyst fails to address and analyze the incipient transference, he does so to a large extent because of his own "'passion'—a primary, drive-like affect aroused by this situation."

The great strength of Cesio's paper is in his rendition of "a play of transferences" that may set the stage for an "incestuous enactment in which the oedipal drama, with the violence which characterizes incest, becomes established in the analytic situation." He further argues that one must differentiate the oedipal tragedy, which results in cases of actualized transference love, from the Oedipus complex. Insofar as what emerges in the analytic situation becomes reality rather than virtuality, both the analysis and the analyst are destroyed.

Jorge Canestri contextualizes the transference love paper (of which, he tells us, the author was justly proud) by relating it to some of Freud's correspondence that reveals the unique semantic field within which Freud addressed erotic love. As Canestri says, Freud apparently was compelled to run "the entire gamut of fire analogies." He points, for example, to Freud's metaphor for the change in the analytic scene: "as, when, for instance, a cry of fire is raised during a theatrical performance." Canestri cites other examples of the fire metaphor and says there is no doubt that Freud was aware of his semantic choices, as evidenced in a letter to Jung. Thus, in part, the paper can be read as a warning to the analyst to control his temptation to countertransference. The metaphor "a cry of fire" has particular meaning because it evokes an imaginary/real discriminant that implies conceptual and technical differences. As Canestri puts it, "the example of fire . . . is part of a semantic field concerning passions."

Very important in Canestri's wide-ranging paper is his explicit formulation that transference love, like transference in general, is treated differently by the various psychoanalytic schools. But there is one thing all these schools agree about: they "all consider the theory of transference a precise and fundamental discriminant among the various analytic theories." Canestri reminds us of an important caveat—namely, that it is bad practice to look at an element of theory except within the context of the entire theory. Freud himself broadened his entire theory when he introduced aggression as on a par with libido. The questions that may be conceptualized differently according to one's theoretical proclivities include gender variations; the belief that "the amorous phenomenon is an effect of the analytic situation in itself . . . or emanates from the patient's internal object world and is merely highlighted in analysis"; the role of narcissism in transference; the degree to which transference is "real," "illusory," "imaginary," or "fictional"; whether transference is merely "the shadow of preceding experience, or ancient deceits or trickeries of love" or an encounter between the analyst's and the patient's desires that creates a new entity; different formulations about the therapeutic alliance and the unobjectionable positive transference; differing concepts of truth; the function of fantasy and the function of the object of the fantasy; "passions" and "madness" in analysis. Canestri's sweep is broad, and he alludes to many theoretical positions including those of Klein, Lacan, and Ferenczi.

In "Amae and Transference Love," Takeo Doi moves in a different direction. Doi explains that amae, a Japanese concept, refers to a kind of "indulgent dependency" like that which the infant experiences when it seeks its mother. Amae does not disappear in adults but remains integral to a variety of emotions. While Doi acknowledges that Freud's delineation of transference love is accurate, he suggests that "the kernel of the transference love" may be amae and that understanding it in this way makes it less tempting for the analyst to respond erotically. In a very sensitive discussion of the psychoanalytic interchange, Doi suggests that amae can be acknowledged nonverbally and that "something quite like an insight into amae on the part of the patient and its acknowledgment on the part of the analyst will take place in a successful analysis." To make the point, he cites several clinical vignettes reported by Evelyne Schwaber that illustrate the analyst's sensitivity to amae (though Schwaber had not so labeled the interactions). Doi makes the interesting suggestion that Freud's unfamiliarity with this concept, which is an important ingredient in any interpersonal relationship, may explain why he was unable to conceive of any real-life model for a recommended course of action for the analyst.

Daniel Stern, too, turns his attention to what one might call the ground of transference love. Writing from the developmental perspective, Stern focuses on the difference between acting (out) and remembering in relation to both the past versus the present and transference love versus normal love. He makes the important point that for Freud, infantile love was not simply the point of origin of transference love but isomorphic with it. Stern's point is that although Freud views other clinical phenomena (for example, memories) as rooted in the past, he does not regard the remembered phenomenon as an *exact* duplicate of the earlier lived one. The present version is always reconstructed in some way. Acting out, on the other hand, is antithetical to remembering in that it brings the past into the present in a directly replicated way: "Accordingly, acting out does not undergo the same transforming process of serial (re)constructions that a memory inevitably does." Transference love is a kind of oddity because it falls on the border between remembering and acting out. As Stern points out, Freud himself never constructed a developmental sequence of love but left the door open for others to do so.

Stern proceeds to a rather dazzling counterpoint between certain behaviors of infant-mother dyads and lovers, pointing out behaviors that are virtually identical—for example, "maintaining very close proximity . . . performing special gestures such as kissing, hugging, touching." He concludes that "not only is the point of origin for this physical language of love very early and preverbal, but the language itself is one of action."

Stern moves from overt behavior to a consideration of the intrapsychic experience of love, relating intersubjectivity in the infant's life to the intimacy of adult lovers. He finds that "the infantile 'roots' and 'prototypes'" encompass far more than the object choice. . . . They include at least the particularities of the physical language of love; the range and depth of intersubjective sharing; the way in which meaning is mutually created, and the intensity of the need to negotiate shared meanings; the degree of singularity occupied by the chosen object; and the temporal and intensity dynamics of the falling-in-love process." Most of these are registered as motor memories, as procedural knowledge, as sensory-motor schemas, as episodic events rather than as symbolic ones. Given these components of love, some of which never reach consciousness, Stern views love and transference love on a continuum, suggesting that "it is not so clear that a theoretical boundary line exists between transference and acting out in the situation of transference love." He follows Laplanche and Pontalis in suggesting that Freud failed to distinguish clearly—or show the connections—between the repetition phenomenon and acting out in the transference. Stern concludes that while acting out may be a resistance, "psychoanalysis has overstated . . . this division into acting and remembering by not distinguishing different kinds of actions of which Freud was well aware." Stern suggests that to some degree the analyst must permit the enactment of action patterns, as the only "path to remembrance [may lie] in the performance of the motor action." He ends with a series of very important theoretical questions, including the all-important one of how memories are packaged, the role of motor memory vis-à-vis other forms, the difference between action and actualization, and, perhaps most important to his paper, the basic difference between repeating (or remembering) in the transference versus repeating via acting out.

These brief summaries cannot come close to portraying the rich array of "readings" presented in this volume. Each of these essays demonstrates the profound insights and conundrums that are sometimes buried in Freud's simplest sentences. At the same time, they also reveal continuing discoveries in our evolving field. As an added benefit—though this was not the explicit intent of this volume—these chapters shed additional light on what continues to be a major problem in all modalities of psychotherapy: unfortunate, often tragic, enactments of erotic transference and countertransference.

REFERENCES

Jones, E. 1953. *The life and work of Sigmund Freud*. Vol. 1. London: Hogarth. New York: Basic.
Sulloway, F. 1979. *Freud: Biologist of the mind*. New York: Basic.
Szasz, T. 1963. The concept of transference. *Int. J. Psycho-Anal.* 44:432–443.

PART ONE

Observations on Transference-Love (1915)

SIGMUND FREUD

OBSERVATIONS ON
TRANSFERENCE-LOVE

(FURTHER RECOMMENDATIONS ON THE TECHNIQUE OF PSYCHO-ANALYSIS III)

EVERY beginner in psycho-analysis probably feels alarmed at first at the difficulties in store for him when he comes to interpret the patient's associations and to deal with the reproduction of the repressed. When the time comes, however, he soon learns to look upon these difficulties as insignificant, and instead becomes convinced that the only really serious difficulties he has to meet lie in the management of the transference.

Among the situations which arise in this connection I shall select one which is very sharply circumscribed; and I shall select it, partly because it occurs so often and is so important in its real aspects and partly because of its theoretical interest. What I have in mind is the case in which a woman patient shows by unmistakable indications, or openly declares, that she has fallen in love, as any other mortal woman might, with the doctor who is analysing her. This situation has its distressing and comical aspects, as well as its serious ones. It is also determined by so many and such complicated factors, it is so unavoidable and so difficult to clear up, that a discussion of it to meet a vital need of analytic technique has long been overdue. But since we who laugh at other people's failings are not always free from them ourselves, we have not so far been precisely in a hurry to fulfil this task. We are constantly coming up against the obligation to professional discretion—a discretion which cannot be dispensed with in real life, but which is of no service in our science. In so far as psycho-analytic publications are a part of real life, too, we have here an insoluble contradiction. I have recently disregarded this matter of discretion at one point,[1] and shown how this same transference situation held back the development of psycho-analytic therapy during its first decade.

---

[1] In the first section of my contribution to the history of the psychoanalytic movement (1914d). [This refers to Breuer's difficulties over the transference in the case of Anna O. (*Standard Ed.*, **14**, 12).]

159

To a well-educated layman (for that is what the ideal civilized person is in regard to psycho-analysis) things that have to do with love are incommensurable with everything else; they are, as it were, written on a special page on which no other writing is tolerated. If a woman patient has fallen in love with her doctor it seems to such a layman that only two outcomes are possible. One, which happens comparatively rarely, is that all the circumstances allow of a permanent legal union between them; the other, which is more frequent, is that the doctor and the patient part and give up the work they have begun which was to have led to her recovery, as though it had been interrupted by some elemental phenomenon. There is, to be sure, a third conceivable outcome, which even seems compatible with a continuation of the treatment. This is that they should enter into a love-relationship which is illicit and which is not intended to last for ever. But such a course is made impossible by conventional morality and professional standards. Nevertheless, our layman will beg the analyst to reassure him as unambiguously as possible that this third alternative is excluded.

It is clear that a psycho-analyst must look at things from a different point of view.

Let us take the case of the second outcome of the situation we are considering. After the patient has fallen in love with her doctor, they part; the treatment is given up. But soon the patient's condition necessitates her making a second attempt at analysis, with another doctor. The next thing that happens is that she feels she has fallen in love with this second doctor too; and if she breaks off with him and begins yet again, the same thing will happen with the third doctor, and so on. This phenomenon, which occurs without fail and which is, as we know, one of the foundations of the psycho-analytic theory, may be evaluated from two points of view, that of the doctor who is carrying out the analysis and that of the patient who is in need of it.

For the doctor the phenomenon signifies a valuable piece of enlightenment and a useful warning against any tendency to a counter-transference which may be present in his own mind.[1] He must recognize that the patient's falling in love is induced

---

[1] [The question of the 'counter-transference' had already been raised by Freud in his Nuremberg Congress paper (1910d), *Standard Ed.*, **11**,

by the analytic situation and is not to be attributed to the charms of his own person; so that he has no grounds whatever for being proud of such a 'conquest', as it would be called outside analysis. And it is always well to be reminded of this. For the patient, however, there are two alternatives: either she must relinquish psycho-analytic treatment or she must accept falling in love with her doctor as an inescapable fate.[1]

I have no doubt that the patient's relatives and friends will decide as emphatically for the first of these two alternatives as the analyst will for the second. But I think that here is a case in which the decision cannot be left to the tender—or rather, the egoistic and jealous—concern of her relatives. The welfare of the patient alone should be the touchstone; her relatives' love cannot cure her neurosis. The analyst need not push himself forward, but he may insist that he is indispensable for the achievement of certain ends. Any relative who adopts Tolstoy's attitude to this problem can remain in undisturbed possession of his wife or daughter; but he will have to try to put up with the fact that she, for her part, retains her neurosis and the interference with her capacity for love which it involves. The situation, after all, is similar to that in a gynaecological treatment. Moreover, the jealous father or husband is greatly mistaken if he thinks that the patient will escape falling in love with her doctor if he hands her over to some kind of treatment other than analysis for combating her neurosis. The difference, on the contrary, will only be that a love of this kind, which is bound to remain unexpressed and unanalysed, can never make the contribution to the patient's recovery which analysis would have extracted from it.

It has come to my knowledge that some doctors who practise analysis frequently[2] prepare their patients for the emergence of the erotic transference or even urge them to 'go ahead and fall in love with the doctor so that the treatment may make progress'. I can hardly imagine a more senseless proceeding.

144-5. He returns to it below, on pp. 165 f. and 169 f. Apart from these passages, it is hard to find any other explicit discussions of the subject in Freud's published works.]

[1] We know that the transference can manifest itself in other, less tender feelings, but I do not propose to go into that side of the matter here. [See the paper on 'The Dynamics of Transference' (1912*b*), p. 105 above.]

[2] ['*Häufig.*' In the first edition only, the word here is '*frühzeitig*' ('early').]

In doing so, an analyst robs the phenomenon of the element of spontaneity which is so convincing and lays up obstacles for himself in the future which are hard to overcome.[1]

At a first glance it certainly does not look as if the patient's falling in love in the transference could result in any advantage to the treatment. No matter how amenable she has been up till then, she suddenly loses all understanding of the treatment and all interest in it, and will not speak or hear about anything but her love, which she demands to have returned. She gives up her symptoms or pays no attention to them; indeed, she declares that she is well. There is a complete change of scene; it is as though some piece of make-believe had been stopped by the sudden irruption of reality—as when, for instance, a cry of fire is raised during a theatrical performance. No doctor who experiences this for the first time will find it easy to retain his grasp on the analytic situation and to keep clear of the illusion that the treatment is really at an end.

A little reflection enables one to find one's bearings. First and foremost, one keeps in mind the suspicion that anything that interferes with the continuation of the treatment may be an expression of resistance.[2] There can be no doubt that the outbreak of a passionate demand for love is largely the work of resistance. One will have long since noticed in the patient the signs of an affectionate transference, and one will have been able to feel certain that her docility, her acceptance of the analytic explanations, her remarkable comprehension and the high degree of intelligence she showed were to be attributed to this attitude towards her doctor. Now all this is swept away. She has become quite without insight and seems to be swallowed up in her love. Moreover, this change quite regularly occurs precisely at a point of time when one is having to try to bring her to admit or remember some particularly distressing and heavily repressed piece of her life-history. She has been in love, therefore, for a long time; but now the resistance is beginning to make use of her love in order to hinder the continuation of

---

[1] [In the first edition only, this paragraph (which is in the nature of a parenthesis) was printed in small type.]

[2] [Freud had already stated this still more categorically in the first edition of *The Interpretation of Dreams* (1900a), *Standard Ed.*, **5**, 517. But in 1925 he added a long footnote to the passage, explaining its sense and qualifying the terms in which he had expressed himself.]

the treatment, to deflect all her interest from the work and to put the analyst in an awkward position.

If one looks into the situation more closely one recognizes the influence of motives which further complicate things—of which some are connected with being in love and others are particular expressions of resistance. Of the first kind are the patient's endeavour to assure herself of her irresistibility, to destroy the doctor's authority by bringing him down to the level of a lover and to gain all the other promised advantages incidental to the satisfaction of love. As regards the resistance, we may suspect that on occasion it makes use of a declaration of love on the patient's part as a means of putting her analyst's severity to the test, so that, if he should show signs of compliance, he may expect to be taken to task for it. But above all, one gets an impression that the resistance is acting as an *agent provocateur*; it heightens the patient's state of being in love and exaggerates her readiness for sexual surrender in order to justify the workings of repression all the more emphatically, by pointing to the dangers of such licentiousness.[1] All these accessory motives, which in simpler cases may not be present, have, as we know, been regarded by Adler as the essential part of the whole process.[2]

But how is the analyst to behave in order not to come to grief over this situation, supposing he is convinced that the treatment should be carried on in spite of this erotic transference and should take it in its stride?

It would be easy for me to lay stress on the universally accepted standards of morality and to insist that the analyst must never under any circumstances accept or return the tender feelings that are offered him: that, instead, he must consider that the time has come for him to put before the woman who is in love with him the demands of social morality and the necessity for renunciation, and to succeed in making her give up her desires, and, having surmounted the animal side of her self, go on with the work of analysis.

I shall not, however, fulfil these expectations—neither the first nor the second of them. Not the first, because I am writing not for patients but for doctors who have serious difficulties to contend with, and also because in this instance I am able to trace the moral prescription back to its source, namely to

[1] [Cf. pp. 152-3.]　　　　　　　[2] [Cf. Adler, 1911, 219.]

expediency. I am on this occasion in the happy position of being able to replace the moral embargo by considerations of analytic technique, without any alteration in the outcome.

Even more decidedly, however, do I decline to fulfil the second of the expectations I have mentioned. To urge the patient to suppress, renounce or sublimate her instincts the moment she has admitted her erotic transference would be, not an analytic way of dealing with them, but a senseless one. It would be just as though, after summoning up a spirit from the underworld by cunning spells, one were to send him down again without having asked him a single question. One would have brought the repressed into consciousness, only to repress it once more in a fright. Nor should we deceive ourselves about the success of any such proceeding. As we know, the passions are little affected by sublime speeches. The patient will feel only the humiliation, and she will not fail to take her revenge for it.

Just as little can I advocate a middle course, which would recommend itself to some people as being specially ingenious. This would consist in declaring that one returns the patient's fond feelings but at the same time in avoiding any physical implementation of this fondness until one is able to guide the relationship into calmer channels and raise it to a higher level. My objection to this expedient is that psycho-analytic treatment is founded on truthfulness. In this fact lies a great part of its educative effect and its ethical value. It is dangerous to depart from this foundation. Anyone who has become saturated in the analytic technique will no longer be able to make use of the lies and pretences which a doctor normally finds unavoidable; and if, with the best intentions, he does attempt to do so, he is very likely to betray himself. Since we demand strict truthfulness from our patients, we jeopardize our whole authority if we let ourselves be caught out by them in a departure from the truth. Besides, the experiment of letting oneself go a little way in tender feelings for the patient is not altogether without danger. Our control over ourselves is not so complete that we may not suddenly one day go further than we had intended. In my opinion, therefore, we ought not to give up the neutrality towards the patient, which we have acquired through keeping the counter-transference in check.

I have already let it be understood that analytic technique

requires of the physician that he should deny to the patient who is craving for love the satisfaction she demands. The treatment must be carried out in abstinence. By this I do not mean physical abstinence alone, nor yet the deprivation of everything that the patient desires, for perhaps no sick person could tolerate this. Instead, I shall state it as a fundamental principle that the patient's need and longing should be allowed to persist in her, in order that they may serve as forces impelling her to do work and to make changes, and that we must beware of appeasing those forces by means of surrogates. And what we could offer would never be anything else than a surrogate, for the patient's condition is such that, until her repressions are removed, she is incapable of getting real satisfaction.

Let us admit that this fundamental principle of the treatment being carried out in abstinence extends far beyond the single case we are considering here, and that it needs to be thoroughly discussed in order that we may define the limits of its possible application.[1] We will not enter into this now, however, but will keep as close as possible to the situation from which we started out. What would happen if the doctor were to behave differently and, supposing both parties were free, if he were to avail himself of that freedom in order to return the patient's love and to still her need for affection?

If he has been guided by the calculation that this compliance on his part will ensure his domination over his patient and thus enable him to influence her to perform the tasks required by the treatment, and in this way to liberate herself permanently from her neurosis—then experience would inevitably show him that his calculation was wrong. The patient would achieve *her* aim, but he would never achieve *his*. What would happen to the doctor and the patient would only be what happened, according to the amusing anecdote, to the pastor and the insurance agent. The insurance agent, a freethinker, lay at the point of death and his relatives insisted on bringing in a man of God to convert him before he died. The interview lasted so long that those who were waiting outside began to have hopes. At last the door of the sick-chamber opened. The free-thinker had not been converted; but the pastor went away insured.

[1] [Freud took this subject up again in his Budapest Congress paper (1919a), *Standard Ed.*, **17**, 162-3.]

If the patient's advances were returned it would be a great triumph for her, but a complete defeat for the treatment. She would have succeeded in what all patients strive for in analysis —she would have succeeded in acting out, in repeating in real life, what she ought only to have remembered, to have reproduced as psychical material and to have kept within the sphere of psychical events.[1] In the further course of the love-relationship she would bring out all the inhibitions and pathological reactions of her erotic life, without there being any possibility of correcting them; and the distressing episode would end in remorse and a great strengthening of her propensity to repression. The love-relationship in fact destroys the patient's susceptibility to influence from analytic treatment. A combination of the two would be an impossibility.

It is, therefore, just as disastrous for the analysis if the patient's craving for love is gratified as if it is suppressed. The course the analyst must pursue is neither of these; it is one for which there is no model in real life. He must take care not to steer away from the transference-love, or to repulse it or to make it distasteful to the patient; but he must just as resolutely withhold any response to it. He must keep firm hold of the transference-love, but treat it as something unreal, as a situation which has to be gone through in the treatment and traced back to its unconscious origins and which must assist in bringing all that is most deeply hidden in the patient's erotic life into her consciousness and therefore under her control. The more plainly the analyst lets it be seen that he is proof against every temptation, the more readily will he be able to extract from the situation its analytic content. The patient, whose sexual repression is of course not yet removed but merely pushed into the background, will then feel safe enough to allow all her preconditions for loving, all the phantasies springing from her sexual desires, all the detailed characteristics of her state of being in love, to come to light; and from these she will herself open the way to the infantile roots of her love.

There is, it is true, one class of women with whom this attempt to preserve the erotic transference for the purposes of analytic work without satisfying it will not succeed. These are women of elemental passionateness who tolerate no surrogates. They are children of nature who refuse to accept the psychical

[1] See the preceding paper [p. 150].

in place of the material, who, in the poet's words, are accessible only to 'the logic of soup, with dumplings for arguments'. With such people one has the choice between returning their love or else bringing down upon oneself the full enmity of a woman scorned. In neither case can one safeguard the interests of the treatment. One has to withdraw, unsuccessful; and all one can do is to turn the problem over in one's mind of how it is that a capacity for neurosis is joined with such an intractable need for love.

Many analysts will no doubt be agreed on the method by which other women, who are less violent in their love, can be gradually made to adopt the analytic attitude. What we do, above all, is to stress to the patient the unmistakable element of resistance in this 'love'. Genuine love, we say, would make her docile and intensify her readiness to solve the problems of her case, simply because the man she was in love with expected it of her. In such a case she would gladly choose the road to completion of the treatment, in order to acquire value in the doctor's eyes and to prepare herself for real life, where this feeling of love could find a proper place. Instead of this, we point out, she is showing a stubborn and rebellious spirit, she has thrown up all interest in her treatment, and clearly feels no respect for the doctor's well-founded convictions. She is thus bringing out a resistance under the guise of being in love with him; and in addition to this she has no compunction in placing him in a cleft stick. For if he refuses her love, as his duty and his understanding compel him to do, she can play the part of a woman scorned, and then withdraw from his therapeutic efforts out of revenge and resentment, exactly as she is now doing out of her ostensible love.

As a second argument against the genuineness of this love we advance the fact that it exhibits not a single new feature arising from the present situation, but is entirely composed of repetitions and copies of earlier reactions, including infantile ones. We undertake to prove this by a detailed analysis of the patient's behaviour in love.

If the necessary amount of patience is added to these arguments, it is usually possible to overcome the difficult situation and to continue the work with a love which has been moderated or transformed; the work then aims at uncovering the patient's infantile object-choice and the phantasies woven round it.

I should now like, however, to examine these arguments with a critical eye and to raise the question whether, in putting them forward to the patient, we are really telling the truth, or whether we are not resorting in our desperation to concealments and misrepresentations. In other words: can we truly say that the state of being in love which becomes manifest in analytic treatment is not a real one?

I think we have told the patient the truth, but not the whole truth regardless of the consequences. Of our two arguments the first is the stronger. The part played by resistance in transference-love is unquestionable and very considerable. Nevertheless the resistance did not, after all, *create* this love; it finds it ready to hand, makes use of it and aggravates its manifestations. Nor is the genuineness of the phenomenon disproved by the resistance. The second argument is far weaker. It is true that the love consists of new editions of old traits and that it repeats infantile reactions. But this is the essential character of every state of being in love. There is no such state which does not reproduce infantile prototypes. It is precisely from this infantile determination that it receives its compulsive character, verging as it does on the pathological. Transference-love has perhaps a degree less of freedom than the love which appears in ordinary life and is called normal; it displays its dependence on the infantile pattern more clearly and is less adaptable and capable of modification; but that is all, and not what is essential.

By what other signs can the genuineness of a love be recognized? By its efficacy, its serviceability in achieving the aim of love? In this respect transference-love seems to be second to none; one has the impression that one could obtain anything from it.

Let us sum up, therefore. We have no right to dispute that the state of being in love which makes its appearance in the course of analytic treatment has the character of a 'genuine' love. If it seems so lacking in normality, this is sufficiently explained by the fact that being in love in ordinary life, outside analysis, is also more similar to abnormal than to normal mental phenomena. Nevertheless, transference-love is characterized by certain features which ensure it a special position. In the first place, it is provoked by the analytic situation; secondly, it is greatly intensified by the resistance, which dominates the situation; and thirdly, it is lacking to a high degree in a regard for reality, is less sensible, less concerned about consequences and more blind in its valuation of the loved person than we are prepared to admit in the case of normal love. We should not forget, however, that these departures from the norm constitute precisely what is essential about being in love.

As regards the analyst's line of action, it is the first of these three features of transference-love which is the decisive factor. He has evoked this love by instituting analytic treatment in order to cure the neurosis. For him, it is an unavoidable consequence of a medical situation, like the exposure of a patient's body or the imparting of a vital secret. It is therefore plain to him that he must not derive any personal advantage from it. The patient's willingness makes no difference; it merely throws the whole responsibility on the analyst himself. Indeed, as he must know, the patient had been prepared for no other mechanism of cure. After all the difficulties have been successfully overcome, she will often confess to having had an anticipatory phantasy at the time when she entered the treatment, to the effect that if she behaved well she would be rewarded at the end by the doctor's affection.

For the doctor, ethical motives unite with the technical ones to restrain him from giving the patient his love. The aim he has to keep in view is that this woman, whose capacity for love is impaired by infantile fixations, should gain free command over a function which is of such inestimable importance to her; that she should not, however, dissipate it in the treatment, but keep it ready for the time when, after her treatment, the demands of real life make themselves felt. He must not stage the scene of a dog-race in which the prize was to be a garland of sausages but which some humorist spoilt by throwing a single sausage on to the track. The result was, of course, that the dogs threw themselves upon it and forgot all about the race and about the garland that was luring them to victory in the far distance. I do not mean to say that it is always easy for the doctor to keep within the limits prescribed by ethics and technique. Those who are still youngish and not yet bound by strong ties may in particular find it a hard task. Sexual love is undoubtedly one of the chief things in life, and the union of mental and bodily satisfaction in the enjoyment of love is one of its culminating peaks. Apart from a few queer fanatics, all the world knows

P-A.N.—XII   M this and conducts its life accordingly; science alone is too delicate to admit it. Again, when a woman sues for love, to reject and refuse is a distressing part for a man to play; and, in spite of neurosis and resistance, there is an incomparable fascination in a woman of high principles who confesses her passion. It is not a patient's crudely sensual desires which constitute the temptation. These are more likely to repel, and it will call for all the doctor's tolerance if he is to regard them as a natural phenomenon. It is rather, perhaps, a woman's subtler and aim-inhibited wishes which bring with them the danger of making a man forget his technique and his medical task for the sake of a fine experience.

And yet it is quite out of the question for the analyst to give way. However highly he may prize love he must prize even more highly the opportunity for helping his patient over a decisive stage in her life. She has to learn from him to overcome the pleasure principle, to give up a satisfaction which lies to hand but is socially not acceptable, in favour of a more distant one, which is perhaps altogether uncertain, but which is both psychologically and socially unimpeachable. To achieve this overcoming, she has to be led through the primal period of her mental development and on that path she has to acquire the extra piece of mental freedom which distinguishes conscious mental activity—in the systematic sense—from unconscious.[1]

The analytic psychotherapist thus has a threefold battle to wage—in his own mind against the forces which seek to drag him down from the analytic level; outside the analysis, against opponents who dispute the importance he attaches to the sexual instinctual forces and hinder him from making use of them in his scientific technique; and inside the analysis, against his patients, who at first behave like opponents but later on reveal the overvaluation of sexual life which dominates them, and who try to make him captive to their socially untamed passion.

The lay public, about whose attitude to psycho-analysis I spoke at the outset, will doubtless seize upon this discussion of transference-love as another opportunity for directing the attention of the world to the serious danger of this therapeutic method. The psycho-analyst knows that he is working with highly explosive forces and that he needs to proceed with as much caution and conscientiousness as a chemist. But when

[1] [This distinction is explained below, p. 266.]

have chemists ever been forbidden, because of the danger, from handling explosive substances, which are indispensable, on account of their effects? It is remarkable that psycho-analysis has to win for itself afresh all the liberties which have long since been accorded to other medical activities. I am certainly not in favour of giving up the harmless methods of treatment. For many cases they are sufficient, and, when all is said, human society has no more use for the *furor sanandi*[1] than for any other fanaticism. But to believe that the psychoneuroses are to be conquered by operating with harmless little remedies is grossly to under-estimate those disorders both as to their origin and their practical importance. No; in medical practice there will always be room for the '*ferrum*' and the '*ignis*' side by side with the '*medicina*';[2] and in the same way we shall never be able to do without a strictly regular, undiluted psycho-analysis which is not afraid to handle the most dangerous mental impulses and to obtain mastery over them for the benefit of the patient.

[1] ['Passion for curing people.']
[2] [An allusion to a saying attributed to Hippocrates: 'Those diseases which medicines do not cure, iron (the knife?) cures; those which iron cannot cure, fire cures; and those which fire cannot cure are to be reckoned wholly incurable.' *Aphorisms*, VII, 87 (*trans.* 1849).]

PART TWO

Discussion of "Observations on Transference-Love"

A Rereading of Freud's
"Observations on Transference-Love"

FRIEDRICH-WILHELM EICKHOFF

Lead the way for Europe's kings!
Give freedom of thought!
—Friedrich Schiller,
Don Karlos

Freud's inspired paper of 1915, originally entitled "Further Recommendations on the Technique of Psychoanalysis," is scarcely ten pages long, but to this day it occupies an outstanding place in the debate on the curative significance of the interpretation of psychical conflicts versus direct emotional experience. Freud, in this paper, methodically establishes—in the context of discussing a countertransference resistance in the face of the "socially untamed passion" of the "erotic transference" of a fictitious female patient—the "fundamental principle of the analytic treatment being carried out in abstinence," tracing this "moral prescription back to its source, namely to expediency." Freud sees this fundamental principle as closely linked with the "neutrality" acquired "by keeping the countertransference in check." He formulates the aim of psychoanalysis as achieving "the extra piece of mental

This essay was translated by Roderick Koeltgen from the original German.

freedom which distinguishes conscious mental activity . . . from unconscious." Finally, he attributes a special status to transference love. The desire
for direct gratification in the transference points to a clinical category of
borderline pathology not yet known on a nosological level in 1915. Freud's
allusion at the end of "Observations on Transference-Love" to the quotation
from Hippocrates which Schiller used as an epigraph for his drama *Die
Rauber* ("Quae medicamenta non sanant, ferrum sanat, quae ferrum non
sanat, ignis sanat"[1]) suggests that he was well aware of his own revolutionary
impetus. He wrote to Karl Abraham on 29 July 1914, "I have become more
honest, bolder and more reckless" (Freud and Abraham, 1965).

THE DISCOVERY OF TRANSFERENCE LOVE

The discovery of transference love belongs to the historical context of the
cathartic treatment of Anna O. by Josef Breuer (Freud and Breuer, 1893–95,
21–47) between 1880 and 1882, on which Freud, from the perspective of a
supervisor, so to speak, gave an "interpretive reconstruction" in 1893. With
the passing of time this interpretation had come more and more under the
influence of his theory of transference (Hirschmüller, 1978, 170). In his
lectures at Clark University he pays detailed attention to the preliminary
phase of the treatment, in which he had not been involved, and interprets the
young woman's symptoms as signs of the memory of her father's illness and
death: "Thus they correspond to a display of mourning" (Freud, 1910a). In
"On the History of the Psychoanalytic Movement" (1914) he cites the transference of Anna O. as the "untoward event" that alarmed Breuer—who had
failed to notice the "universal nature of this unexpected phenomenon"—and
caused him to break off the treatment. In the "Autobiographical Study"
(1925) Freud writes of the patient's "condition of transference love," which
Breuer "had not connected with her illness"; he had "therefore retired in
dismay." In a letter to Stefan Zweig in 1932 (Freud, 1960a, 428) he finally
mentions that after the conclusion of the treatment the transference love had
expressed itself in a false pregnancy: "On the evening of the day on which all
her symptoms had been overcome he [Breuer] was called to her again, found

---

1. "Those diseases which medicines do not cure, iron (the knife?) cures; those
which iron cannot cure, fire cures; and those which fire cannot cure are to be reckoned
wholly incurable" (Attributed to Hippocrates, *Aphorisms* VII, 87 [trans. 1849]. See
Freud, 1915, 171n.) In Freud's version: "No; in medical practice there will always be
room for the *'ferrum'* and the *'ignis'* side by side with the *'medicina.'*"

her confused, writhing with abdominal convulsions. Asked what was the matter with her, she answered: 'Now the baby I'm expecting from Dr. B. is coming.' At that moment he had the key in his hand that would have opened the way . . . but he dropped it. He had, with all his great intellectual gifts, nothing Faustian in him." (Translation by R. K.) Freud never officially published this reconstruction but wrote respectfully in an obituary for Breuer (1925b) that "a purely emotional factor" had "given him an aversion to further work on the elucidation of the neuroses. He had come up against something that is never absent—the patient's transference onto her physician—and he had not grasped the impersonal nature of the process." However, in the "Observations on Transference-Love" Freud blames Breuer's "retirement from our common work" for holding back the "development of psycho-analytic therapy during its first decade" (159).

In line with Freud's remark in *The Interpretation of Dreams* (1900) that "Everything that can be an object of our internal perception is *virtual*, like the image produced in a telescope by the passage of light-rays" (611), the universal, impersonal nature of transference can be characterized as virtual (Eickhoff, 1987). There is evidently a conceptual identity between the transference of the intensity of unconscious ideas onto preconscious ones, as defined in *The Interpretation of Dreams* (562), and the "transference on to the physician . . . through a false connection" referred to in "Studies on Hysteria" (Freud and Breuer, 1893–95, 302). Freud remarks on the former view: "Here we have the fact of 'transference,' which provides an explanation of so many striking phenomena in the mental life of neurotics (1900, 562–63). According to Laplanche and Pontalis (1973), transference is the repetition of "infantile prototypes . . . experienced with a strong sense of immediacy" (455). Sandler, Dare, and Holder (1973) define it as "a specific illusion which develops in regard to the other person, one which, unbeknown to the subject, represents in some of its features a repetition of a relationship towards an important figure in the person's past" (47).

Freud writes most unequivocally on the therapeutic indispensability and universal character of transference love in his "Delusions and Dreams in Jensen's 'Gradiva'" (1907): "The process of cure is accomplished in a relapse into love, if we combine all the many components of the sexual instinct under the term 'love'; and such a relapse is indispensable, for the symptoms on account of which the treatment has been undertaken are nothing other than precipitates of earlier struggles connected with repression or the return of the repressed, and they can only be resolved and washed away by a fresh high tide of the same passions" (90). He compares the cure in Jensen's novella of the archaeologist Norbert Hanold by the forgotten playmate of his childhood—of whom the ancient relief of Gradiva reminded him—with the more modest "expedients and substitutes of which the doctor . . . makes use to help him to approximate with more or less success to the model of a cure by love which has been shown us by our author."

An intermediate stage relevant for the understanding of transference love in the development of the theory of transference is the "Fragment of an Analysis of a Case of Hysteria" (1905), in which Freud characterizes transference as the final production of the patient's persistent illness: "It may be safely said that during psycho-analytic treatment the formation of new symptoms is invariably stopped. But the productive powers of the neurosis are by no means extinguished; they are occupied in the creation of a special class of mental structures, for the most part unconscious, to which the name of 'transferences' may be given" (116).

In the postscript Freud attributes Dora's premature breaking off of the treatment to his own failure to interpret the transference ("I did not succeed in mastering the transference in good time"). Freud had begun to perceive this as a technical problem. Dora acted out instead of remembering: "In this way the transference took me unawares, and, because of this unknown quantity in me which reminded Dora of Herr K., she took her revenge on me as she wanted to take her revenge on him, and deserted me as she believed herself to have been deceived and deserted by him." Problematizing the interpersonal distance of his method, and without considering the complicity with Dora's father, which might have answered his question as to the "unknown quantity," Freud wonders: "Might I perhaps have kept the girl under my treatment if I myself had acted a part, if I had exaggerated the importance to me of her staying on, and had shown a warm personal interest in her—a course which, even after allowing for my position as her physician, would have been tantamount to providing her with a substitute for the affection she longed for?" In a footnote Freud subsequently laments his failure "to discover in time and to inform the patient that her homosexual (*gynaecophilic*) love for Frau K. was the strongest unconscious current in her mental life."

The concept of transference undergoes a technical extension in "Remembering, Repeating and Working Through" (1914), namely to that of the "transference neurosis" as "an artificial illness which is at every point accessible to our intervention. . . . Provided only that the patient shows compliance enough to respect the necessary conditions of the analysis, we regularly succeed in giving all the symptoms of the illness a new transference meaning and in replacing his ordinary neurosis by a 'transference-neurosis' of which he can be cured by the therapeutic work. The transference thus creates an intermediate region between illness and real life through which the transition from the one to the other is made." There is a very similar presentation in the twenty-eighth lecture in *Introductory Lectures on Psychoanalysis* (1916/17, 455) of the "transference illness" as a repetition in the analysis of pathogenic object relations to important persons from the past, from which the patient should be liberated in the struggle for the "new object," the analyst. The art of "managing the transference" consists, Freud says in "Remembering, Repeating and Working Through," of "giving" the repetition compulsion "the right to assert itself in a definite field. We admit it into the transference as a playground in which it is expected to display to us everything in the way of pathogenic instincts that is hidden in the patient's mind" (154). Finally, Freud concedes that working through the resistances has the greatest effect on changing the patient.

The concept of the transference neurosis has occasionally been ideologically overloaded. In contrast, Loewald (1971) recognizes in it the significance of an ideal construction which organizes a complex array of occurrences and gives a certain order to an otherwise chaotic constellation of events; it functions as a principle of order. Loewald (1975) also has reflected on the intermediate region of the transference neurosis and the transference illness and of the new production of the inner life history of the patient (whose co-authors are the analyst and the patient) and compared this intermediate region to the creation of an illusion, a game, whose specific impact depends on its being experienced simultaneously as reality and as a creation of the imagination. This double-facedness becomes an important component in the patient's experience. Loewald sees his formulations in these reflections as very close to Winnicott's (1967) "third sphere, that of the game, which covers creative life and the whole of human cultural experience." Regarding this concept of illusion, the art historian Ernst Gombrich (1960) writes of the "intermediate region between truth and deception . . . in which we consciously and freely surrender ourselves to illusion."

INTERPRETATION VERSUS GRATIFICATION AND APPEASEMENT

Several decades after the partly productive, partly disappointing experiences he shared with Breuer, Freud notes in "Observations on Transference-Love" the "vital need of psycho-analytic technique" to identify the management of the transference as the only really serious therapeutic difficulty. A few years after the founding of the International Psychoanalytical Association, he addresses this issue with presumably numerous beginners, without making any reference to published cases.[2] He seizes on a special situation "because it occurs so often and is so important in its real aspects and partly because of its theoretical interest"—namely, that "a woman patient shows by unmistakable indications, or openly declares, that she has fallen in love, as any other mortal woman might, with the doctor who is analysing her" (159).

He describes the situation as distressing, comical, serious, and finally unavoidable and difficult to resolve, hence tragic. In glorious rhetoric Freud demonstrates the possible outcomes: forming a lasting legal union, breaking off the work, or entering into an illicit love-relationship. The first and last of these possibilities seem compatible with the treatment but are made impossible by bourgeois morality and professional standards. Freud continues convincingly: the psychoanalyst should look at things from a different point of view. The fact that repetitions of the transference love are to be expected if the treatment is broken off is "a valuable piece of enlightenment [for the doctor] and a useful warning against any tendency to a counter-transference which may be present in his own mind." The "analytic situation" forces the patient to fall in love; this event cannot be "attributed to the charms of his [the analyst's] own person; so that he has no grounds whatever for being proud of such a 'conquest'" (160–61).

For the patient there are two alternatives: either abandoning the treatment or accepting "falling in love with her doctor as an inescapable fate." In a footnote, Freud goes on to say, "We know that the transference can manifest itself in other, less tender feelings, but I do not propose to go into that side of the matter here" (161n). This footnote conveys Freud's intentional neglect of other kinds of transference. Doctors practicing analysis may engage in "blood and tears" speeches as a preparation for disappointments in the introductory phase of the analysis, and these are by no means rare, but Freud is quick to point out the absurdity of expressly preparing for the occurrence of love transference. He also distinguishes more extreme cases of transference love, what many now refer to as erotized transference.

The serious difficulty of making something useful out of the woman patient's falling in love—or out of the so-called erotized transference—is dem-

2. For the significance of the passionate climate of the time, which did not allow the small group of the first psychoanalysts the necessary detachment we today call neutrality, see Appendix A.

onstrated by Freud in the example of the patient's demand that her love be returned. The scene of the psychoanalytic situation seems to change, "as when, for instance, a cry of fire is raised during a theatrical performance" (162). This metaphor reminds one of Loewald's comparison of the analytic situation with aesthetic experience. Kohut (1971) may also be referring to it when he writes:

> In its central aspects the analytic situation is not real, in the usual sense of the word. It has a specific reality, which resembles to a certain extent the reality of the artistic experience, such as that of the theater. . . . Analysands whose sense of their own reality is comparatively intact will, with the appropriate transitional resistances, allow themselves the requisite regression in the service of the analysis. They will thus be able to experience the quasi-artistic, indirect reality of transference feelings which once related to a different (then current and direct) reality in their past. (210–211)

No doctor who experiences this disturbance (transference love, or the erotized transference) for the first time, Freud continues, will find it "easy to retain his grasp on the analytic situation and to keep clear of the illusion that the treatment is really at an end." To demonstrate the possible expression of resistance in the passionate demand for love, he describes the change from the affectionate transference (which has appeared to be of such benefit to the treatment) to a lack of insight at the very point when the patient might be expected to "admit or remember some particularly distressing and heavily repressed piece of her life-history." The resistance thus makes use of a love that has existed for a long time. One can recognize the influence of "motives which further complicate things" in the form of "the patient's endeavour to assure herself of her irresistibility, to destroy the doctor's authority by bringing him down to the level of a lover." As an "agent provocateur" the resistance "heightens the patient's state of being in love and exaggerates her readiness for sexual surrender in order to justify the workings of repression all the more emphatically, by pointing to the dangers of such licentiousness" (162–63).

Freud then discusses how the treatment can be carried on in spite of this erotic transference in a detailed argument supporting the demand for abstinence, according to which the analyst should neither satisfy nor reject the patient's unconscious drive wishes but should interpret them. He thus excludes any implication of action in the psychoanalytic situation and adopts a metaposition shared by such modern philosophers as Hans Reichenbach. This principle is formulated as a fundamental generalization: "The treatment must be carried out in abstinence." The analyst's duty not to return the offered affection thus is based on considerations of analytic technique—namely, the need to treat the situation as "something unreal," to understand and interpret the transference in its virtuality. Freud's central interest is in avoiding professional errors, not moral transgressions. To answer the patient's admission of a love transference with a demand that she sublimate it would be as absurd as if, "after summoning up a spirit from the underworld by cunning spells, one were to send him down again without having asked him a single question"—a metaphor Freud adapted from *The Interpretation of Dreams*. To the "middle course" probably advocated by some of his pupils—returning "the patient's fond feelings" but at the same time "avoiding any physical implementation of this fondness"—Freud replies emphatically that "psycho-analytic treatment is founded on truthfulness," and therein "lies a great part of its educative effect and its ethical value." For Freud it is a matter of course that "anyone who has become saturated in the analytic technique will no longer be able to make use of the lies and pretences which a doctor normally finds unavoidable" (164).

These pronouncements represent an invariant of Freud's work. Having written of "education to truth" in the *Introductory Lectures on Psycho-Analysis* (1916/17, 434) and of "submission to the truth" in *New Introductory Lectures on Psycho-Analysis* (1933, 182), he expresses this credo in particularly moving terms in "A Comment on Anti-Semitism" (1938), in which, in protest against the persecution of the Jews, he puts the defense of a "religion of truth" into the mouth of a fictitious non-Jew.

It is noteworthy that the theme pervading the search for the truth is countertransference, which in his 1915 paper was not yet defined as an instrument for understanding transference. By rejecting the so-called middle course, Freud connects the "neutrality . . . which we have acquired through keeping the counter-transference in check" with "the fundamental principle of the treatment being carried out in abstinence."

Strachey's rendering of the German *Indifferenz* as "neutrality" paved the way for the entry of that concept into the vocabulary of psychoanalysis. Without reflecting on the "continuance of [the analyst's] sympathy and respect after the confession has been made," as emphasized in the *Studies on Hysteria* (Freud and Breuer, 1893–95) and the insight conveyed by interpretation as the giving side of the technique, Freud restricts the principle of frustrating satisfaction demanded in the love transference to "appeasement by means of surrogates"; deprivation of everything the patient desires could perhaps not be tolerated by a sick person. Yet need and longing have to be allowed to persist as forces impelling her to do work.

To illustrate the failure of an analysis due to the analyst's agreeing to false compromises, to surrogates, Freud recounts the enigmatic anecdote (retold in "The Question of Lay Analysis: Conversations with an Impartial Person" [1926]) of the pastor who is asked by the relatives of an unbelieving insurance agent to convert this ailing man before his death. The unbeliever is not converted, but the pastor leaves the sickroom with a new insurance policy (65). Freud warns the analyst who is seduced into stilling the patient's need for affection and becomes "insured" in the sense of the anecdote with a second suggestive image: the doctor should not, as in a dog race, put up "a garland of sausages" as a prize, for if some humorist were to throw "a single sausage on to the track" the dogs "would throw themselves upon it and forget all about the race" (169). Freud is evidently resorting to a joke to interpret the countertransference resistance of the overinvolved analyst, an intervention which Eissler (1958), with references to the interpretation of transference resistance, described as a "pseudoparameter." With the help of this pseudoparameter, he writes, one can smuggle interpretations into the arena and thus temporarily avoid the resistance. A patient who might offer the most stubborn resistance to an interpretation containing a rationally argued statement may accept it in the form of a well-chosen joke.

Four years after his first formulation, Freud, in the Budapest lecture "Lines of Advance in Psycho-Analytic Therapy" (1919), extended the principle of abstinence to include an "opposition to premature substitutive satisfactions. . . . Cruel though it may sound, we must see to it that the patient's suffering, to a degree that is in some way effective, does not come to an end prematurely." Yet he adds a modification to his warning about the patient's search for a substitutive satisfaction in his transference relationship to the doctor "for all the other privations laid upon him." He writes, "Some concessions must of course be made to him, greater or less, according to the nature of the case and the patient's individuality." Remembering the limited practicability of demanding total abstinence, Freud concentrates in the paper on transference love on the implicit problem in the countertransference of appeasing the need and longing that she shows, or of even returning the affection. In the latter case the patient may "bring out . . . the pathological reactions of her erotic life," but "the distressing episode would end in remorse and a great strengthening of her propensity to repression," an outcome which Herbert Marcuse (1966) has described in a nontechnical sense as "repressive desublimation." The need for neutrality, "for which there is no model in real life," also requires the renunciation of rejection: "He [the analyst] must take care not to steer away from the transference-love, or to repulse it or to make it distasteful to the patient. . . . He must . . . treat it as something unreal, as a situation which has to be gone through in the treatment and traced back to its unconscious origins. . . . The patient . . . will then feel safe enough to allow . . . all the detailed characteristics of her state of being in love, to come to light" (166).

From the beginnings of psychoanalysis Freud attached central importance to this fundamental step toward self-knowledge, which represents the precondition for a psychoanalytic concept of insight. In *The Interpretation of Dreams* he writes: "If we look at unconscious wishes reduced to their most fundamental and truest shape, we shall have to conclude, no doubt, that psychical reality is a particular form of existence not to be confused with material reality."

LOVE TRANSFERENCE VERSUS TRANSFERENCE LOVE

In a brief passage that in the paper as a whole has the effect of an incidental observation, Freud mentions "one class of women" with whom the "attempt to preserve the erotic transference for the purposes of analytic work without satisfying it" cannot succeed. "These are women of elemental passionateness who tolerate no surrogates. They are children of nature who refuse to accept the psychical in place of the material, who, in the poet's words, are accessible only to 'the logic of soup, with dumplings for arguments'" (166–67).

Before it was revealed by the meticulous editorial work for the supplementary volume of the *Sigmund Freud Studienausgabe* (1975), most readers were probably not aware that this formulation appears in a poem in the form of a political parable by Freud's "fellow-unbeliever" Heinrich Heine, entitled "Die Wanderratten" ("The Roving Rats"). As the expression "the logic of soup, with dumplings for arguments" is not a familiar one in the German language, and in view of the many Heine quotations in his work, it can be assumed that Freud was acquainted with the Heine poem and that he took his hardly flattering, misogynistic, extremely curious definition of a category of women patients from it. The poem is reproduced here by permission of the translator, Hal Draper.

The Roving Rats

There are two kinds of rat;
One hungry, and one fat.
The fat ones stay content at home,
But hungry ones go out and roam.

They rove for miles away,
Without any stop or stay,
Straight on along their bitter track—
No wind or weather holds them back.

They climb on heights that freeze,
They swim through brimming seas;
Some drown, some fall and crack their head—
The living go on and leave their dead.

These queer old birds are louts
With fearsome-looking snouts;
Their heads are shorn, as rats are bald,
So radical, so ratty called.

This radical rodent squad
Is ignorant of God.
Their whelps unbaptized as can be,
The wives are common property.

This sensual rat pack will
Think only to stuff and swill;
They swill and stuff without control
And forget we have an immortal soul.

These wild and savage rats
Fear neither hell nor cats;
They have no property, or money too,
So they want to divide the world anew.

These roving rats, alas!
Are near us now en masse;
I hear their squeaks—straight on they press—
Their multitude is numberless.

We're lost—O woeful fate!
They're already at the gate!
The mayor and Council shake and pray,
They don't know what to do or say.

The burghers spring to arms,
The priests ring out alarms.
The bulwark of the state, you see,
Is periled—namely, Property.

No blaring bells or priestly prayers,
No councillors or decrees of theirs,
No cannon, nor the biggest guns,
Can help you now, my pretty ones!

No finespun talk can help, no trick
Of old outdated rhetoric.
Rats are not caught with fancy isms—
They leap right over syllogisms.

When bellies are hungry, they only make sense
Of soup-bowl logic, breaded arguments.[3]
Of reasoning based on roast beef or fish,
With sausage citations to garnish the dish.

A codfish, silently sauteed in butter,
Delights that radical gang of the gutter
Much more than the speeches of Mirabeau
And all orations since Cicero.

Heine's ominous vision of the triumph of the hungry over the fat rats—of the proletariat over the bourgeoisie—contains oral-sadistic metaphors of exceptional impact and reflects horror in the face of terror. Dolf Sternberger (1976) calls it "magnificent in its perception, passion and malicious wit" and remarks that the words of the penultimate verse, serving as a detached and sarcastic commentary, drastically reveal Heine's rejection of utopian motives and his awareness of the futility of his search for a religious revolution.

Freud's connotative allusion to Heine's depiction of the inaccessibility to political arguments, which is itself perfectly comparable to the implicit interpretation of a countertransference resistance by a pseudoparameter, is impres-

3. This, of course, is Draper's version of the line in question.

sively perceptive. He thereby characterizes a clinical category of patients who demand direct gratification in the transference without the element of virtuality and who are impervious to interpretations. He resorts to the denotative level insofar as the concept of a borderline state is not yet developed; he writes repeatedly of love-transference rather than transference-love and beyond that, indirectly, of a violent state of being in love. In the 1915 paper he continues doubtingly: one can "turn the problem over in one's mind of how it is that a capacity for neurosis is joined with such an intractable need for love" (167). He did not explicate this incompatibility of neurosis and the craving for love, but it has been a frequent subject of reflection by later authors.

Bion (1962), without expressly referring to love transference, called "undigested facts"—facts that are suitable only for projective identifications and are not transformed—*beta elements* and differentiated them from *alpha elements*, which can be used for a transformation process by waking and dream thoughts and are dependent on the "capacity to contain." In a personal communication to the author (Bion, 1978), he agreed that there is a connection between Freud's characterization of a category of patients with a concretizing transference (the "logic of soup" women) and his own characterization of patients with a preponderance of what he called loose beta elements.

He also called to mind "this very dark area" of which Freud wrote to Lou Andreas Salome on 25 May 1916: "I know I have made myself artificially blind in my work in order to cast all light on the only dark area; I have renounced connection, harmony, elevation and all that you call the symbolic, alarmed by the one experience that every demand of that kind, every expectation, involves the danger of seeing what is to be revealed in a distorted, albeit embellished, way." (Translation by R. K.) This statement clearly goes beyond the recommendation for "evenly suspended attention" and comes very close to Bion's (1967) view that one should behave as if one were "without memory, without desires, without comprehension . . . in order to make possible and facilitate the intuition of the dreamlike psychical reality." This has been characterized by Loch (1981) as second-degree abstinence. It allows the therapist to withdraw from preoccupation with the patient's verbal and nonverbal statements and to renounce the pressure of having to understand the patient, instead of trusting that he is capable of developing mental life, the prerequisite for the evolution of the ultimate truth.

The *Liebesübertragung* ("love transference"),[4] despite and throughout

4. Strachey repeatedly, but by no means logically, usually translates this as "erotic

which the treatment must be continued—but which in the case of the "children of nature" with "elemental passionateness" can also cause it to fail—is not allocated by Freud to a particular clinical type, although, as mentioned above, he is doubtful of its compatibility with neurosis. He also restricts himself, evidently for the historical reasons discussed in Appendix A, to warning male colleagues—especially "those who are still youngish and not yet bound by strong ties"—against evoking erotic transference in their female patients, one of the four possible "treatment dyads" depending on the sex of the analyst and analysand (see Person, 1985). He makes no sharp distinction between love transference and transference love, but in the former instance he makes clear the difficult task of interpretation as revealed in possible countertransference problems (not named by him as such).

This "love transference" has subsequently been extensively investigated as a part of various "transference illnesses" and linked with different kinds of psychopathology. Etchegoyen (1991) writes: "There can, then, be psychotic [delusional, manic] forms, perverse forms and psychopathic forms of the transferential link with the so-called love transference." According to Hanna Segal (1977) the projective identifications defined by beta elements turn the countertransference into a particularly important part of the analytic process and affect patients who have been the object of massive parental projections, inducing in the analyst experiences of past helplessness with regard to violent projections.[5]

ABSTINENCE, FREEDOM OF THOUGHT, AND THE SPECIAL STATUS OF TRANSFERENCE LOVE

Beyond the demand for abstinence in terms of refusing to "give love," Freud's discussion of the task of interpretation betrays the inner attitude corresponding to second-degree abstinence, calling on analysts to make themselves "artificially blind" in order to "cast all light on the only dark area." It may seem authoritarian when he writes of making those who are "less violent in their love" than the women of uncompromising passionateness adopt the analytic attitude by emphasizing the "unmistakable element of

transference." He sometimes gives preference to "transference-love" while irritatingly avoiding "love-transference."

5. For erotized transference, see Appendix B.

resistance in this 'love' " and questioning its genuineness. But after using the image of a "cleft stick" (*"Zwickmuhle"*) to illustrate the confusion of communicative functions as a consequence of the patient's threatening to withdraw from the treatment—either because she feels scorned or because of being in love—and after considering a continuation of the work with a love which has evidently been "moderated or transformed" by the exaction of unavoidable pain and whose aim is to uncover "the patient's infantile object-choice and the phantasies woven round it," he asks: "Can we truly say that the state of being in love which becomes manifest in analytic treatment is not a real one?" In Freud's eloquent presentation the "whole truth regardless of the consequences" is twofold: the state of being in love which occurs during the analytic treatment cannot be denied the character of a "genuine love," and being in love outside analysis is also an abnormal phenomenon. The genuineness is not disproved by the resistance, which aggravates its manifestations, and the repetition of infantile prototypes is "the essential character of every state of being in love"; its dramatic quality in fact stems from its "infantile determination." Yet "transference-love has perhaps a degree less of freedom . . . it displays its dependence on the infantile pattern more clearly and is less adaptable and capable of modification" (167–68).

In the end Freud attributes a "special position" to transference love: "In the first place, it is provoked by the analytic situation; secondly, it is greatly intensified by the resistance, which dominates the situation; and thirdly, it is lacking to a high degree in a regard for reality, is less sensible, less concerned about consequences and more blind in its valuation of the loved person than we are prepared to admit in the case of normal love" (168–69). The second aspect implies the defense character of transference love, which Freud always emphasized. Although Freud concentrates more, under the aspect of abstinence, on the dangers of countertransference, by emphasizing the "special position" of transference love in the analytic process, he acknowledges its essentiality, its therapeutic indispensability, without expressly identifying its counterpart—namely, the analyst's continuing obligation, inherent in the "treatment," to be aware of the patient and to interpret her mental processes. The "limits prescribed by ethics and technique" make it possible "to extract from the situation its analytic content." Freud continues, "The patient, whose sexual repression is of course not yet removed but merely pushed into the background, will then feel safe enough to allow all her preconditions for loving, all the phantasies springing from her sexual desires, all the detailed characteristics of her state of being in love, to come to light; and from these she will herself open the way to the infantile roots of her love" (166). The patient will find this way with certainty only if the analyst adequately interprets the unconscious processes whose object he has become and does not react in an angry, frightened, or seductive way. Freud does not tire of warning that the woman patient must not "dissipate in the treatment" her capacity for love (169). At worst her initial transference fantasy that "she would be rewarded at the end by the doctor's affection" (169) may last beyond the end of the treatment and resist transformation. In an incidental remark Freud comments that the difficulty of regarding sensual desires "as a natural phenomenon" requires "all the doctor's tolerance," a problem to which an "erotic horror" (Kumin, 1985/86) of woman patients may correspond. Although Freud reflected in 1910 on the countertransference "which arises in [the analyst] as a result of the patient's influence on his unconscious feelings," he does not consider that the analyst's "aim-inhibited wishes" to "forget his technique and his medical task for the sake of a fine experience" might be specifically provoked by the patient. He emphasizes in only a normative way that it is quite out of the question for the analyst to give way.

Strachey (1934) was the first to describe the mutative transference interpretation—by which the understanding, tolerant superego elements are internalized in place of the archaic ones—as the central curative factor. Freud's final formulation of the aim of the treatment is by no means "value-abstinent" but contains a clear plea for sublimation: the patient "has to learn from him [the analyst] to overcome the pleasure principle, to give up a satisfaction which lies to hand but is socially not acceptable, in favour of a more distant one, which is perhaps altogether uncertain, but which is both psychologically and socially unimpeachable. To achieve this overcoming, she has to be led through the primal period of her mental development and on that path she has to acquire the extra piece of mental freedom which distinguishes conscious mental activity—in the systematic sense—from the unconscious" (170). While most of Freud's statements on transference love sound as if they refer to the reproduction of oedipal conflicts, the reference to the "primal period" makes one think of preoedipal fixations or of the reexperiencing of deep regression, emphasized by Ferenczi and Balint, in the analytic situation and of emerging from it by way of a "new beginning" (Haynal, 1989).

Freud restricts his observation in the paper on transference love to "affectionate attachment by the patient to the doctor," which, according to the twenty-seventh lecture in *Introductory Lectures on Psycho-Analysis,* "comes to light again and again, under the most unfavourable conditions and where there are positively grotesque incongruities, even in elderly women and in relation to grey-bearded men." In the case of male patients, he continues, one—he means the male analyst—might hope "to escape the troublesome interference caused by difference of sex and sexual attraction." But he finds "the same attachment to the doctor, the same overvaluation of his qualities, the same absorption in his interests, the same jealousy of everyone close to him in real life" in elderly patients. And, he continues: "The sublimated forms of transference are more frequent between one man and another and straightforward sexual demands are rarer in proportion as manifest homosexuality is unusual as compared with the other ways in which these instinctual components are employed."

Chasseguet-Smirgel (1988), who does not unreservedly accept the "elegant asymmetry" of the male and female Oedipus complex as an explanation for transference love in women and men, finds that the complete picture of transference love, irrespective of the sex of the analyst, coincides with the state of being in love more rarely in men than in women and that men's transference love is "better disguised"; men less frequently exhibit resistance by means of transference love but rather exhibit signs of opposition to it; men defend themselves, in her view, by mobilizing their anality against incestuous desires. Similarly, Person (1985), building on the distinction between the transference as resistance and resistance to the transference, suggests that while women use the erotic transference as resistance, men more readily display resistance to experiencing the erotic transference. According to Person, the most intensive mother-transferences from women patients onto female analysts, even if erotic feelings can be freely expressed, reflect the emergence of rage, envy, rivalry, and fear as a part of the oedipal constellation. Quite in line with the thesis presented above of the connection between Freud's concretizing love transference and Bion's beta elements, the direct transference onto the body of the woman analyst described by Lea Goldberg (1979) does not seem to be sex-specific.

Freud's principle of abstinence—which must be seen as separate from his rules for treatment, even though it has often been reformulated into a "rule of abstinence" (e.g., Nerenz, 1985)—emphasizes the necessity for frustration in situations which are determined by transference and countertransference resistances. He notes the need for a "certain amount of real suffering" by the patient (Freud, 1937), so that she will not find any substitutive satisfactions for her symptoms, and for the renunciation of any noninterpreting activity on the part of the analyst. Some years after the paper on transference love Freud warned against turning "a patient who puts himself into our hands in search of help into our private property, to decide his fate for him, to force our own ideals upon him, and with the pride of a Creator to form him in our own image and see that it is good." The categorical differences of this warning from the "technical rules," of which Freud said (1912) that "(at least many of them) may be summed up in a single precept," that the analyst show everything "the same 'evenly suspended attention,' " adjust himself to the patient "as a telephone receiver is adjusted to the transmitting microphone," is without question significant. Utilizing the metaphor of "constant detachment," out of which the analyst should direct his attention to the unconscious parts of the id, the ego, and the superego, Anna Freud (1946) commented in a clear way on the principle of abstinence.

The principle of abstinence is manifestly linked with neutrality, which signifies a utopian ideal of impartiality and noninterference, the analyst's aim not to become a real character in the life of the patient. It is connected in the closest possible way with the values implicit in the analytic attitude, the ethic of truthfulness, respect for freedom of thought, and the therapeutic aim of psychoanalysis, "to handle the most dangerous mental impulses and to obtain mastery over them for the benefit of the patient."

APPENDIX A

HISTORICAL BACKGROUND

The historical background of Freud's paper on transference love was probably formed by both the "confused, passionate countertransference" (Eissler, 1982) of C. G. Jung in the analysis of Sabina Spielrein and the eminently more complex personal and scientific dialogue between Freud and Ferenczi (Falzeder and Haynal, 1989). Freud wrote to Jung on 7 July 1909: "I myself have never been taken in quite so badly, but I have come very close to it a number of times and had a narrow escape. I believe that only the grim necessities of my work and the fact that I came to psycho-analysis a decade later than you have saved me from the same experiences. But it does no harm. One acquires the necessary thick skin, one comes to master the 'countertransference' which really does arise in one every time, and one learns to shift one's own emotions and place them with expedience. It is a blessing in disguise." (Translation by R. K.) Jung's letters to Spielrein having come to light (Carotenuto, 1980), we know that his relationship to her was considerably more intense than Freud could possibly have concluded from the letters written to him by Jung. Thanks to Falzeder and Haynal, we have been able to see in the correspondence between Freud and Ferenczi the very complicated conflict caused by the interrupted analyses of Elma Palos (who was later to become Ferenczi's stepdaughter!) by Ferenczi, who had fallen in love with her, and by Freud, who, despite great reservations, had given in to Ferenczi's urging to accept her for analysis. Haynal (1989) sums up: "Thus the most crucial questions of psychoanalytic technique were asked in an atmosphere of conflicts, sometimes of sadness, of injured narcissisms and violent emotions" (60). The discussion of the different conceptions of abstinence represents a fundamental aspect of the Freud-Ferenczi controversy, so significant for the history of psychoanalysis; the reader is referred to A. Hoffer's (1991) fine investigation of this controversy.

On the one hand, Ferenczi was a particularly zealous champion of the principle of abstinence in his "active technique" and, on the other hand, he advocated in his relaxation experiments spoiling the patient, even to the point of exchanging physical caresses characteristic of the mother-child-relationship. "We must admit, therefore, that psycho-analysis employs two opposite methods; it produces heightening of tension by the frustration it imposes and relaxation by the freedom it allows" (Ferenczi, 1930, 115).

Freud's warning against the degeneration of psychoanalysis became well known through Jones' publication (1962) of Freud's crucial letter to him of 13 December 1931: "Looking at the fashionable scene he has created, Godfather Ferenczi may well say to himself: with my technique of motherly affection perhaps I should have stopped before the kiss after all" (translation by R. K.). There is every reason to believe that the *furor sanandi* which Freud turns against at the end of his essay on transference love also referred to Ferenczi's "passionate need to help and heal" (Grubrich-Simitis, 1980, 273). The "affirmative presence" of the analyst emphasized by Loch (1991) may surely be regarded as a legitimate equivalent of Ferenczi's "motherly affection."

APPENDIX B
EROTIZED TRANSFERENCE

The description "erotized transference" for the special form of transference that is closest to Freud's "love transference" goes back to an unpublished comment of Lionel Blitzsten, which E. Rappaport (1956) quotes: "Blitzsten noted that in a transference situation the analyst is seen *as if* he were the parent, while in erotization of the transference he *is* the parent. The patient does not even acknowledge the 'as if'." In a 1959 paper, Rappaport quotes Blitzsten's conception of the unfavorable prognostic significance of the undisguised appearance of the analyst in the patient's first dream (which indicates an inability to differentiate between the analyst and a significant person of the past) and of the erotization of the transference with its excess of the erotic components as an expression, not of the capacity to love, but rather of an excessive need to be loved. In Rappaport's view such an erotization of the transference signifies a grave disturbance of the sense of reality and is a sign of serious illness, in particular of a fantasy of omnipotence. As early as the Lucerne Congress in 1934, Grete Bibring had already reported on a patient who acted out "the transference relationship in all its aspects. He made vehement demands on me to take him on my lap, carry him about and feed him, because his mother, wicked woman that she was, had never done so herself. He wanted to strike me, he heaped abuse on his mother as well as on myself, and would no longer address me except with the familiar 'Du'—all this to the accompaniment of severe outbreaks of anxiety and sweating, and with such intense emotion that he would cling to the sofa to avoid putting his impulses into action" (Bibring-Lehner, 1935). Nunberg (1951) attributed the behavior of a woman patient who tried to reeducate him and turn him into her father to her nonrealized readiness for transference and the futility of her efforts to establish a "working transference."

In a comprehensive overview Blum (1973) emphasized that the predisposition to the erotization of the transference as a subspecies of the transference was facilitated by a number of factors: disturbed ego functions (frequently but not invariably); childhood seductions that really took place, but which adults failed to validate; the seductive style of the defense; the confluence of transference and reality; the importance of narcissistic and preoedipal pathology with an oedipal façade, and the frequency of feeling "exceptional," in Freud's sense of the word. He concedes, however, that the erotized transference can be a part of an analyzable transference neurosis and can represent a distorted attempt to master a trauma by means of active repetition. Blum finally leaves no doubt that the erotized transference can be anchored in inadequate (for example, sadistic) countertransference, even though it is not created by this countertransference.

Gitelson (1952), demonstrating a special sensitivity for the restrictions of abstinence, points out unequivocally the danger the analyst can transfer onto the patient, in the mask of a positive assumed countertransference. This is true, for instance, if the analyst reacts to him as a person, introducing something into the analytic situation which for the patient means the repetition of an old relationship—above all, in a negative respect—for which the early undisguised appearance of the analyst in the patient's dream is an indication.

Neyraut (1976) does not follow the American example by describing this transference as erotized but instead classifies it as "direct transference." He considers it impossible to equate those analysands who even in the first sessions ask for something to eat, demand direct sexual gratification, want books from the analyst's library, immediately ask the analyst to entrust his children to them—in a word, want the analyst to exhibit here and now the most tangible proofs of his unique and incomparable love—with a second category of patients, those who after the long process of analysis make the same demands, but with an element of virtuality. According to Neyraut such cases constitute a touchstone for the analyzability of borderline patients and the character neuroses. The technical side of psychoanalytic work with a so-called borderline patient with a very distorted transference love is convincingly presented by Fonagy (1991) as "developmental help," implying the analyst's active involvement in the psychical processes of the patient, with the aim of reactivating inhibited—not deficient—functions based on the ability to consider one's own psychical states as well as those of others.

REFERENCES

Bibring-Lehner, G. 1936. A contribution to the subject of transference resistance. *Int. J. Psycho-Anal.* 17:181–89.

Bion, W. R. 1962. *Learning from experience.* London: Heinemann.

———. 1967. Notes on memory and desire. *Psychoanal. Forum* 2:272–73.

———. 1978. Personal communication.

Blum, H. P. 1973. The concept of erotized transference. *J. Amer. Psychoanal. Assn.* 21:61–76.

Carotenuto, A. 1982. *A secret symmetry: Sabina Spielrein between Jung and Freud.* New York: Pantheon.

Chasseguet-Smirgel, J. 1988. Ein besonderer Fall: Zur Übertragungsliebe beim Mann. In *Zwei Bäume im Garten.* Munich: Verlag Internationale Psychoanalyse.

Eickhoff, F.-W. 1987. A short annotation to Sigmund Freud's "Observations on transference-love." *Int. J. Psycho-anal.* 14:103–09.

Eissler, K. R. 1958. Remarks on some variations in psychoanalytic technique. *Int. J. Psycho-anal.* 39:222–29.

———. 1982. *Psychologische Aspekte des Briefwechsels zwischen Freud und Jung.* Jahrbuch der Psychoanalyse, Supplement 7. Stuttgart–Bad Cannstatt: Verlag Frommann-Holzboog.

Etchegoyen, R. H. 1991. *The fundamentals of psychoanalytic technique.* London: Karnac.

Falzeder, E., and Haynal, A. 1989. "Heilung durch Liebe?": Ein aussergewöhnlicher Dialog in der Geschichte der Psychoanalyse. In *Jahrbuch der Psychoanalyse* 24:109–27.

Ferenczi, S. 1930. The principle of relaxation and neo-catharsis. In *Final contributions to the problems and methods of psycho-analysis,* ed. M. Balint. London: Hogarth, 1955.

Fonagy, P. 1991. Thinking about thinking: Some clinical and theoretical considerations in the treatment of a borderline patient. *Int. J. Psycho-anal.* 72:639–56.

Freud, A. 1946. *The ego and the defence mechanisms.* London: Imago.

Freud, S. 1900. *The interpretation of dreams. SE* 4–5.

———. 1905a. Jokes and their relation to the unconscious. *SE* 8.

———. 1905b. *Fragment of an analysis of a case of hysteria. SE* 7.

———. 1907. Delusions and dreams in Jensen's "Gradiva." *SE* 9.

———. 1910a. *Five lectures on psycho-analysis. SE* 11.

———. 1910b. The future prospects of psycho-analytic therapy. *SE* 11.

———. 1912. Recommendations to physicians practising psycho-analysis. *SE* 12.

———. 1914a. On the history of the psycho-analytic movement. *SE* 14.

———. 1914b. Remembering, repeating and working-through (Further recommendations on the technique of psycho-analysis, II). *SE* 12.

———. 1916/17. *Introductory lectures on psycho-analysis. SE* 15–16.

———. 1919. Lines of advance in psycho-analytic therapy. *SE* 17.

———. 1925a. An autobiographical study. *SE* 20.

———. 1925b. Josef Breuer. *SE* 19.

———. 1926. The question of lay analysis: Conversations with an impartial person. *SE* 20.

———. 1933. *New introductory lectures on psycho-analysis. SE* 20.

———. 1937. Analysis terminable and interminable. *SE* 23.

———. 1938. A comment on anti-Semitism. *SE* 23.

———. 1975. *Sigmund Freud Studienausgabe: Ergänzungsband.* Frankfurt: S. Fischer Verlag.

———. 1960. *Briefe.* Ed. E. L. Freud. Frankfurt: S. Fischer Verlag.

Freud, S., and Abraham, K. 1965. *Sigmund Freud/Karl Abraham: Briefe, 1907–1926.* Ed. H. C. Abraham and E. L. Freud. Frankfurt: Suhrkamp Verlag.

Freud, S., and Andreas-Salome, L. 1966. *Sigmund Freud/Lou Andreas-Salome: Briefwechsel.* Frankfurt: S. Fischer Verlag.

Freud, S., and Breuer, J. 1893–95. *Studies on hysteria. SE* 2.

Freud, S., and Jung, C. G. 1974. *Briefwechsel*. Frankfurt: S. Fischer Verlag.

Gitelson, M. 1952. The emotional position of the analyst in the psychoanalytic situation. *Int. J. Psycho-Anal.* 33:1–10.

Goldberg, L. 1979. Remarks on transference-countertransference in psychotic states. *Int. J. Psycho-Anal.* 60:347–56.

Gombrich, E. H. 1967. *Art and illusion.* London: Phaidon.

Grubrich-Simitis, I. 1980. Six letters of Sigmund Freud and Sandor Ferenczi on the interrelationship of psychoanalytic theory and practice. *Int. J. Psycho-Anal.* 13:259–77.

Haynal, A. 1989. *Die Technik-Debatte in der Psychoanalyse: Freud, Ferenczi, Balint.* Frankfurt: S. Fischer Verlag.

Hirschmüller, A. 1978. *Physiologie und Psychoanalyse in Leben und Werk Josef Breuers.* Jahrbuch der Psychoanalyse, Supplement 4. Bern: Verlag Hans Huber.

Hoffer, A. 1991. The Freud-Ferenczi controversy: A living legacy. *Int. Rev. Psycho-Anal.* 18:465–72.

Jones, E. 1957. *Sigmund Freud: Life and work.* Vol. 3. London: Hogarth; and New York: Basic.

Kohut, H. 1971. *The analyses of the self.* New York: International Universities Press.

Kumin, I. 1985/86. Erotic horror: Desire and resistance in the psychoanalytic situation. *Int. J. Psycho-Anal. Psychoth.* 2:3–20.

Laplanche, J., and Pontalis, J. B. 1973. *The language of psychoanalysis.* New York: W. W. Norton.

Loch, W. 1981. Die Frage nach dem Sinn: Das Subjekt und die Freiheit, ein psychoanalytischer Beitrag. *Jahrbuch der Psychoanalyse* 15:68–99.

———. 1991. Therapeutische Monologe—Therapeutik des Dialogs—Einstellungen zur Seele. *Luzifer-Amor* 4:9–23.

Loewald, H. 1971. The transference neurosis: Comments on the concept and the phenomenon. *J. Amer. Psychoanal. Assn.* 1954–66.

———. 1975. Psychoanalysis as an art and the fantasy character of the psychoanalytic situation. *J. Amer. Psychoanal. Assn.* 23:277–99.

Marcus, S. 1974. Freud und Dora: Roman, Geschichte, Krankengeschichte. *Psyche* 28:32–79.

Marcuse, H. 1966. *Repressive toleranz.* Edition suhrkamp 181.

Nerenz, K. 1985. Zu den Gegenübertragungskonzepten Freuds. *Psyche* 39:501–18.

Neyraut, M. 1976. *Die Übertragung.* Frankfurt: Suhrkamp Verlag.

Nunberg, H. 1951. Transference and reality. *Int. J. Psycho-Anal.* 32:1–9.

Person, E. S. 1985. The erotic transference in women and men: Differences and consequences. *J. Amer. Acad. Psychoanal.* 13:159–80.

Rappaport, E. 1956. The management of an erotized transference. *Psychoanal. Q.* 25:515–29.

————. 1959. The first dream in an erotized transference. *Int. J. Psycho-Anal.* 40:240–46.

Sandler, J.; Dare, C.; and Holder, A. 1973. *The patient and the analyst: The basis of the psychoanalytic process.* London: Allen and Unwin.

Segal, H. 1977. Countertransference. *Int. J. Psycho-Anal. Psychoth.* 6:31–37.

Sternberger, D. 1976. *Heinrich Heine und die Abschaffung der Sünde.* Frankfurt: Suhrkamp Taschenbuch.

Strachey, J. 1934. The nature of the therapeutic action of psychoanalysis. *Int. J. Psycho-Anal.* 15:127–59.

Szasz, T. 1963. The concept of transference. *Int. J. Psycho-Anal.* 44:432–43.

Winnicott, D. W. 1967. The location of cultural experience. *Int. J. Psycho-Anal.* 48:368–72.

On Transference Love:
Revisiting Freud

ROBERT S. WALLERSTEIN

It has become a truism in psychoanalytic scholarship that there are continuing, and apparently endless, advantages to be gained from a rereading of Freud's pivotal papers, even those that are seemingly the most transparent. Reassessment of those papers in the light of new developments over the years in theory and technique enables us to see both the alterations in conceptualization since Freud and also, surprisingly, how fundamental concepts have stood the test of analytic time, even alongside today's more complex and subtly honed formulations.

This is very much the case with Freud's "Observations on Transference-Love," one of the half-dozen short papers on technique published between 1911 and 1915 and brought together in volume 12 of the *Standard Edition*. This small group of papers, together with the technical prescriptions implicit in the five major case histories; a few chapters in the *Introductory Lectures* and *New Introductory Lectures* and in the (1940) *Outline;* and of course Freud's late, great, summarizing clinical credo, reprise, and reassessment, "Analysis Terminable and Interminable," essentially constitutes the entirety of Freud's technical writings within the grand corpus of the twenty-four-volume *Standard Edition*.

Perhaps more than any of the other papers of technical prescription, the transference-love paper may seem by today's lights to be quaintly dated, perhaps even naive, essentially of only historic interest as part of the developmental unfolding of our discipline. Yet, curiously, at the same time it conveys the feeling of imparting a fundament of our professional life, something to be slighted or by-passed only with real risk. Actually, of course, the apparent simplicity and self-evident quality of this paper are deceptive indeed. The theme (or at least the import) is not unitary but several-fold, with interlocking threads.

It is, to be sure, a paper about a particular kind of transference development, which Freud called "transference love" (others have since labeled its extreme form "erotized transference"—as a more difficult and pathological extension beyond the ordinarily expectable "erotic transference" (more about this later), and also a warning about the countertransference risks that such a transference development can pose. It is, relatedly, a paper about the vital psychoanalytic technical principles of abstinence and neutrality, but without the distinction between these two concepts made subsequently. And finally, it is a statement of Freud's thinking on an issue that troubled him at that time and that has continued to trouble psychoanalytic discourse: the issue of how to view and encompass the simultaneous unity and diversity of human mental functioning—the synthesized unity that gives us our consistencies of character in the face of the diverse and antagonistic trends that we know as intrapsychic conflict. Should we view this in terms of dichotomies and dualisms and oppositions (for which Freud had a well-known penchant), or as a continuum shifting over an entire spectrum with perhaps nodal crystallizations around major positions (as in the fundamental continuum that Freud came to see and declare between normal and abnormal behaviors), or as a "complemental series" of varying contributions to particular behavioral manifestations from quite distinct sources (as in the famous footnote in "The Dynamics of Transference" [99n.] where he spoke to the additive contributions of constitutional and experiential elements to the formation of the neurotic outcome)?

Before enlarging on each of these themes in Freud's paper on transference love, I want to try to locate where the impression of datedness and naivete seems rooted. It is true, of course, that Freud wrote this paper as if the erotic efflorescence within the transference were always a (seemingly) mature heterosexual phenomenon between an emotive, hysterical, female patient and a male analyst, who was particularly susceptible to countertransference activation and involvement if he was "still youngish and not yet bound by strong [marital] ties" (169). It is also true that there is an implication throughout this paper and the other technical papers of its period that these intense transference manifestations are artifacts, creations specifically of the psychoanalytic treatment process, though Freud also conveys here and elsewhere (pointedly in "The Dynamics of Transference") that transference is ubiquitous in human life, that it shapes behaviors and relationships in everyday living and in nonanalytic treatments as well. Its special character in psychoanalytic treatment stems from the creation in the treatment of both conditions and a mental focus that highlight it explicitly as transference so that it can then be made into an object of interpretive activity. And it is also true that there is a clear implication in Freud's paper that these transferences (at least the intense or excessive transferences) are a hallmark of the (hysterical) neurotic state much more than of any other state or of so-called normal people. But this was before Freud had firmly developed his concept, so fundamental to the psychoanalytic understanding of mental functioning, of the continuum between what we call normality and neurosis—the view that all our minds operate in comparable ways, that we all have intrapsychic conflicts that arise out of the maturational unfolding of constitutional givens in interplay with experiential vicissitudes, that we each have to reach the best possible compromise-solutions to the conflicts that inevitably arise out of life's developmental tasks and milestones (plus all the traumatic happenings and interactions along the way), and that those solutions we designate as neurotic rather than normal have happened to arise in more strained, more behaviorally disturbed, and more symptomatic ways.

Most prominent among the places where the impressions of psychoanalytic naivete or datedness can arise in modern readings of the transference-love paper is Freud's categorization of transference phenomena, actually stated most clearly in "The Dynamics of the Transference." There, in trying to explain how the transference could become the most powerful resistance in analysis, Freud said:

> We find in the end that we cannot understand the employment of transference as resistance so long as we think simply of "transference." We must make up our minds to distinguish a "positive" transference from a "negative" one, the transference of affectionate feelings from that of hostile ones, and to treat the two sorts of transference to the doctor separately. Positive transference is then further divisible into trans-

ference of friendly or affectionate feelings which are admissible to consciousness and transference of prolongations of those feelings into the unconscious. As regards the latter, analysis shows that they invariably go back to erotic sources. And we are thus led to the discovery that all the emotional relations of sympathy, friendship, trust, and the like, which can be turned to good account in our lives, are genetically linked with sexuality and have developed from purely sexual desires. (p. 105)

In trying to turn these formulations into technical advice, Freud went on to say: "Thus the solution of the puzzle is that transference to the doctor is suitable for resistance to the treatment only insofar as it is a negative transference or a positive transference of repressed erotic wishes. If we 'remove' the transference by making it conscious, we are detaching only these two components of the emotional act from the person of the doctor; the other component, which is admissible to consciousness and unobjectionable, persists and is the vehicle of success in psychoanalysis exactly as it is in other methods of treatments" (105). It is this phrase, about the component of unobjectionable positive transference, that has led to all the technical prescriptions about not interpreting the transference until it becomes a resistance, about "riding" on the positive (trusting, affectionate, cooperative) transference, and the like. It has also given rise to a whole literature on the therapeutic alliance (see Zetzel, 1956) or the working alliance (see Greenson, 1965) as well as to a counterliterature (see Brenner, 1979; Curtis, 1979; and, especially, Stein, 1981).

Freud took as his chief focus in the transference-love paper the more "objectionable" repressed erotic transference, and as a central resistance over which the analytic treatment could well founder as a central danger to the susceptible countertransference. Today we no longer speak in this simple dichotomous fashion of the negative (hostile) versus the positive (libidinal) transference, or of the subdivision of the latter into a sublimated and unobjectionable (mostly conscious) component and a directly sexual, resistant (mostly unconscious) component. We see many more—in fact, most—sets of psychic phenomena as points on continua rather than as sharply dichotomized dualisms, whether we are talking about primary and secondary process thinking; about conscious, preconscious, and unconscious phenomena; or even about drive-instinctual (id) and defensive-adaptive (ego) determinants of behavior.[1]

But Freud also saw admixture and continuum and was not completely

1. See especially in this connection, Rapaport, 1960; Gill, 1963; and Schur, 1966.

caught in dichotomized, clearly demarcated, either-or thinking. He wrote of the unconscious erotic transference as "genetically linked" to the more acceptable and more conscious "emotional relations of sympathy, friendship, trust, and the like," implying a process of gradation and transition. And in the same 1912 paper he referred to the coexistence of various transference manifestations in the context of Bleuler's term *ambivalence*.

> In the curable forms of psychoneurosis it [the negative transference] is found side by side with the affectionate transference, often directed simultaneously towards the same person. Bleuler has coined the excellent term "ambivalence" to describe this phenomenon. . . . Ambivalence in the emotional trends of neurotics is the best explanation of their ability to enlist their transferences in the service of resistance. Where the capacity for transference has become essentially limited to a negative one, as is the case with paranoiacs [that is, an extreme case at one end of the continuous spectrum], there ceases to be any possibility of influence or cure. (pp. 106–07)

Today, of course, we think in a more complexly nuanced way. We see the transference position of the patient at each moment in the analysis as being predominantly colored by a particular object-relationship in his or her experience and as having a particular emotional valence with whatever characterizes the complex mixture or fusion of affects mobilized at that moment by that relationship.

Let us turn now to the major enduring contributions to psychoanalytic theory and praxis advanced in the transference-love paper. First, of course, is the theme announced in the title, the warning to new analysts of the technical and moral dangers that can stem from the analyst's faulty technical and human response to the patient's feeling of truly "falling in love" with the analyst, whether it be a countertransference-driven response of mutual romantic involvement or, its opposite, an adjuration to the patient to suppress or renounce these sentiments in the interest of the continuation of the treatment. Both responses are wrong on technical grounds as counterproductive to the purpose of the analysis, and the first is also wrong on moral grounds, as an unconscionable exploitation of the patient's transference-heightened vulnerability. Freud's prescription—and a universal fundament of the technique he innovated that has continued to be the touchstone of psychoanalysis ever since—was to treat the outpourings of love as transference manifestations, to be interpreted and analyzed in both their defensive (resistance) and drive components.

That Freud felt it necessary to devote one of his few papers of technical prescription to this issue is an indication of his awareness, even in those earliest years of psychoanalysis, of the potentially serious nature of this problem for the proper practice of psychoanalysis—and not just for those he called "still youngish and not yet bound by strong ties." Among other cases, he must have had in mind Breuer's treatment of Anna O., the patient whose therapy in 1880 gave rise to the very first psychoanalytic ideas—the concept of "the talking cure" by "chimney sweeping." This was alluded to by Freud both in "On the History of the Psycho-analytic Movement" (1914) and in his obituary of Josef Breuer (1925). In the "History" Freud wrote: "Now I have strong reasons for suspecting that after all her [Anna O.'s] symptoms had been relieved Breuer must have discovered from further indications the sexual motivation of the transference, but that the universal nature of this unexpected phenomenon escaped him, with the result that, as though confronted by an 'untoward event,' he broke off all further investigation. He never said this to me in so many words, but he told me enough at different times to justify this reconstruction of what happened" (12).

It was Jones (1953), in the first volume of his biography of Freud, who first elucidated the nature and interpretation of the "untoward event" and filled in a hiatus in Breuer's account of the case in *Studies on Hysteria,* (Freud and Breuer, 1893–95; see footnote by Strachey, *SE* 2:40). Jones wrote of Breuer's obsessional preoccupation with this fascinating patient and his endless recounting of the dramatic treatment happenings to his wife, which finally aroused her intense jealousy and made her severely unhappy and morose. Breuer reacted to his wife's remonstrations with acute feelings of love and guilt, and he decided to abruptly terminate the treatment of Anna O., who was, in any case, by now much better. But on the very evening of Breuer's announcement to his patient he was fetched back to find her in a full-blown revival of her illness state and in the throes of an hysterical childbirth (pseudocyesis) as well. Jones called this "the logical termination of a phantom pregnancy that had been invisibly developing in response to Breuer's ministrations" (224–25).

Breuer was profoundly shocked, but he managed to calm Anna O. down by hypnosis and then fled the house; he and his wife left the very next day for a second honeymoon in Venice. When describing in his obituary note Breuer's reluctance to publish this case history, Freud said:

A kind of reserve which was characteristic of him, an inner modesty, surprising in a man of such a brilliant personality, had led him to keep his astonishing discovery secret for so long that not all of it was any longer new. I found reason later to suppose that a purely emotional factor, too, had given him an aversion to further work on the elucidation of the neuroses. He had come up against something that is never absent—his patient's transference onto her physician—and he had not grasped the impersonal nature of the process. At the time when he submitted to my influence and was preparing the Studies for publication, his judgement of their significance seemed to be confirmed, "I believe," he told me, "that this is the most important thing we two have to give to the world." (p. 280)

Nor was Freud immune to the same countertransference pressures. In further discussion of Breuer's reluctance to collaborate with Freud in publishing this thinking about hypnosis, hysteria, and the talking cure—a reluctance that Freud overcame only with real difficulty—Jones (1953) wrote:

It gradually dawned on Freud that Breuer's reluctance was connected with his disturbing experience with Frl. Anna O. related earlier in this chapter. So Freud told him of his own experience of a female patient suddenly flinging her arms around his neck in a transport of affection, and he explained to him his reasons for regarding such untoward occurrences as part of the transference phenomenon characteristic of certain types of hysteria. This seems to have had a calming effect on Breuer who evidently had taken his own experience of the kind more personally and perhaps even reproached himself for indiscretion in the handling of his patient. (p. 250)

And Eickhoff (1987), in his annotation of Freud's transference-love paper, quoted Freud's remark to Jung (in reference to Jung's relation with Sabina Spielrein) that these experiences are a sort of "blessing in disguise. . . . I myself have never been taken in quite so badly, but I have come very close to it a number of times and had a 'narrow escape'" (107).

But Freud did more than warn about these ubiquitous countertransference risks. In his transference-love paper he also tried to place the phenomenon in terms of psychopathology and explain its sometimes overriding intensity and tenacity. He identified this erotic transference as a powerful treatment resistance: the patient presses the analyst to act out in the countertransference and thus collude with her in deflecting the healthy treatment goal of cure by analysis to the (inevitably doomed) neurotic goal of "cure by love." Freud felt that this was a particular transference phenomenon in female hysterical patients, most of whom were very amenable to analysis—by those who understood the situation and could refrain from countertransference enactments—except for "one class of women with whom this attempt to preserve the erotic transference for the purposes of analytic work without satisfying it will not succeed. These are women of elemental passionateness who tolerate no surrogates. They are children of nature who refuse to accept the psychical in place of the material. . . . With such people one has the choice between returning their love or else bringing down upon oneself the full enmity of a woman scorned. In neither case can one safeguard the interests of the treatment. One has to withdraw, unsuccessful" (166–67).

In all this discussion, incidentally, of the nature, conditions, and hazards of transference love to the patient and the analyst, Freud did not refer to the complementary issue and danger: the sexual exploitation of the hapless patient by the impulse-ridden or unscrupulous therapist, a problem that is unhappily so much a center of attention in today's professional (and journalistic) literature regarding all the mental-health occupations. Freud simply took for granted the ethical intentions of the psychoanalytic practitioner of his day, much as he was so fond of quoting F. T. Vischer's "What is moral is self evident" (see Hartmann, 1960, 121).

The very small body of analytic literature since Freud focused specifically on transference love or erotic transference and the risks of countertransference collusive enactment has elaborated Freud's consideration of the "class of women . . . of elemental passionateness." Ernest Rappaport (1956) developed this in two directions: drive and ego. The drive considerations had to do with the intensity of the preoedipal and dependent attachment hunger of these patients, the oral yearning for the nurturant parent. The ego considerations had to do with the disturbance of the sense of reality, the fading of the "as-if" quality of the transference illusion, so that the analyst actually becomes the reincarnated idealized (and/or diabolized) parent, and the consequent borderline character of the patient's ego functioning. Both sets of dynamic considerations feed the patient's strong conviction of the ego-syntonic nature of her behaviors and attitudes; the analyst is the one who is perceived as stubborn and inconsiderate in not accepting the patient's protestations of love at their true (face) value. Rappaport stated that these transference resistances could be so tenacious that often the analyst's only recourse was to refer the patient to another analyst, at times even over the patient's protests (though later in the same article he indicated that this might only serve to reactivate deformative childhood traumata).

In a later article, Rappaport (1959) quoted Blitzsten's well-known dictum about the ominous prognosis when the analyst appears undisguised in the patient's initial dream. Even if an analytic process can ensue, "the analysis is going to be erotized right from the start" (240), and again the erotic transference resembles the preoedipal and oral demandingness of the child upon the parent. He added, "Blitzsten postulated that an erotized transference must be worked through quite early or the patient must be sent to another analyst" (242). All this, of course, explicitly shifted the ground from the phallic-oedipal and heterosexual transference between adults postulated by Freud to the preoedipal, oral-dependent transference of infant to mother which is perhaps implicit as an underlying dynamic in "women of elemental passionateness." Freud clearly was not so explicit.

After Rappaport, it is Blum (1973) who has written the most comprehensive paper on this subject, systematically extending these elaborations first made implicitly by Freud and then much more explicitly by Rappaport. Blum drew a far sharper distinction between the erotic transference described by Freud as an expectable transference development, temptation, and risk and what Blum characterized as the "erotized transference"—again, recalling Freud's "women of elemental passionateness." Blum wrote, "The erotized transference is a particular species of erotic transference, an extreme sector of a spectrum. It is an intense, vivid, irrational, erotic preoccupation with the analyst, characterized by overt, seemingly ego-syntonic demands for love and sexual fulfillment from the analyst. The erotic demands may not seem unreasonable or unjustified to the patient. . . . Disturbance of the relationship to reality may be primary or represent a regressive alteration" (63). Patients with this transference, Blum said, "can resemble intractable love addicts" (64); thus he linked them conceptually (metapsychologically and nosologically) with those having impulse neuroses and addictive disorders. Like Rappaport, Blum saw these persons as sicker-than-neurotic patients, with the constant threat of the regressive loss of reality testing and of a dramatically urgent transference psychosis eruption.[2]

In terms of drive dynamics Blum painted a broader canvas than Rappaport did. He talked of a possible homosexual dynamic masked by an exaggerated heterosexual erotization; of frequent childhood sexual seductions and over-stimulations with failures of phase-appropriate parental protection and sup-

2. See Wallerstein, 1967, for a full discussion of the transference psychosis as a treatment development in sicker-than-neurotic but not overtly psychotic individuals and its relation to the conception of the "hysterical psychosis."

port; of traumatic primal-scene exposures with parental exhibitionism and intrusions into children's privacy; of the narcissism of the "exception"; of preeminent oral insatiability, dependent clutching, and object-hunger with vulnerability to disappointment and defensive detachment; of severe sado-masochistic trends; of a malignant erotomania with severe ego impairment; of a constant thirst for both revenge and reparation for all real and fantasied disappointments and loss of objects or objects' love.

In contrast to this erotized transference, which "resembles a vehemently distorted form of expectable erotic transference," Blum considers the expect-able erotic transference to be "a relatively universal, though variably intense and recurrent phase of analysis. There is a continuum from feelings of affec-tion to strong sexual attraction" (69). Here Blum makes the continuum con-cept explicit in relation to psychic phenomena, a point of view which has just about become a given of modern psychoanalytic thinking. As we have noted, Freud's thinking was evolving toward this conception over his lifetime, al-though it always was balanced against the attractions of dualisms and po-larities, with the greater clarity and simplicity in theorizing that they can make possible. Anchored more firmly in the continuum concept, Blum could say, "The erotization may be transient or persistent, mild or malignant, accessible to analysis or indicative of ego defect. I do not believe these patients are necessarily all borderline or psychotic" (70). All this, of course, is completely compatible with nodal-point crystallizations along the contin-uum from those (more neurotic, more amenable to analysis) he designated "erotic transference" to those (sicker, less amenable) he designated "erotized transference."

Though he claimed that "analysis is usually impossible" (70) with the malignant erotomanias or the severely ego-impaired, Blum carefully bal-anced his therapeutic predictions: "Falling in love with the analyst is not a requirement for therapeutic success, nor is erotized transference always a harbinger of analytic failure" (71). The first half of the sentence is an allusion to the current revisionist view that the full unfolding of a regressive trans-ference neurosis, with its re-creation of the infantile neurosis interactions and the thorough resolution of this transference neurosis through interpretation and insight, is no longer a sine qua non of psychoanalytic success. In terms of countertransference dangers, Blum simply echoed Freud: "Counter-transference can divert the tensions of transference into shared erotic fanta-sies or frightened flight. It can anchor the patient's fantasies and transference reactions in the reality of actual seductive responses of the analyst. Analysis can be deadlocked in the embracing arrest of countertransference" (74). In his annotation of Freud's paper, Eickhoff (1987) referred to the clinical category highlighted by Freud of "patients who demand direct gratification in the transference without the element of virtuality" (105)—again the loss of the safeguarding "as-if" quality. He felt that Freud seemed here implicitly to be describing almost "delusional forms of transference."

All these changes, from the hysterical-oedipal to the preoedipal orally demanding and oral-dependent; from the neurotic to the sicker-than-neurotic, the borderline, the transference psychotic; from the love demands of a (neurotic) woman upon a man to the more intense demands of the sicker and/or more infantile and childlike upon the containing and holding parent—all these can be looked upon as significant extensions of Freud's conceptions in the transference-love paper or merely as more explicit renditions of what was implicit even then, though it emerged more clearly over Freud's subsequent scientific career. Certainly a substantial literature has grown up around each of Freud's great case histories, and a major theme in much of that literature has been the discerning of evidence—already made available by Freud, though not explicitly categorized in that way by him—indicative of sicker-than-neurotic (that is, more borderline) aspects of character functioning, although the manifest focus was on the more classically neurotic features.

This perspective, incidentally, is comparable to the conceptions advanced by Zetzel (1968) in the cognate realm of the psychopathology and psychoanalytic therapy of the so-called hysterical patient. In her paper "The So-Called Good Hysteric" Zetzel parceled out the realm of hysteric character formation and symptomatic manifestations into four major crystallizations, ranging from, on one end, those best integrated and functioning on the phallic-oedipal level, with the triangular fixations and inhibitions characteristic of classically neurotic hysteric functioning, to, on the other, the predominantly orally fixated, with an absence of meaningful, sustained object investments with either sex, genuinely incapable of meaningful distinctions between external and internal reality, and almost completely refractory to true analytic work. This continuum comprises an almost identical patient population to that described in Blum's 1973 article and present, at least implicitly, in Freud's 1915 transference-love paper. In all these ways we have built on and developed beyond Freud's legacy and at the same time still have his work and his thinking very much with us.

Another major theme in Freud's paper—and this is what marks it as a paper of technical prescription as well as moral warning—has to do with the "rule of abstinence" or neutrality as a technical fundament of the psychoanalytic method. As Eickhoff (1987) has put it, "Rejection of the implication of action [by the analyst] is an essential part of the rule of abstinence as we have known it since Freud's (1915) paper 'Observations on transference love'" (104). Actually, in that paper Freud used the word *neutrality* once and *abstinence* three times, and as if the meanings were quite interchangeable. For example: "In my opinion, therefore, we ought not to give up the neutrality towards the patient, which we have acquired through keeping the counter-transference in check" (164) and "The treatment must be carried out in abstinence. By this I do not mean physical abstinence alone, nor yet the deprivation of everything that the patient desires, for perhaps no sick person could tolerate this. Instead, I shall state it as a fundamental principle that the patient's need and longing should be allowed to persist in her, in order that they may serve as forces impelling her to do work and to make changes" (165). (There is a third appearance of the word *abstinence,* in a completely comparable sense.)

This paper was of course written in the era of the topographic model of mental functioning articulated in the seventh chapter of *The Interpretation of Dreams* (Freud, 1900) and more than a decade before "Inhibitions, Symptoms and Anxiety" (1926), with its recasting of mental functioning into the tripartite model of id, ego, and superego. It was this structural model that established the proper conceptual basis for disentangling the closely related but distinct concepts of abstinence and neutrality. Novey (1991), in an article entitled "The Abstinence of the Psychoanalyst," has put this differentiation clearly and tersely. After stating that the two concepts were blurred and then confused in the psychoanalytic literature, she goes on to say: "The word *neutrality,* although used by Freud (1915 [1914]) almost synonymously with *abstinence* before he developed the structural theory, later usually referred to a position 'equidistant from the id, the ego and the super-ego' (A. Freud, 1936, p. 30). Abstinence, however, has a libidinal significance, referring to gratification or frustration of libidinal drives" (344).[3] That is, the analyst, in being neutral, refrains from aligning himself with the drive or ego or superego pressures or strictures. This is what Novey contrasts with the refusal to gratify (or the frustration of) the patient's libidinal and, she should have

3. The complete quotation from Anna Freud's monograph (1936) defining analytic technical neutrality within the framework of structural theory is "He [the analyst] directs his attention equally and objectively to the unconscious elements in all three institutions. To put it another way, when he sets about the work of enlightenment he takes his stand at a point equidistant from the id, the ego and the superego" (30).

added, aggressive, drives. The two concepts together address different aspects of the technical and human dangers represented by the challenge of the transference-love manifestations to the analyst. As Eickhoff has stated, all this stems from the transference-love paper and has been an unswerving component of psychoanalytic technique ever since, though there have been major reconsiderations of the meanings and implementations of the concepts of abstinence, gratification, and frustration over the years,[4] as well as major questionings of the values of technical neutrality via the Alexandrian notions of the place of the "corrective emotional experience" in the work of analysis (see Alexander and French, 1946).[5]

The third major facet of Freud's paper that I wish to discuss is one that has stood the test of time (and enlarging experience) less well. This comes from the classification system of transference phenomena that Freud actually presented in "The Dynamics of Transference," the neat division into negative and positive transferences and the further division of the latter into the (repressed) erotic transference and the so-called unobjectionable positive transference. The negative transference and the erotic transference, repressed or not, Freud saw from the first as resistances demanding explicit interpretive attention. Of the two, the negative transference would make fewer (or less obvious) collusive countertransference demands and in that sense would pose the lesser technical problem to the analytic practitioner; therefore the special focus in the transference-love paper on the peculiar hazards posed by the erotic emotional constellation to the analytic work and to analysts, especially to those "still youngish and not yet bound by strong ties" and, more broadly, to those less seasoned in general.

All this left—explicitly in the "Dynamics of Transference" paper, and by implication in the transference-love paper—"unobjectionable" positive transference as a phenomenon to be accepted and utilized—rather than one that itself required analytic attention—unless and until it in turn became a resistance. Such a resistance, one would assume, would become manifest via an emerging negative coloration or by indications of its repressed childhood erotic roots—for Freud already, to some extent, envisioned a continuum from the most archaic, sexual, and repressed to the most sublimated, de-eroticized, and acceptable. More precisely, he had in mind the derivation of

4. Stone's 1961 monograph *The Psychoanalytic Situation* is the most subtly and complexly nuanced of these contributions.
5. For a reconsideration in contemporary terms of the concept of the corrective emotional experience, see Wallerstein, 1990.

the sublimated form from the archaic, as well as the ambivalent admixtures of negative and positive colorations.

It is this classification of the transference into three compartments—two of them clearly resistances requiring analytic interpretation and one considered "unobjectionable"—that led to the technical prescriptions (so long taken for granted as givens, at least within the ego-psychology literature) about letting the transference unfold, not interpreting transferences until they take on manifest resistance colorings, not just "riding" on the positive transference as long as possible but being willing at times to allow it to persist essentially unexamined and therefore unaltered throughout the whole analytic course. It is this set of ideas that provided the impetus not only for the evolving psychoanalytic literature on the therapeutic alliance, starting with Zetzel (1956), and on the related, or synonymous, working alliance, starting with Greenson (1965), but for an even greater body of psychoanalytically influenced psychodynamic psychotherapy literature in which the construct of the therapeutic alliance has become almost a reified entity, both the essential condition and the guarantor of psychotherapeutic success. This in turn has spawned an entire area of empirical psychotherapy research literature dedicated to measuring the "strength" of the therapeutic alliance, relating this assessment to treatment course and outcome, and devising interventions to strengthen the therapeutic alliance in order to improve the treatment prognosis.

There has, of course, been another side to this set of theoretical and technical developments: an opposing body of literature questioning the clinical usefulness of this juxtaposition of therapeutic alliance and transference as two separate, necessary, complementary, and interacting components of the evolving psychoanalytic process. Discussion of the pros and cons of that controversy would be a digression; I mention it here only to illustrate once again the wealth of theoretical and clinical directions that resulted from the germinal insights in Freud's small cluster of papers on technique. For my purposes I want to focus on only one pivotal article, that by Stein (1981) called "The Unobjectionable Part of the Transference." While solidly aligned with those who question the concept ("I share . . . a serious concern about the usefulness of the concept and, even more, about its capacity to be misleading by encouraging the blurring of important transference elements and impeding our search for the nature of the 'unobjectionable' component to which Freud referred" [871]), this paper focuses specifically not on its putative conceptual or technical usefulness but rather on the danger presented in the last part of the sentence just quoted, of "impeding" or blocking altogether the psychoanalytic uncovering of the dynamics and genetics of even the most innocuous or banal (realistically friendly and appropriate) transference elements and thereby limiting the thoroughness of the analytic work. Set this way, Stein's focus becomes in turn almost unobjectionable since even those who enthusiastically support the usefulness of the therapeutic- or working-alliance concept will acknowledge that this phenomenon, too, carries meanings and a developmental dynamic whose elucidation would add to the fullness of the analytic uncoverings of the sources of the patient's mental life.

Stein develops his thesis by drawing a composite picture of a characteristic "good patient," even a seemingly "ideal analytic patient," easily recognizable as a character type. Such patients "do not, alas, constitute the majority of patients we see in practice, but [they] are by no means so rare as some would claim" (873). They are normal-neurotic people with well-defined and circumscribed classically neurotic illness pictures; they are intelligent, articulate, and cooperative in playing the analytic game—that is, in free-associating, giving respectful, thoughtful attention to interpretations, and developing a widening arc of insights in the context of an unfolding and enlarging life history. Most of them present exactly the kind of positive, affectionate transference that Freud called unobjectionable. The danger that Stein develops explicitly is of a mutually admiring and seductive transference-countertransference interplay. Stein put it this way

One has a tendency to fall into a comfortable situation dominated by mutual teasing, appreciation, and intellectual competition. It is likely, therefore, that such patients will evoke on the part of the analyst what corresponds to the "unobjectionable" component of the transference. He finds himself regarding the patient as if he or she were a favorite child, going out of his way to be kindly and protective, taking considerable pride in the patient's accomplishments, and so on. (p. 874)

This, of course, leads to the great risk of a serious analytic incompleteness.

What is generally obscure is the role of this positive, overtly nonerotic transference in maintaining a powerful resistance, not only to the resolution of inhibitions, but also to the analytic exploration of hidden springs of defiance and revenge. . . . What seems altogether unobjectionable may after a time constitute the most difficult aspect of the transference neurosis. (p. 876)

And then a summary statement:

> There is a vast difference in accepting a phenomenon as reality-based, conflict-free, representing only itself, and, on the other hand, treating it more properly as a surface manifestation of a complex set of opposing forces, most of which operate outside of conscious awareness, and which require explanation sooner or later in the course of analysis. (p. 886)

This becomes, then, one of those places where Freud's technical advice has been, for good reason, much modified and substantially superseded by our widened and more finely honed understandings of today. Freud, after describing the unobjectionable part of the transference, went on in his next paper on technique (1913) to say: "So long as the patient's communications and ideas run on without any obstruction, the theme of transference should be left untouched." Stein's comment on this is, "Solving the problem of analyzing the transference neurosis, necessary for more than purely abstract reasons, would have been impossible, I should judge, had we adhered literally to Freud's (1912) principles" (875). The key word is *literally*. Here, to be sure, we are reminded of formulations and prescriptions grounded in a particular historical-developmental matrix that should no longer be taken literally. Every science, of course, has to grow and to surpass even the greatest of its contributors. The undiminished tribute to Freud is that he gave us singlehandedly the structure of a functioning science of the mind and a foundation upon which we could all build so productively and in so many directions.

By now I seem to have wandered far from the explicit focus on the central statement of the transference-love paper, the manifestations of an untoward transference development that, if not handled properly, can have unhappy consequences for the patient, not to speak of the analyst, and beyond that— certainly in Freud's mind during those early days in which psychoanalysis struggled so hard for the establishment and recognition of its legitimacy—for the public repute of psychoanalysis as a helpful therapeutic enterprise. I can plead, of course, the interlocking nature of the whole group of papers on technique, each necessary to the overall understanding of the network of premises and technical prescriptions, and I can plead further that each line of discussion I have touched upon is represented at least implicitly, either in precursor form or in more fully developed fashion, in the transference-love paper. At least I hope that I have been reasonably persuasive to that effect. The paper certainly takes its place among the writings of Freud that warrant the kind of regularly updated reconsideration to which this series of volumes is devoted.

REFERENCES

Alexander, F., and French, T. M. 1946. *Psychoanalytic therapy: Principles and application.* New York: Ronald.

Blum, H. 1973. The concept of erotized transference. *J. Amer. Psychoanal. Assn.* 21:61–76.

Brenner, C. 1979. Working alliance, therapeutic alliance, and transference. *J. Amer. Psychoanal. Assn.* (Suppl.) 27:137–57.

Curtis, H. C. 1979. The concept of therapeutic alliance: Implications for the "widening scope." *J. Amer. Psychoanal. Assn.* (Suppl.) 27:159–92.

Eickhoff, F.-W. 1987. A short annotation to Sigmund Freud's "Observations on transference-love." *Int. Rev. Psycho-Anal.* 14:103–09.

Freud, A. 1936. *The ego and the mechanisms of defense.* New York: International Universities Press, 1946.

Freud, S. 1900. *The interpretation of dreams. S.E.* 5.

————. 1912. The dynamics of transference. *S.E.* 12.

————. 1913. On beginning the treatment (Further recommendations on the technique of psycho-analysis, I). *S.E.* 12.

————. 1914. On the history of the psycho-analytic movement. *S.E.* 14.

————. 1925. Josef Breuer. *S.E.* 19.

————. 1926. Inhibitions, symptoms and anxiety. *S.E.* 20.

Freud, S., and Breuer, J. 1893–95. *Studies on Hysteria. S.E.* 2.

Gill, M. M. 1963. *Topography and systems in psychoanalytic theory.* Psychol. Issues 10. New York: International Universities Press.

Greenson, R. R. 1965. The working alliance and transference neurosis. *Psychoanal. Quart.* 34:155–81.

Hartmann, H. 1960. *Psychoanalysis and moral values.* New York: International Universities Press.

Jones, E. 1953. The life and work of Sigmund Freud. Vol. 1. New York: Basic.

Novey, R. 1991. The abstinence of the psychoanalyst. *Bull. Menn. Clinic* 55:344–62.

Rapaport, D. 1960. *The structure of psychoanalytic theory: A systematizing attempt.* Psychol. Issues 6. New York: International Universities Press.

Rappaport, E. A. 1956. The management of an eroticized transference. *Psychoanal. Q.* 25:515–29.

————. 1959. The first dream in an erotized transference. *Int. J. Psycho-Anal.* 40:240–45.

Schur, M. 1966. *The id and the regulatory principles of mental functioning.* New York: International Universities Press.

Stein, M. H. 1981. The unobjectionable part of the transference. *J. Amer. Psychoanal. Assn.* 29:869–92.

Stone, L. 1961. *The psychoanalytic situation.* New York: International Universities Press.

Wallerstein, R. S. 1967. Reconstruction and mastery in the transference psychosis. *J. Amer. Psychoanal. Assn.* 15:551–83.

———. 1990. The corrective emotional experience: Is reconsideration due? *Psychoanal. Inq.* 10:288–324.

Zetzel, E. R. 1956. Current concepts of transference. *Int. J. Psycho-Anal.* 37:369–76.

———. 1968. The so-called good hysteric. *Int. J. Psycho-Anal.* 49:256–60.

Five Readings of Freud's
"Observations on Transference-Love"

ROY SCHAFER

Like so many other of Freud's works of genius, "Observations on Transference-Love" is wide in scope, deep in understanding, and forceful in the way it challenges conventional modes of thought. But it is a short piece, and the price of its brevity is that it deals with each of its major topics in only an introductory or cursory fashion. It is also a relatively early work. Consequently, the essay calls for clarification, amplification, coordination of its various propositions, interpretation of implied or latent content, and methodological and epistemological reconsideration. And in responding to this call, we should express our own views and concerns as contemporary psychoanalysts now that more than seventy-five years have passed since the essay was written; we should not simply try to establish exactly what Freud "had in mind," for the topic is now and will always be of great concern to all analysts.

I shall present five perspectives on or readings of "Observations on Transference-Love." These readings supplement one another, each bringing out different aspects of Freud's text. In certain respects my readings empha-

I wish to express my gratitude to Dr. William I. Grossman for his penetrating, thorough, and helpful critique of an earlier version of this essay.

size the major contributions of the essay; in other respects, its limitations and its controversial aspects. The essay's difficulties derive either from its having been written during the relatively early years of the development of psycho-analysis or from Freud's philosophical, social, and personal commitments, values, and biases. My five readings are entitled "The Demolition of Conventional Boundaries," "Managing the Erotic Transference," "Counter-transference," "Freud's Patriarchal Outlook," and "Positivism, Perspectivism, and Narration."

THE DEMOLITION OF CONVENTIONAL BOUNDARIES

Even today most people draw sharp lines between the normal and abnormal, between childhood and adulthood, and between psychoanalysis and "real life." By "most people" I refer not only to the general public and many patients undergoing treatment but also to many people who work in the helping professions. Dichotomous thinking has wide appeal; it satisfies a need for simplicity and a sense of clear structure. We can see in many places that dichotomous thinking appealed greatly to Freud too (for example, Pain-Pleasure, Pleasure Principle–Reality Principle, Life Instinct–Death Instinct).

It is, however, an outstanding feature of Freud's writings that, at bottom, they continuously challenge conventional beliefs. Rejecting simplistic conventional dichotomies, Freud is steadily identifying and articulating transitional phenomena, transformations, and the dynamics of change: tracing the retention of the old in the new without denying the new; demonstrating the benefits of thinking in terms of differences of degree rather than of kind; seeing people as occupying mixed, internally contradictory or conflicting positions. In his dream book (1900), for example, we encounter him arguing for the continuity of mental life in sleep and waking; in the "Three Essays" (1905b), undermining any hard and fast distinction between perversion and normal sexuality; in various papers on sexuality, such as "On Transformations of Instinct as Exemplified in Anal Erotism" (1917), approaching psychosexual development as a series of transformations rather than sharply delineated phases and portraying the interpenetration of these phases in a most subtle fashion. And there is no need any longer to dwell on Freud's not accepting an absolute normal-abnormal distinction but rather insisting that the same fundamental issues shape the lives of normals and neurotics.[1]

Many of those who reject Freud's work do so because they mistake his search for continuity within transformations over time as simple-minded reductionism. Typically they cite statements torn out of the total context of Freud's writings and the mode of thought they stand for. In using these citations as warrants for their rejection, they miss the point of Freud's inspired breaks with those conventions of his time that governed the construction of psychological knowledge.

The breaking of various conventional conceptual boundaries can be discerned in "Observations on Transference-Love." I select for special emphasis one piece of demolition that, on my reading, Freud accomplished more impressively and explicitly in this essay than anywhere else. Viewed narrowly, it is the demolition of the boundary between transference love and "real love"; viewed broadly, the demolition of the boundary between the analytic relationship and "real-life" relationships.

In this essay, Freud seems content for some time to develop his technical thesis that transference love must be handled as something unreal, that is, as an irrational, unconsciously motivated repetition of repressed desire and conflict that takes the form of resistance. Only well into the argument (168) does he pause and, with his ever-restless and self-questioning genius, challenge his own insistence on transference-love's *un*reality. It is as though he has just recognized that he had become so involved in technical concerns with differences that he had lost his cherished perspective on continuities in mental life. His perspective regained, he goes on to assert that the difference between normal love and transference love is not so great after all; at most, this difference is a matter of degree, and while it remains useful technically to bear in mind and interpret transference love's exaggerated nature and unrealistic features, doing so should not limit the recognition that normal love, too, has many of the same unrealistic aspects. Normal love, like transference love, has its infantile prototypes; it, too, is repetitive, idealizing, and replete with conflictual transferences; it, too, is a complex mix and not simply a new and pure experience.

1. Elsewhere (1970) I have taken up ways in which Freud never did free himself *entirely* from dichotomous thinking. There, I tried to show that it was Heinz Hartmann in particular who developed more fully and systematically the freer aspect of Freud's analytic thinking. It would be unreasonable for us to expect Freud to have done the whole job singlehandedly.

In developing this position on love, Freud is actually asserting three fundamental continuities simultaneously: that between the infantile and the adult, that between the normal and the neurotic (the rational-realistic and the irrational-unrealistic), and that between psychoanalysis and real life. It is the last of these that we can read as a major step forward in psychoanalytic understanding of the total personality and its development in the context of human relatedness. The other important continuities I just mentioned had already figured for some time in Freud's thought about development, psychopathology, and the treatment process.

Although we could piece together clues in Freud's previous writings to show that he had already reached these interpretive conclusions concerning love as transference and transference as love, and although we could also argue that he had already conveyed this understanding in other writings, in pursuing that course we would, I think, be mistaking tacit knowledge and fragmentary insight for express conviction in a developed and integrated context. Further, we would be overlooking Freud's own sense of fresh awareness in "Observations on Transference-Love" and his pointed emphasis on and implicitly pleased interest in this further contribution to his theories of both love and the psychoanalytic process.

Notwithstanding these various merits, it could be argued that Freud's essay taken as a whole is an indecisive and incomplete document. He presented transference love as both unreal and "genuine" and suggested that, technically, it should be treated simply as unreal, even if it is basically genuine. For technical purposes, transference love is to be regarded as repetition, merely a "new edition" of an old text of love. And yet, because of its continuity with genuine love, our analytic approach could or should allow for new attachment—that is, for the analysand's relating to the analyst as a "new object."

Much later, Loewald (1960) argued just this point when he discussed the theory of the therapeutic action of psychoanalysis. Loewald focused attention on the new and higher levels of organization made possible by analysis and on the possibility of new modes of experience of self and others in relation that attests to the structural changes. This new mode of relatedness and of the experience of self and others is no longer kept excessively rigid or fluid, overwhelming or indifferent by primitive suspicion, depression, ambivalence, and the like. In this context, one may encounter "new" objects and so experience "new" love.

On this point, however, Freud remained conspicuously silent. Out of respect for his perspicacity, I would like to think that he decided not to take on the difficulties of theorizing about the "new" in the same essay in which he was warning the presumably young, inexperienced, or even unanalyzed analyst not to be misled and certainly not to be carried away by the patient's declaration of new-found love. Freud was surely right to be steadily concerned that any significant relaxation of the properly detached analytic attitude might easily lead one to slide into an ethically and therapeutically compromised role in the course of doing analysis. Today more than ever, we are aware of how often therapists do lapse into having affairs with their patients or at least approaching them sexually. Very much in the eye of the alert public, these scandals are no longer considered occasional and isolated. In the far more frequent case, the analyst who gets carried away emotionally but refrains from sexual overtures or responses is still in no position to interpret the patient's conflictual love helpfully.

We cannot, however, be sure of this pragmatic explanation of Freud's silence on "real" love in the therapeutic relationship. Consequently, we must allow for an alternative—namely, that in 1915 Freud may well have been both *personally and theoretically unprepared* to think further about the implications of the real aspects of transference love for technique and the theory of the analytic process. I shall return to Freud's personal unpreparedness when I consider his discussions of technique and countertransference and when I comment on his patriarchal orientation. Concerning his theoretical unpreparedness, it may be inferred from Freud's zeal in developing his central theses that he sensed that taking up the real elements in transference love would or could compromise his thoroughgoing emphasis on the determining of the present by the past. This determinism is seen in the compulsion to repeat, in transference and acting out, and in other signs of the inextinguishable infantile unconscious. His first order of business, in addition to economy of explanation, was demonstrating the unconscious continuity of human lives over time.

An additional limiting factor in this connection may be derived from a consideration of historical context. In 1915, Freud had not yet developed his ego psychology, which, as Hartmann (1939, 1964) was to argue later on, does allow a theoretical place for the new and the autonomous and can do so without rejecting Freud's theoretically precious premises of determinism and continuity.

MANAGING THE EROTIC TRANSFERENCE

Freud repeatedly experienced himself as forcibly confronted by the erotically charged romantic feelings and demands of his female analysands. Some women manifested these feelings and demands quite plainly while others seemed to show only subtle signs of them and were instead engaged urgently, though often unconsciously, in combating or defending against them. Characteristically, and to the lasting benefit of all of us, analysand and analyst alike, Freud set about working out what could be learned from these emotional developments. What could these phenomena reveal about the depths of his analysands' mental lives and the sources of their neuroses?

Freud came to view the female analysand's outpouring of romantic and passionate feelings and demands in two ways. On the one hand, it was a resistance insofar as it enacted the patient's pressure on the analyst to change the analytic relationship into a love affair: By inducing a shift away from the psychical sphere toward the physical, she could substitute neurotic action for therapeutic remembering. With the same stroke, Freud explained, she could "bring down" the analyst from his position of authority in the relationship and prove to herself that the treatment is dangerous and warrants determined resistance. On the other hand, Freud regarded the resistance-serving erotization of the therapeutic relationship as a gateway to the analysand's repressed infantile libidinal desires and conflicts. Once analyzed, that resistant maneuver could reveal her unconsciously maintained "preconditions for loving" and "all the detailed characteristics of her state of being in love" (166). In this view, transference love is like dreams: on the one hand, a complex set of disguises; on the other, a royal road to the therapeutically essential memories of childhood. These are the memories by which Freud could hope to demonstrate to the analysand the origins and driving forces of her neurosis and at the same time demonstrate to the world the truth of his theories.

We can see that Freud viewed the erotic transference as a way of blocking analysis that is motivated unconsciously by all that is essential to the analytic cure. On this understanding, the analysis of transference love as opposition is invaluable. Here lies much of the sense of Freud's remark, "The only really serious difficulties . . . lie in the management of the transference" (159). Freud emphasized that the carrying out of this delicate task depends on the analyst's remembering that this transference love is created by the analytic situation itself. It is a product of the observational field and method, not a simple, direct response of one person to another; in other words, there is no reason to expect the analyst to carry a special transference valence.

We shall soon come to consider the implications of Freud's apparent failure to consider the possibility that, in both form and content, analysands unconsciously collaborate with the analyst through transference love; specifically, they employ it as a communication in the form of a showing rather than a conscious remembering and verbal telling. His focus remained on opposition and the overcoming of inaccessibility.

Today we encounter a special, situationally provoked defensive use of transference-love: women who, on the basis of a smattering of analytic knowledge, enter analysis with the conviction that they are supposed to fall in love with their male analyst; if they do not, this only proves to them that they are bad, rebellious, or otherwise unfit analysands. In these cases, the analyst must first find opportunities to interpret their conflicts over being "good" and "bad" and their fears of spontaneity in what are for them the as-yet-uncharted waters of psychoanalysis. In 1915, however, Freud had to be concerned instead with those ill-prepared analysts who encouraged analysands to fall in love with them or at least thought it necessary to alert them to that eventuality (161).

In this essay, Freud tries to lay the groundwork for consistent reliance on interpretation in overcoming the resistance expressed in the erotic transference. In some places, however, Freud seems to rely on rational argument and pressure as well. For example (167), he seems ready to argue with the analysand about the unreality of her love, asserting that she would be compliant rather than oppositional if she truly loved the analyst. In statements of this sort, and despite his pointing out how important it is that the analyst be patient, Freud comes across partly as a rationalist technician, working rather closer to the intellectually persuasive than the emotional end of the continuum (Schafer, 1992, chap. 14). Although we can appreciate the fact that Freud is portraying an extreme version of an erotic transference and is appropriately concerned to protect the treatment from an untimely and mutually painful ending, upon reflection we can also realize that that very fact serves better the argument *against* resorting to or relying too heavily on intellectual explanation and exhortation. Furthermore, Freud himself emphasized early in his essay that, in this overheated context, rational explanations fall on deaf ears. To Freud's emphasis we might now add that, if anything, those explanations and exhortations usually only add fuel to the fire, in part by seeming to the analysand to confirm her transference fantasies that the analyst *is* attached to her.

In this oscillation on the question of the uses of reason and pressure, Freud may have been exposing some personal discomfort with respect to transference love that I shall soon be discussing. First, however, we must return to the subject of Freud's theoretical readiness for conceptualizing real love in the transference. Freud wrote "Observations on Transference-Love" almost ten years before he presented his ego psychology in developed form. In 1915, he still believed that it was the lifting of repression and the recovery of memories in early childhood—"making the unconscious conscious"—that is the essential curative factor in the therapeutic process. That belief was based theoretically on his topographic conception of the mind. It does, however, necessarily slant technique in a direction that is simultaneously pressuring and rationalistic; it fosters an adversarial slant on resistance and too great reliance on conscious understanding as the route to mastery.

In contrast, Freud's later structural formulations emphasized the need to modify defenses, reduce superego pressures, and in general strengthen the ego: "Where id was, there shall ego be" (1923). By then Freud had realized that the total personality is involved in neurotic problems. Consequently, he induced a considerable shift of emphasis in the direction of insight based on emotional experiencing as essential in bringing about deep and lasting change in the mind as a whole. This new role of emotional experience extends beyond the emotions of transference love itself; it is the kind of experience that is possible only in a prepared structural context, developed through analytic interpretations of repetitions within life history. This shift from topography to structure underlies many of the advances in psychoanalytic technique that have been made subsequent to 1915; especially to be noted about this shift is the analyst's constant and heightened concern with preparing the ground for transference interpretations rather than just seeming to read the unconscious straightaway.

When considering Freud's ideas in historical context, we must also be alert to what seem to be intimations of the future, for Freud was, in a sense, always catching up with himself. Already in such papers as "Formulations on the Two Principles of Mental Functioning" (1911), "On Narcissism" (1914), and "Mourning and Melancholia" (1917 [1915]), he gives the appearance of straining toward that formal theory of the ego that could lead to a decisive break with rationalistic pressuring and a shift toward consistent interpretation.

Meanwhile, the inconsistency or vacillation persisted, and we must be impressed by how large a part of "Observations on Transference-Love" is devoted to cautioning the young, inexperienced, or unanalyzed analyst against the temptation to yield to the patient's entreaties. For Freud, however, more was involved than reinforcing the doctor's sense of ethical responsibility. He was not only urging the analyst not to forfeit any of his public dignity and therapeutic authority by responding in kind but developing his general theory, in this instance emphasizing the point that romantic or sexual gratification could have no therapeutic value because the patient's neurosis, rooted as it is in the highly conflictual infantile past, renders her incapable of genuine gratification in the here and now (165).

I have already suggested, however, that one cannot rest easy with the belief that Freud was simply intent on remaining realistic and practical as he went on developing his clinical insights and their theoretical context. I believe that he was also manifesting some unresolved countertransference of his own. It is, for example, noteworthy that, despite his having argued in an earlier essay (1914a, 150) that repetition and acting out can be understood as forms of remembering, in this essay he emphasizes almost exclusively the here-and-now function of transference love as a resistance—that is, its blocking of remembering by insistence on repeating. Although, as I mentioned earlier, Freud realized that this resistance could be analyzed down to its infantile roots, the split-off aspect of this realization conveys no recognition that the analysand might also be collaborating by communicating, via enactments, something of value. Elsewhere (1992, chap. 14), I have attempted to show that Freud's continued concentration on the oppositional aspects of resistance in all its forms can be considered as a manifestation of an adversarial countertransference. To deal effectively with the question of Freud's countertransference, specifically to transference love, we must next look at his explicit discussion of countertransference in "Observations on Transference-Love": what he says, how he says it, and what he neglects to say.

It will, however, help pave the way to pause here to consider enactment as communication. One finds special emphasis on this point in the writings of leading modern Kleinians, such as Betty Joseph (1989). But there the argument is not adequately developed, for it does not follow that whatever is interpretable, as an enactment may be, is intended as a communication. The analyst can learn from observing noncommunicative behavior, too, and that point is not ignored by Joseph. The issues involved are too complex to go into here, but I must at least say that, when the analyst is keeping a steady focus on transference-countertransference dynamics, constantly seeking to define the object-related, interactive aspects of the events of the analytic session, it is heuristically useful to regard the analysand as always experiencing simply being, as well as using words, as a means of relating to another, hence of getting something across to someone else. I further believe that most analysands respond well to an atmosphere in which *how* they are as well as *what* they say is taken to be an active part of relating to the analyst in an informative way.

COUNTERTRANSFERENCE

In a footnote to "Observations on Transference-Love" (160–61n.), James Strachey comments that this is one of the very few essays in which Freud referred explicitly to countertransference. It seems self-evident why this is so. In 1915 Freud was working with a theory framed almost entirely in terms of the driving force of libido. Although he took account of the ego instincts, as he then called them; although he had already developed his ideas about the secondary process, reality testing, and the reality principle; and although he was consistently cognizant of aggression and guilt in human relations, he still had no general and systematized theory of aggression and restraining psychic structure. In 1915, conflict was pretty much a matter of repression versus the libidinal drives; and, of course, the very roots of Freud's theory are embedded in the idea that the flesh is weak and repression is never accomplished once and for all. Additionally, with Freud's development of his ideas on narcissism already under way (1914b), we can understand his taking up specifically the narcissistic aspects of the analyst's erotic countertransference—that is, the analyst's temptation to accept and enjoy being idealized by the aroused patient.

From the standpoint of today's analyst, however, Freud's approach to countertransference, while groundbreaking, is clearly rudimentary. Numerous countertransferential factors that now figure prominently in our thinking are not even mentioned, nor are there signs that Freud appreciated the usefulness of countertransference for the analyst's interpretive work. It seems that, in part, it was Freud's positivistic scientific ideal of total objectivity, founded on personal detachment, that led him to advocate that one should try to expunge all countertransference by personal analysis, self-analysis, and a sound grasp of his theories of development, psychopathology, and the therapeutic process. Already at this point we can infer the presence of some characterological countertransference, for it is inherent in Freud's general theory that all human relationships are more or less colored by infantile transferences. Yet Freud seems to want to exempt the analyst from this fundamental proposition. Again, as in dealing with transference love, we encounter some split-off rationalistic bias in Freud's simply negative attitude toward countertransference—one might say a countertransference to countertransference.

It may be objected that it is unwarranted to think of countertransference in this connection, that it might be quite enough to refer to characterological tendencies that can become sources of countertransference in specific relationships. I believe that this objection stems from preference for the traditional conceptions of both character and countertransference; these conceptions are narrower and more split off from each other than those I regard as more useful. The first difference to consider here is that traditionally countertransference has been looked on with disfavor, whereas in the broader usage pioneered by Kleinian object-relations theorists countertransference is a routinely expectable phenomenon, a phenomenon in which the influence of unconscious inner-world dynamics can always be discerned by psychoanalytic means. Consequently, to attribute countertransference to Freud seems not at all to charge him with a fault but rather to face him squarely as, in principle, no different from anyone else engaged in analytic work.

A second difference to consider pertains to character. Traditionally, although lacking a uniform definition, character is a term used to refer somehow to an array of stable and interrelated traits or modes of action (broadly defined); it is an array that can be analyzed as compromise formations made up of id, ego, and superego tendencies. In contrast, from the object-relations standpoint, character would refer to the patterning of preferred, customary, real, and fantasied relations with others; these patternings could still be analyzed as expressing enduring aspects of inner-world dynamics.

Taking these two differences into account, one may go on to think of generalized or characterological countertransferences. This way of thinking was adopted long ago and usefully developed, though not precisely in these terms, by Annie Reich (1951). In her articulation of types of countertransference, she intended to emphasize how characterological countertransference inevitably pervades the work of every analyst owing to her or his distinctive life history of conflict, compromise formation, sublimation, and consequent modes of relating to others.

On this basis, I surmise that in Freud's case we are witnessing a characterological countertransference with regard to countertransference itself. He viewed countertransference in a manner that reflects the idealization of reason buttressed by some moralistic leanings; this view eventuates in putting more emphasis on the scope of rational control than can be supported by psychoanalytic experience. Such an emphasis may itself indicate that over-estimation of rationality is rooted in unconscious conflict. That is why at this point we hear echoes of what I took up earlier as consequences of Freud's topographic orientation, such as his pressuring suggestions that conscious-ness can be effective in combating resistances.

Although many contemporary analysts continue to take Freud's problem-atically narrow and negative position on countertransference, it seems correct to say that the trend in contemporary psychoanalysis is for analysts to ap-proach countertransference more broadly and positively. In one respect, they use countertransference as a way to monitor the patient's unconsciously enacted communications. Here they are actually following Freud's advice to analysts in another of his papers on technique (1912, 115–16): Bend your unconscious toward the analysand's on the understanding that it is a finer instrument for receiving information about the analysand than focused, con-scious attention. The contemporary extension of Freud's advice goes further, however; now analysts also attend to their own emotional reactions to an analysand as containing useful information about the analysand. Freud did not develop his recommendations along this line, and I believe that we have to thank especially the Kleinian object-relations school of analysis for having done so (see, e.g., Heimann, 1950; Racker, 1968; Segal, 1986; Joseph, 1989).

Today, countertransference is viewed as a significant element in another way as well. This view also resembles Freud's without being identical to it. Analysts tend currently to be constantly alert to the possibility that they may be provoking the analysand's immediate feelings. They do not regard them-selves as exempt from enacting their own conflictual desires in the way they conduct each analysis. With regard to transference love specifically, male analysts will be alert to how they might be fanning the flames of the female analysand's desires. They already know many of the reasons why they might do so—to avoid problems of aggression; to engage in guilty reparative efforts by romanticizing the relationship; to seek to charm or dominate a woman in order to bolster their own flagging self-esteem; to ward off recognition that they are dealing with an analysand who at that time is emotionally "dead"; or to ward off recognition of the analysand's maternal transference by heating up the heterosexual, apparently paternal transference. It seems to me that male analysts frequently resort to countertransference on this last-mentioned prov-ocation. As I shall argue soon, it may be that Freud did too.

I have already indicated, however, that Freud did not approach this complex conception of countertransference in his writings. He was committed to developing and forcefully advocating his idea of the analyst as a scientific healer and an ethical man objectively observing a specimen of irrationality and inductively coming to purely rational conclusions, albeit with the help of his own unconscious mental processes. During the analysis, the observer's personal feelings other than respect and responsibility are to be kept "in check," if not eliminated, for they corrupt the treatment. Freud's personal and theoretical rationalist constraints and overestimation of conscious reason pushed the more or less fluid experiential aspects of analytic work into the margins or off the page altogether.

In addition to its narrow and negative view of countertransference, the rudimentary nature of Freud's approach is also evident in his neglect of the role of aggression in the analyst's erotized *counter*transference. Today, we would be alert to parallels in the countertransference to the constitution of the analysand's transference, and in particular to parallel hostility; for we are careful now not to neglect the insight that the analysand's seductive efforts also, and perhaps primarily, express the hostility of negative transference: hostility in the guise of "intractable" love and desire. In this respect, we seem to concur with Freud's alertness to hostility in transference-love, as when he pointed out how it may be used in an effort to undermine the analyst's professional authority. But Freud was viewing this hostility as part of a strategy designed to block access to infantile libidinal memories; that is, it is the "fight" aspect of the patient's sexual repressions. We, on the other hand, might view transference love as being pushed forward in order to block access to negative transference; alternatively, we might suspect the female analysand is making desperately forced efforts to feel something, anything, as a cover or "cure" for feeling herself to be dead or an emptied-out victim; and finally, not to go on too long about it, we might emphasize the analysand's willingness in therapy, as in the rest of her life, to offer romantic and sexual feelings to a man in order to be held and soothed, in which case we could be focusing on a defensively deaggressivized, unconscious maternal transference. We are likely to see transference love as a fluid combination and layering of more than one of these factors, and perhaps others. In any case, we would be constantly attending to the vicissitudes of both aggression and relations with the mother.

We can believe that Freud was being influenced by his sensitivity to the criticisms of psychoanalysis by the public and other professionals for its scandalous openness about sexual matters. We can accept that he was sensitive as well to similar objections raised by family members of his analysands, those critics who were always in a position to undermine the continuation of Freud's treatments and his scientific explorations. Also, a footnote reference (159) suggests that Freud still had an acute memory of Josef Breuer's countertransferential flight from Anna O. and its disruptive effect on their scientific collaboration. To all this we might add the surmise that Freud was smarting from the relatively recent scandal surrounding Carl Jung's affair with his patient Sabina Spielrein and its continuing reverberations.

By placing this paper in historical and personal context as well as in the context of Freud's dedication to making psychoanalysis a pure empirical science and an effective scientific therapy, we can understand his paternalistically narrow approach to countertransference, the warning and admonishing tone and content of this essay, and so on. But making sense of the direction and limits of his discussion does not invalidate our inference concerning the operation of characterological countertransference in Freud's thinking. Indeed, it goes some way toward understanding the role of Freud's own countertransferences. Just because he was concerned with struggles and worries about the public, his professional standing, the conduct of his followers, and his need to make a rational science out of what he was doing as an analyst, he was relating to his patient with culturally well-established attitudes that were in keeping with his own characterological countertransferences and the extratherapeutic aims they entailed. How else could it be? For present purposes, cultural and historical contexts explain away nothing; actually, they alert us to and fill in our understanding of repetitive conflictual behavior.

We have additional reason to infer the controlling influence of countertransference on Sigmund Freud's thinking about countertransference. Freud's own writings show that, for internal reasons, he felt it necessary to be dismissive of mothers and to remain preoccupied with fathers, and so to dwell throughout his writings on paternal transference in male and female patients alike. A number of analysts who have examined Freud's major clinical case studies have shown that maternal and preoedipal transference and countertransference are not well-developed ideas in his writings (see, e.g., Blum, 1980; Silverman, 1980; Bernheimer and Kahane, 1985; Mahony, 1986; Frankiel, 1992). In his view these were oedipal transferences and, in the case of women, primarily were positive in nature. But we know now that the male analyst must always be prepared to recognize that he is also serving as a female, probably maternal, figure in the transference. Freud, however, when pressed finally by female colleagues to take more account of maternal transference, could only say that he left it to them, as women, to explore that issue (1931, 226–27). Similarly, in "The Ego and the Id" (1923), after portraying the Oedipus complex of boy and girl alike as bisexual, Freud went on to present a predominantly patriarchal conception of the superego as the heir of that complex.

Today we see how difficult it would have been for Freud to have remained, as he did, primarily on the oedipal level if he had opened his work wider to include signs of maternal transference, for we understand much of that transference to be preoedipal in nature. We may, therefore, surmise that a patriarchal bias was one of Sigmund Freud's countertransferences. It is to this specific countertransferential factor that we now turn. It will be useful, I think, to single out this patriarchal factor, because it has come to occupy a prominent place in certain telling feminist critiques of Freud's work (see, e.g., Bernheimer and Kahane, 1985).

FREUD'S PATRIARCHAL ORIENTATION

Freud gave serious and frank consideration to female psychology at a time when the culturally normative position was one of shame disguised as modesty or tact. It was a time and a setting when a hush-hush attitude and false dignity were expected. In his insightful way, he made fundamental contributions to the psychoanalytic psychology of female development and psychopathology. Many of these contributions, such as those pertaining to the female Oedipus complex and bisexual factors in the personality, have stood the test of time, even though today we would present a more complex picture of these matters and of women in general. And yet it seems that, with all his dedication and insight and all his creativity and courage, Freud did not recognize and shake off a patriarchal bias in his thinking about women. Here I am using the term *patriarchal* to refer to a mixture of consciously benevolent paternalism, consistent authoritarianism, and pervasive condescension.

I addressed a number of aspects of this bias in some detail in a 1974 paper entitled "Problems in Freud's Psychology of Women." I shall not here offer a full summary of that discussion. Suffice it to say that I questioned Freud's conclusions that the morality and judgment of women are second-rate; I argued against the limitations imposed by his assumption that women's full development depends on their being given a baby, especially a son, by a father-substitute, as compensation for their "castrated" state and as balm for what Freud hastily and narrowly termed their "penis envy"; on linguistic as well as psychological grounds, I characterized as sexist his equating passive, submissive, and masochistic behavior with femininity; and I emphasized his relative disregard of preoedipal development and the centrality therein of the girl's tie to her mother. Before my 1974 essay and certainly since then, many feminist writers, including some who value psychoanalysis, have criticized Freud's orientation to women as patriarchal, masculinist, sexist, and phallocentric—words with overlapping but not identical connotations.

In "Observations on Transference-Love," it is particularly his patriarchal tone and imagery, as well as his limitation of analytic attention, that stimulate critical comment. Freud's tone and imagery are shockingly condescending in several places: for example, when he refers to the "comical" aspect of the woman's transference-love for the male analyst (159); when he is dismissive toward those women who, apparently driven by transference love, do not respond to his interventions, referring to these patients as, "in the [unnamed] poet's words," women who understand only "the logic of soup, with dump- lings for arguments" (167) and throwing up his rhetorical hands in wonder that a woman can be so consumed by elemental passion that her need for love is "intractable" (clearly no longer thinking here as an analyst but rather defensively, I would suggest, and, in effect, no longer referring to women as people); when he makes the simplistic assumption (intended to be relayed to the analysand) that, if it was true love, she would become "docile" and seek to get well in order to "acquire value in the doctor's eyes" (167); when he writes that "when a woman sues for love" the analyst has "a distressing part . . . to play," especially if that woman is refined rather than crudely sensual, Freud seeming here to exempt this bit of gallantry from countertransference anal- ysis (170); and perhaps even when he introduces the metaphor of a dog race with the prize of "a garland of sausages," a race that would be disrupted if a sausage (the analyst's desirous countertransference) were thrown onto the track (169). Freud's resort to this condescending rhetoric complied with the patriarchal norm of his times, but, as I have already pointed out, it must also be approached as manifesting countertransference within the psychoanalytic process.

Equally important in this connection is the question of Freud's selecting for his discussion of transference love a female patient who is in great romantic distress or unreasoning passionate arousal. Is it really enough for Freud to explain that he is selecting only one instance of a problem with a broad scope? Why select just this one, and why discuss it in just this way? And is it enough that he emphasizes the realistic problems I alluded to in the previous sections of my essay? I think not. Where, I ask, is there in his writings any equivalent discussion of the male patient's transference love of the male analyst? Where did Freud sort out that potentially disruptive homosexual love in the interest of furthering objective psychoanalytic work? However similar the issues sometimes may be in male and female transference love, are they not sometimes radically different? Why did Freud deal so consistently and relatively narrowly with male transference in terms of rebelliousness toward the father's authority? Why did he not give careful consideration to lesser, simpler forms of female erotic transference to a male analyst and other forms of love that, whatever their infantile psychosexual origins, can play large parts in the analytic process? And why, finally, pay so little attention to erotically colored maternal transference?

On the basis of these considerations and questions, and others presented elsewhere (1993, in press), I propose that Freud's patriarchal orientation predisposed him to select for discussion of transference love the aroused, importunate, excessive, but somehow attractive woman and to portray her as the sole initiator of all the significant, simply sexual currents of the analytic relationship. Consequently, he could feel consciously comfortable in his patriarchal orientation and spend much time in this essay issuing reminders, warnings, and exhortations, meanwhile neglecting to provide detailed and balanced coverage of transference love in all its forms and with all its functions. Even had he not covered these issues comprehensively, he could have done what he did so often in other contexts: raised searching questions and pointed out persisting ambiguities and the need for further study.

POSITIVISM, PERSPECTIVISM, AND NARRATION

In the preceding sections of this essay I have presented supplementary observations and various critiques garnered from the subsequent history of the topics touched on in "Observations on Transference-Love." My presentation demonstrates plainly that Freud's essay provides only one limited version of only one facet of the analytic relationship. Since 1915, numerous authors, including Freud himself, have presented modified, extended, or alternative versions of transference love and its mental and situational contexts. As psychoanalysis changes, transference love keeps being retold, as it should be, for new developments in psychoanalysis call for new versions of familiar narratives (Schafer, 1983, 1992). The emphasis shifts even with variations of perspective within ego-psychological Freudian analysis; certainly it shifts between schools of psychoanalysis. Psychoanalysts live now in an age of multiple perspectives, and as yet they have failed to agree on some common ground; it may even be fruitless to search for any such ground (Schafer, 1990).

We have already noted how the telling of transference love changed once analysts broke away from Freud's narrowing approach. If we now take up another example, that of the Kleinian object-relational version of Freudian analysis, some significant further aspects of perspectivism and narration may become accessible. I present here only a schematic version. I suggest that, in the Kleinian narrative, the analyst must try to locate the manifestations of transference love within the framework of the paranoid-schizoid and depressive positions (see, e.g., Segal, 1986). Thus, in one instance, the analyst could approach that love as an attempt to forestall persecution by propitiation of a figure into whom the woman has projected her own rageful self and which she then has defensively idealized as a source of protective love. In another instance, the analyst might approach the erotic transference as the expression of sadomasochistic sexual excitement based on unconscious fantasies that the analytic relationship is an enactment of sadomasochistic practices. Or perhaps the Kleinian analyst would see a particular woman's transference love primarily as manifesting a reparative move, stemming from within the depressive position—that is, as an attempt to cure the object through love (see, e.g., Feldman, 1990). We might recall in this connection that Freud saw transference love as the patient's seeking to cure *herself* through love; reparation of the love-object did not figure prominently in his narratives.

Note that none of these Kleinian versions denies the sexual charge and the romantic fantasy involved in transference love. What they do is situate these factors in the two positions or dynamic configurations that are fundamental to their approach to interpretation: the paranoid/schizoid and the depressive. They do so in order to provide their own developmental contexts and an appropriate array of interpretive storylines to work with. In Freud's perspective, the essential context is the inevitable infantile phases of libidinal development, especially the oedipal phase and, most particularly, the positive oedipal phase. In the Kleinian perspective, the analysis would emphasize the vicissitudes of aggression rather more than libido.

In these two perspectives we see contrasting but not unrelated hierarchies of variables. Associated with each hierarchy are typical narratives and individual storylines such as those I used in giving specific examples in the preceding paragraphs. We cannot avoid seeing the shortcomings of Freud's efforts to establish a science that yields only one definitive account of its constituent subject matter, such as the matter of transference love. For in the event, the practices of psychoanalysts show psychoanalysis to be an interpretive, hermeneutic enterprise that is made manifest in a variety of preferred narratives, some of them significantly different from Freud's. Those preferred narratives enter into method and thereby into the eliciting and shaping of clinical phenomena that will then be interpreted in keeping with these very narratives. This is the hermeneutic circle, and it provides knowledge that is not available to the traditional positivistic approach.

The hermeneutic view of psychoanalytic understanding is just that: a view or a perspective, not a new technical prescription; that is, it describes what analysts do. In this view, Freud's positivistic perspective seems to hold up unmodified only when we arbitrarily rule all other perspectives out of court and when we also go so far as to ignore or minimize the considerable variations even among Freud's close adherents. Indeed, in every section of my essay there are arguments implying a poor fit between Freud's creation and his favoring of the positivistic conception of this creation.

It should be noted, however, that Freud did not always advocate a straightforward positivist conception of psychoanalysis. This we can see, for example, in some of his methodological discussions (e.g., 1909a, 104–05; 1915, 117) and in his clinical examples. There, he did not maintain his "official" scientific position; he did recognize, at least implicitly, the necessarily hermeneutic aspects of this discipline he was creating.

Nevertheless, it is with his usual formal propositions that we must be concerned, for it was by means of these propositions that Freud was trying to establish the conventions for how to constitute and so be able to talk about those subjective experiences that he deemed crucial to the psychoanalytic process. Seen in this light, these conventions are epistemological directives to the analyst as to how to process the ambiguous associative material: how to decide what will count as evidence and insight. But if more than one interpretive method and outcome is, as we see, always possible, then the epistemological propositions must be challenged and the presuppositions on which they are based revised.

I content, therefore, that Freud was not presenting unmediated reports of detached observations. Instead, he could only have been retelling lives, past and present, as they emerged, mediated by linguistic and epistemological assumptions, in his clinical dialogue with his patients. And these were dialogues that had been shaped by his preferred master narratives and the specific storylines they laid down for interpretive work (Schafer, 1992).

If, finally, we ask ourselves, What is transference love? the preceding discussions, taken together, suggest that we can begin to respond to that question only tentatively and only after getting answers to a long series of other questions that have been asked from various related but not identical points of view.

These queries include: Who is asking the question? In connection with which specific clinical example? Which school of psychoanalytic thought has regulated and guided this analysis up to this point? And just which hierarchy of variables or narrative preferences is the questioner prepared to accept as the most useful for psychoanalytic purposes? Questions of this sort were made possible by Freud's "Observations on Transference-Love," by his other papers on technique, and by his entire body of work. They are among his legacies (Schafer, 1992, chap. 9). Fittingly, other psychoanalysts have not been content to rest on Freud's laurels. For his part, he never did either.

REFERENCES

Bernheimer, C., and Kahane, C., eds. 1985. *In Dora's case: Freud-hysteria-feminism.* New York: Columbia University Press.

Blum, H. 1980. The borderline childhood of the Wolf Man. In *Freud and his Patients,* vol. 2, ed. M. Kanzer and J. Glenn, 341–58. New York: Jason Aronson.

Feldman, M. 1990. Common ground: The centrality of the Oedipus complex. *Int. J. Psycho-Anal.* 71:37–48.

Frankiel, R. V. 1992. Analyzed and unanalyzed themes in the treatment of Little Hans. *Int. Rev. Psycho-Anal.*

Freud, S. 1900. *The interpretation of dreams. S.E.* 4–5.

———. 1905a. *Fragment of an analysis of a case of hysteria. S.E.* 7.

———. 1905b. Three essays on the theory of sexuality. *S.E.* 7.

———. 1909a. *Analysis of a phobia in a five-year-old boy. S.E.* 10.

———. 1909b. Notes upon a case of obsessional neurosis. *S.E.* 10.

———. 1911. Formulations on the two principles of mental functioning. *S.E.* 11.

———. 1912a. The dynamics of transference. *S.E.* 12.

———. 1912b. Recommendations to physicians practising psycho-analysis. *S.E.* 12.

———. 1914a. Remembering, repeating and working-through (Further recommendations on the technique of psycho-analysis, II). *S.E.* 12.

———. 1914b. On narcissism: An introduction. *S.E.* 14.

———. 1915. Instincts and their vicissitudes *S.E.* 14.

———. 1917a[1915]. Mourning and melancholia. *S.E.* 14.

———. 1917b. On transformations of instinct as exemplified in anal erotism. *S.E.* 17.

———. 1918. From the history of an infantile neurosis. *S.E.* 17.

———. 1923. *The ego and the id. S.E.* 19.

———. 1931. Female sexuality. *S.E.* 21.

Hartmann, H. 1939. *Ego psychology and the problem of adaptation.* New York: International Universities Press, 1964.

———. 1964. *Essays on ego psychology: Selected problems in psychoanalytic theory.* New York: International Universities Press.

Heimann, P. 1950. On counter-transference. *Int. J. Psycho-Anal.* 31:81–84.

Joseph, B. 1989. *Psychic equilibrium and psychic change: Selected papers on Betty Joseph,* ed. E. G. Spillius and M. Feldman. London: Tavistock/Routledge.

Loewald, H. 1960. On the therapeutic action of psychoanalysis. *Int. J. Psycho-Anal.* 41:16–33.

Mahony, P. 1986. *Freud and the Rat Man.* New Haven: Yale University Press.

Racker, H. 1968. *Transference and countertransference.* New York: International Universities Press.

Reich, A. 1951. On counter-transference. *Int. J. Psycho-Anal.* 32:25–31.

Schafer, R. 1970. An overview of Heinz Hartmann's contributions to psycho-analysis. *Int. J. Psycho-Anal.* 51:425–46. Reprinted in *A new language for psychoanalysis,* 57–101. New Haven: Yale University Press, 1976.

———. 1974. Problems in Freud's psychology of women. *J. Amer. Psychoanal. Assn.* 22:459–85. Reprinted in *Retelling a life: Dialogue and narration in psychoanalysis.* New York: Basic.

———. 1983. *The analytic attitude.* New York: Basic.

———. 1990. The search for common ground. *Int. J. Psycho-Anal.* 71:49–52. Revised version reprinted in *Retelling a life: Dialogue and narration in psychoanalysis.* New York: Basic.

———. 1992. *Retelling a life: Dialogue and narration in psychoanalysis.* New York: Basic.

———. 1993. On gendered discourse. *Psychiatry and the Humanities* 14.

Segal, H. 1986. *The work of Hanna Segal: A Kleinian approach to clinical practice.* London: Free Association.

Silverman, M. 1980. A fresh look at the case of Little Hans. In *Freud and his patients,* vol. 1., ed. M. Kanzer and J. Glenn, 95–120. New York: Jason Aronson.

Footnote to a Footnote to
"Observations on Transference-Love"

MAX HERNÁNDEZ

The first of the recommendations made by Freud (1912b) urged physicians who practice psychoanalysis to maintain an "evenly suspended attention" attuned to the unconscious of the patient. This was a revolutionary technical innovation which corresponded exactly with his metapsychological formulations in chapter 7 of *The Interpretation of Dreams* (Freud, 1900). The last of the "Further recommendations . . . " published by Freud between 1913 and 1915 dealt with something that had happened to, or with, someone who could be called the first psychoanalytic patient, if it were not for the fact that psychoanalysis did not then exist. Freud had not become yet the first psychoanalyst. He had not gone through the painful process of self-analysis or laid out the theoretical and technical foundations of his creation.

Breuer had met difficulties in the treatment of Anna O. Shrouded in a veil of discretion, they had not been submitted to scientific scrutiny. Thus the development of psychoanalytic therapy had been held back. In the last paper of the "Further Recommendations" series, Freud chose those situations that

This essay is based on seminars given at the Instituto de la Sociedad Peruana de Psicoanálisis and at the Centro Psicoanálisis y Sociedad in Lima. The footnote mentioned in the title is that on page 159 in the *S.E.* printing of Freud's article.

arise when "a woman patient shows by unmistakable indications, or openly declares, that she has fallen in love, as any other mortal woman might, with the doctor who is analyzing her" (159) to discuss the "struggle between the doctor and the patient, between intellect and instinctual life, between understanding and seeking to act [which] is played almost exclusively in the phenomena of transference" (1912a). Transference love serves for Freud to exemplify and illustrate the "really serious difficulties" the analyst has to meet in the management of the transference. But there is something else. In his history of the psychoanalytic movement, when referring to his mentors, Breuer, Charcot, and Chrobak, Freud states that all three men had communicated to him "a piece of knowledge which, strictly speaking, they themselves did not possess" (1914a). Therefore, the paper on transference love has a dual aspect. One is technical: how to manage the transference. The other is more ambitious: to transmit to us knowingly some knowledge that was communicated to him unknowingly.

What is it that this paper can tell us about love, transference, female sexuality, and also about *bürgerliche Moral* (conventional morality)? Let us begin with love. As the argument of the paper explains, contrary to general opinion, matters of love are not "written on a special page on which no other writing is tolerated" (160). In this respect, the paper constitutes a hallmark of modern sensibility. Love, like everything else in the psychic realm, is subject to the compulsion to repeat, an axiom that is "one of the foundations of psycho-analytic theory." This notion had appeared as the kernel of a technical paper the year before the transference love essay was published (Freud, 1914b). Accordingly, love is merely a reprint of something inscribed once upon a time in the unconscious.

To be aware of this is for the doctor "a very useful warning against any tendency to a counter-transference." At the time, countertransference was considered to be an unnecessary complication. In this context, it is clearly understood as that which may induce an action on the part of the analyst. So, the analyst had better be prepared. The patient, for *her* part (and let us not forget it is *her* part), either abandons the idea of having an analysis or else accepts her "inescapable fate": falling in love with her doctor.

Freud calls our attention to the fact that neuroses, at least for women, if one adheres to the letter of the paper, interfere with the "capacity for love," whether "the jealous father or husband" knows it or not (161). The analyst knows, though, that if the love interfered with by the neurotic process is expressed and analyzed, it will contribute to the patient's recovery. The link between loving and knowing, shown in the analysis of little Hans (Freud, 1909), is emphasized again. Yet things are more complicated than this. If in actual life neuroses interfere with the capacity for love, in the treatment love interferes with the capacity for that specific form of knowledge called insight. The "outbreak of a passionate demand for love" is the work of resistance. The patient loses her docility, her acceptance of explanations, her comprehension, her intelligence, her insight. She "seems to be swallowed up in her love." Passion has supplanted memory. Even the continuation of treatment is endangered. An essential duality articulates this paradox: love is the motor of the analytic cure as well as the main obstacle to it.

Let us assume that the process of analysis has been developing, so to say, uneventfully. Suddenly "a complete change of scene" occurs, as if "some piece of make-believe had been stopped by the sudden irruption of reality." How are we to understand this apparent inversion of the logic of the argument? Let us stay close to the text, where the emergence of transference love in the midst of an analysis is described as having the quality of a piece of reality impinging on the illusory condition of the process. Transference, compared elsewhere to a playground in which the patient's compulsion to repeat is permitted, is now compared—at any rate, in its effects—with that which stops a theatrical performance from going on. We may surmise that during the phases of an analysis in which transference love is foremost, the subject, the analysand who speaks, and the subject of which "she" speaks seem to have become one. There is no space between them. The space in which analysis is possible has narrowed. But it is not reality that appears. Another subject now occupies the center of the scene, someone to whom the patient actively addresses her passive wishes: the analyst.

Thus we move from love to transference. Or, to put it more exactly, here we are dealing with the composite concept of transference love. Freud (1914b, 154) had spoken of a new *Übertragungsbedeutung* (transference meaning) that the analyst gives the symptoms of the patient. In that fashion, a transferential meaning is attributed to the illness. But that which is a hermeneutical proposal in his 1914 paper, a technical device for the analyst, has the quality of the real from the point of view of the patient. So intense is the patient's feeling that it can lead the analyst to error. He can think of the transference love as love pure and simple. Hence, it can have the quality of reality for him. There seems to be only one way out of this conundrum. The analyst should conduct the analysis along a middle course: between the Scylla of detached hermeneuticism and the Charybdis of analytic "realism." Only then will the virtuality of transference "create an intermediate region between illness and real life through which the transition from the one to the other is made" (Freud, 1914b).

The interpretation of the transference love should thus aim at restoring the space between the patient and her discourse. This is more than working on a resistance. It has to do with recreating the analytic space. To succeed it is necessary to redress the substitution of the analyst for the analysand as the subject of the analysis. It is only when he or she is outside the center of the patient's psychic life that the analyst is in a position to give the symptoms of the neurosis the new "transference-meaning" alluded to in Freud's 1914 paper. The interpretation of the transference may facilitate the patient's insight into the special individuality in the expression of *his* capacity to love (see Freud, 1912a).

The use of the masculine pronoun above may lead us to understand something about the "dark continent" of feminine sexuality. The "his" belongs to the paper "The Dynamics of Transference." There, it is applicable to either male or female individuals. It is not necessary to repeat that the paper with which this "footnote" is concerned deals with the treatment of a woman patient by a male analyst who is furthermore a doctor. No wonder then that the patient is confined to the extreme condition of pure demand and depicted as a begging creature. The first inklings of the yet-to-be-explored aspects of primitive orality are at work here, as are narcissistic preoccupations. It is then that "to assure herself of her irresistibility" [let us pay attention to the intransitivity of the formulation] she will try to "destroy the doctor's authority" and bring him "down to the level of a lover" ("Observations on Transference-Love," 163). The biblical echoes of "the Fall" ring heavily all through the paragraph devoted to this theme: the eternal Eve tempting Adam in the Garden of Eden. To say this today is easy indeed. When we have been sensitized to gender issues, the sociocultural matrix of such expressions as "the animal side of her self," "domination" (*Herrschaft*), "conquest," "women of elemental passionateness," or "the full enmity of a woman scorned" become altogether evident.

Nevertheless, if we transcend both the literality of the text and the circumstances defined by the epoch in which it was written, it becomes possible to follow the tenuous lines of a shape that will become clearer in Freud's subsequent papers. If the "father-imago" seems in some way to "tally with the real relations of the subject to his doctor" (Freud, 1912a), it also underlines a symbolic dimension: that which defines the articulation of the Oedipus complex. The object of the patient's desire is not the analyst. It is not even the wish to be the passive object of the analyst's love. It is rather to possess, without any mediation, the emblematic representation of love and knowledge, of satiety and completeness—in other words, to abolish those differences of sex, gender, and generation predicated upon a successful oedipal solution.

In a way, at least some of the "darkness" of feminine sexuality lies in the eyes of the beholder. In the past few years the social tissue upon which male hegemony was implanted has been infiltrated with feminist issues. This has meant changes in the self-perception of both sexes. Even *bürgerliche Moral* may have changed, but maybe not. All the same, what is really important for us, now as much as when the paper was written, is on the one hand "to replace the moral embargo by considerations of analytic technique" and on the other to hold onto the "ethical value" of psychoanalysis "founded on truthfulness" (164). Neither technical nor ethical considerations allow us to depart from truth. And a basic truth we have learned from our practice is that anything we could offer aside from the truth we can encompass in our interpretations is only a surrogate, "for the patient's condition is such that, until her repressions are removed, she is incapable of getting real satisfaction" (165). This means that those aspects of truth communicated to the patient through our interpretations aim at removing the effects of repression. To be faithful to the spirit of the paper, this refers especially to those repressions that constitute the neurosis and interfere with the capacity for love.

Now, as when the paper was written, analysts have "a threefold battle to wage" (170). Against the forces that conspire to shake us out of our analytic stance, a careful monitoring of countertransference is essential. Against those opponents who, raising the prudish flags of conventional morality, seek to impede the clarification and transmission of a valid knowledge about sexuality—be it infantile or adult, feminine or masculine—we have to gain more understanding, not only about sexuality itself but also about the conditions of our very understanding. And against the reductionist views of those who look for quick therapeutic results through instant therapies, we must gain more insight into the conditions that allow insight to occur.

This is what is at stake in an analysis. Maybe it is the reason those other aspects of transference, consisting of "less tender feelings," are confined to another footnote (161n.). There is not a single word about the distinction between a "positive" and a "negative" transference that appears in the 1912

paper. If transference love aims at the abolition of differences through erotization, negative transference aims at the abolition of difference through
destruction. Any representation of difference—be it language, norm, or
symbol—is felt as a threat to the patient's narcissism that has to be done away
with. Psychoanalysis implies a struggle toward and a resistance against remembering. Remembering implies avoidance as well as an approximation
to reliving. Reliving implies a shortcut, as much as a diversion, to understanding.

That may be why once an analysis is over—one hesitates to say finished—
the memory that the analyst or the analysand has of it, and especially the
written account of it by the analyst or analysand, is but a pale reflection of
what happened during the analysis to either of them or between them. All one
knows is that it occurred once upon a time. Yet it carries a power of persua-
sion. Often, listening to such an account, one finds oneself saying: "The story
was incredible indeed, but convinced everyone, for it was substantially true"
(Borges, 1974, 568). As in Borges' tale, true was the emotional tonality, true
the regard, true the sensitivity, true the rebuttal; "only the circumstances, the
time and a couple of proper names were false."

REFERENCES

Borges, J. L. 1974. *Obras completas*. Buenos Aires: Emecé Editores.
Freud, S. 1900. *The interpretation of dreams*. S.E. 4–5.
——. 1909. *Analysis of a phobia in a five-year-old boy*. S.E. 10.
——. 1912a. The dynamics of transference. S.E. 12.
——. 1912b. Recommendations to physicians practising psycho-analysis. S.E. 12.
——. 1914a. On the history of the psycho-analytic movement. S.E. 14.
——. 1914b. Remembering, repeating and working-through (Further recommendations on the technique of psychoanalysis, II). S.E. 12.

On Transference Love:
Some Current Observations

BETTY JOSEPH

Freud's paper on transference love is, to my mind, not only of very lively interest but of fundamental importance. This I think for two reasons. First, the problems that Freud found analytical psychotherapists of that period struggling with, or failing to struggle with, are problems that all of us, as practicing psychoanalysts, still have to face in our daily work. Second, the paper touches on many points of technique that have subsequently been discussed and elaborated and proved to be the growing edge of analytic work. And as always, with improvements in our understanding of technical issues go, *pari passu,* refinements in our theoretical understanding. My aim in this chapter is to concentrate on a few of these points and what I consider to be some of the main developments from them.

Freud, it is clear, was deeply concerned about the way in which analytical therapists were getting caught up in involved relationships with certain types of patients. The model he had in mind was that of a male analyst and a female patient, the patient either openly or more covertly indicating that she had fallen in love with the therapist, and the therapist drawn into *acting out* with the patient in his behavior or emotionally feeling excited, pleased, or flattered by the patient's signs of affection. I hope to indicate how the issues that emerge in this paper are not limited to this group of patients but are ubiquitous.

Nevertheless, I want to start by looking at the type of patient Freud describes. He shows how the particular element that makes such a patient so difficult to handle in the transference is not only the fact of her falling in love with the therapist but the nature and expression of her loving. He describes how unreal it is, how her apparent insight seems to become *swallowed up in her love* but he also describes the loving in terms of the patient's endeavor to assure herself of her irresistibility, to destroy the doctor's authority by bringing him down to the level of a lover, and he discusses the compulsive character of this love, verging on the pathological. He keeps stressing how the analytic work must aim to uncover the nature of the patient's infantile object-choice, linked with the phantasies around it. He also stresses a point that clearly does not apply only to this kind of case—that a patient, as such, inescapably will fall in love with her therapist and, further, that the nature of the falling in love, the pattern, will repeat itself so that, even if the patient leaves one therapist and eventually finds her way to another, the same pattern of behavior will soon emerge with the second.

With this insight, Freud has taken a very important step, but one that, in this generation, I think we could put in a different way. We would stress that the patient inescapably brings her habitual type of object relationships, especially those with her inner objects, into the relationship with the analyst— the loving, the hating, the ambivalence, the defenses against loving and dependence—the whole gamut of relating. This is what we would mean by *falling in love*. Freud seemed to feel that, particularly in the type of patient he is concerned with in this paper, those who form a powerful erotized transference, it is most important to get to the infantile roots of loving. Surely this would be so with all our patients. But the point I think we especially need to note here concerns, rather, the roots of the infantile love. The infantile personality appears in these cases to be of an ill nature in itself, what Freud later speaks of as *verging on the pathological*. I think that we can take this a step further and see something of the pathological personality of the patient that emerges. The patient believes herself to be irresistible and behaves as if the therapist finds her irresistible. All of us have had patients of this type, some of whom correspond to Freud's description of people of high intelligence, sensitive and subtle, but others of whom are more frankly crude or nearly pathetic. All of these patients have in common the conviction, conscious or unconscious, that the analyst is emotionally involved with them.

We could broadly describe the personality of such a patient in this way. Here is a person with an omnipotent, narcissistic picture of herself, feeling herself to be extremely attractive, convinced that the analyst must be in love with her. She is out of touch with the reality of herself and her object. She struggles to avoid any sense of difference between self and object and cannot allow for the analyst's different qualities or skills, or his superiority. Nowadays we could see this picture as being maintained by the use of projective identification. The patient projects her own desiring of the analyst into the analyst and then really believes that he is in love with her. This she may, as I shall discuss later, actively try to bring about. As already noted, Freud describes how the patient aims to destroy the doctor's authority by bringing him down to the level of a lover (163). We might add that by now any sense she has of his superiority has gone. But Freud, in a slightly tortuous section, discusses whether this attempt should be seen as part of her loving, or as *resistance*. I shall come back to this point in a moment, but I would think that in these examples the patient's attempt to change her analyst into her lover needs to be seen as part of her primitive narcissistic character structure, which will not allow the object—the analyst—to succeed, to be different and separate from herself. It is an aspect of an aggressive, envious, destructive attitude that has been split off and hidden in the earlier part of the analysis (Freud describes the patient as often docile), but it emerges as the analysis progresses, and then one sees the destructiveness as being part of the way the patient relates to people.

To return to the discussion on resistance: Freud very much emphasizes how the patient's demands for love, her erotization of the transference, can be seen as a resistance, as a force *that interferes with the continuation of the treatment*. Of course this is what is unconsciously intended; certainly understanding or being understood plays no part in the patient's wishes at such times. Here, as is usual in Freud's writings, resistance is seen as a force mobilized particularly against remembering repressed material and thus against the treatment as such. Recently some analysts have questioned this limiting use of the word (e.g., Schafer, 1991). Others find that it largely has dropped from their vocabulary and that its place has been taken by more detailed descriptions of the patient's impulses and defenses within the session and as part of his or her general personality structure. Thus, we might consider that, in showing her love, by her docility, the patient Freud describes already was showing her defenses against more critical and negative feelings and impulses.

As I suggested at the beginning of this chapter, one of the fascinating things about Freud's paper is its relevance today. We still occasionally see the extreme type of case that Freud describes in our work, but the same or similar factors also are operating in more subtle ways in many apparently more ordinary but still rather intractable cases. I want to mention a brief example of this: The patient was a young woman, a research scientist, intelligent and with lively interests; she seemed to form a good relationship with the analyst and the analysis and to wish to cooperate and use the analysis constructively. Slowly I built up a picture of her inner world. She had a powerful conviction that people were attracted to her; for example, although a former boyfriend actually married someone else, she was convinced that he was still deeply emotionally attached to her. Regarding the relationship with me, it became quite evident that there was a phantasy that my life was very empty, that I was dependent on my work with my patients, and that I was very much attached to her, needing to have her in treatment for my own sake, and was envious of her achievements, especially of her relationships with men. She managed, in her mind, to keep me at the level of a person envious of her and needing her. Her way of achieving this was partly purely in phantasy, but she subtly, unconsciously, tried to draw me into a kind of acting in with her. For example, she would use almost any interpretation in order to attack herself masochistically; thus in her mind I became a sadistic partner. She would accomplish this outside the session, repeating potential insights and interpretations and using them to beat and torment herself, sometimes for hours on end. Although she appeared docile and cooperative, there was almost no progress, since insight in this way had become a source of perverse sexual excitement. Within the sessions there was a subtle erotization of the transference, aimed quietly at preventing any real difference between us; we were both to be caught up in this acting in, which should prevent my being a real analyst and different from her, and so defeat me, and keep me in thrall. It also afforded her perverse gratification. This is a patient who does not demand love verbally in the way that Freud describes but tries unconsciously to draw or manipulate the analyst into a sort of sadomasochistic loving and at the same time holds the convictions that the analyst is, in a sense, in love with her and dependent on her, and that she is irresistible.

As I noted, Freud discusses the need with these patients to get to the infantile roots of their loving. The patient described above was from very early childhood much involved with a boy cousin who lived with her family most of the time, since his own parents were stationed abroad. This boy was apparently very sadistic and tormenting, and the two children were deeply involved with each other, my patient feeling unable to escape. She had always had a sense of certainty that she was her mother's favorite, preferred even to the father. Family history had it that in infancy she was not weaned but herself turned away from the breast. I am stressing this to indicate that in this patient's erotization of the transference, although it can be seen as a resistance to the analysis, the resistance is only part of her way of loving, hating, controlling, preventing any shift in the structure she has established of omnipotent superiority and avoidance of more realistic and dependent relationships. Freud's patient at first seemed cooperative and docile; my patient at first, as she responded to interpretations, seemed to be coming to terms with insight and guilt. But, in fact, the guilt was being exploited for sadomasochistic purposes, to control the analyst and prevent the analysis from coming alive.

Returning then to Freud's discussion, we can today see how patients who erotize the transference are bent on nullifying or actually defeating the treatment. Freud, however, in this paper of 1915, still saw this destructiveness either as a resistance to the emergence of impulses or memories from the unconscious or as an aspect of loving—that is, of the sexual instincts. It was not until five years later, in "Beyond the Pleasure Principle," that he saw these highly aggressive aspects to be in conflict with life instincts, including sexuality, and subsumed them under the name of death instincts. This new classification opened up the whole area of aggression and destructiveness in analysis and in life. The notion of patients being determined to destroy progress was then further worked out with the concept of the negative therapeutic reaction. In the transference-love paper we get a marvelous picture of such negativism using erotization as its main weapon, but the reasoning—as, for example, when Freud tries to sort out the different motives, some connected with love, others with resistance—is somewhat tortuous. This, I believe, often happens when he is moving toward a new discovery but is tied to ideas that he cannot yet abandon. Here, he is unable quite to face the radical step he was soon to take in seeing the power and distinctiveness of the destructive drives. In the patient I have just described we can see how the erotization of the transference was aimed, in large part, at destroying my work, my separateness as a human being, my capacity to help her—the very stuff of progress and life.

The kind of behavior Freud is discussing in this paper is a classic example of acting rather than thinking or remembering. I find his discussion here of great interest. He stresses the importance of using action instead of thought, a topic with which he was very much concerned at this period, as we can see from the previous paper in this series, "Remembering, Repeating and Working Through" (1914). This remains of great significance in analytic thinking today, especially when we are considering patients who use very primitive mental mechanisms, such as a great deal of projection or projective identification, and whose thinking is very concrete. To them thinking and reality are so close that acting rather than thinking is inevitable. But quite apart from these more severely disturbed patients, I think nowadays we would see this sharp dichotomy as, in a sense, false, since we could say that all patients bring their habitual attitudes and behavior into the relationship with the analyst, and not just their minds.

Our understanding of the subtlety of acting out, or acting in, in this transference is perhaps one of the more significant developments in technique over the recent years. We would take it for granted not just, as Freud describes here, that the patient's falling in love with the therapist is inescapable, but that the characteristic nature of the patient's loving will inevitably be enacted in the relationship with the therapist. It may be acted out noisily, with protestations, demands, or threats, as in the cases described by Freud. Or it may not appear as falling in love at all, but, as I have stressed, the nature of the patient's way of loving, or not loving, will inevitably emerge in the transference. The patient may be rejecting, silent, withdrawn, determinedly independent. Alternatively, the loving may be more silent, subtle, and perverse, as in the case I described. It might indeed be better, instead of using the term *falling in love* to describe the nature of the object relationships the patient brings into the transference.

What is also striking in the transference-love paper is the way in which the patient acts on the analyst to get him involved with her, cajoling, flattering, teasing, threatening. This is, of course, where Freud came in—clearly concerned that analytic therapists were being drawn into some kind of actual or emotional behavior with the patients rather than remaining neutral. We could say that to some extent all patients do this; they try unconsciously and usually more delicately to draw us into mental or emotional activity, to play on our concern or guilt, to humor us or gratify our assumed expectations. They try to manipulate us to fit in with and act out according to their unconscious demands and phantasies. To look for a moment at my patient: she would present some piece of material in such a way as unconsciously to try to push me into making a critical remark or interpretation, or one that could be experienced as such, and thus would try to build up a sadomasochistic relationship. Or she would carefully tell me about her work, but in a way that would tend ordinarily to make the listener feel rather an outsider, a bit inferior. We know that we need to listen not just to the content of what is being told but to the way in which it is being said, the atmosphere that is being created; this is likely to give us a clue as to how we are being manipulated. The importance of this kind of acting in has been stressed recently by a number of writers, including Sandler (1976), O'Shaughnessy (1989), and Joseph (1985). The understanding of this phenomenon has been greatly helped by the notion of projective identification, with the patient unconsciously in phantasy projecting parts of the self or impulses into the analyst. I am suggesting that sometimes these projective identifications are purely within the patient's phantasy. Sometimes the patient tries to stimulate the analyst to behave accordingly, as I indicated with my patient. It may well happen, as O'Shaughnessy has pointed out, that we do not realize the existence or understand the nature of the projective identification until we find ourselves drawn into some subtle kind of behavior or indicating some attitude rather than remaining detached and neutral.

All this, of course, is linked to the recent developments and current thinking about countertransference, a term that Freud uses in this paper but in very few other writings. As has been much discussed, he used the term to describe the feelings that arise in the analyst *as a result of the patient's influence on his unconscious feelings*. He used it to denote something pathological, something to be guarded against, as, for example, when the therapist actually feels flattered by the patient's love for him. But many people now feel that to restrict the meaning of the term to some pathological response on the part of the analyst is too limiting, though this aspect should always be kept in mind. In Freud's cases, one can see how, for example, the therapist who was flattered or seduced by the patient's love not only was responding from a highly personal need to feel flattered and loved but was out of touch with the patient's pathology. But we can also say that the feelings aroused in the session can act as a very important guide to what is going on in the session— provided that the analyst can monitor his feelings as they arise or shift during the hour. He needs to be able to check on what and how much comes from him, his impulses and personality, and how much from the patient's acting on him. It would be necessary, for instance, in the case of the woman I described to be able to listen to such a remark as "Everything went wrong again after the last session" and to see whether this remark should be taken as indicating that the patient felt worried and concerned that she had slipped back, or whether, instead, the analyst was supposed to be pushed into a mood of anger, hopelessness, or impatience. This kind of awareness can best be achieved by the use of what one might call countertransference, though some people would prefer to use a term like *empathy*. In any case, if the analyst felt resentment and impatience, it would be very important to sort out whether this was due to his or her own bad mood and actual irritation that the patient did not seem to progress or whether the patient wanted or needed to push the analyst into feeling this, and perhaps had tried to do so.

Although Freud's paper appears to express concern, admonition, warning, and advice to therapists, the more we study it, the more we can see that major aspects of a psychoanalytic approach to treatment are emerging. Freud takes as basic to the issue he is discussing that the acting-out, erotizing patient presents a real problem for the therapist. He sees that the therapist will be cajoled and harassed, that he can easily give in and act out sexually with the patient or abandon the case and let her go to another therapist in due course. But then the old problem, Freud warns, will only be repeated. Neither of these alternatives is a solution, but they highlight the fact—not discussed in this paper, but one we would very much recognize today—that not every practitioner will be able to stand up to the stresses that treating patients analytically involves. Issues about the selection of future analysts are implicit in this.

If the therapist does try to continue real analytic work, Freud has real sympathy for the problem he confronts. He is aware that the patient must, by the very nature of things, bring her problems into the treatment and must harass and flatter the therapist, try to make him useless and pressured, but the analyst must not lose his professional stance. Freud looks at some of the issues involved, which are highly relevant to every analyst today. He indicates that the therapist has to guard against his narcissism and not imagine that the patient's apparently having fallen in love with him has anything to do with his personality. Rather, he must see it as part of the analytic process, part of what the patient brings with her into treatment.

Freud's discussion in itself raises a very important issue that has been developed consistently over recent years: What does the patient bring into the relationship? Following particularly the work of Strachey (1937) and Klein (1952), there has been more understanding that what is transferred is not just figures from the past, from the patient's actual history, but complex internal phantasy figures that have been built up from earliest infancy, constructed from the interaction between real experiences and the infant's phantasies and impulses toward them. Recognizing the complexity of what is transferred is of course basic to the analytic process itself and the understanding of the patient's internal world, anxieties, and defenses. But it also helps the therapist to recognize more deeply that what emerges in the relationship with him is really a transference from the patient's internal world, and this helps him to keep a more detached and professional stance.

Freud, in going on to examine the problems for the therapist, touches on further issues that not only concern working with the erotizing kind of patient but are fundamental to the proper analytic approach. He discusses the senselessness of a moralizing attitude toward the patient—such as urging the patient to suppress feelings and instincts that have been aroused—saying "the passions are little affected by sublime speeches" (164). Nowadays, it is, to my mind, not so much a question of the analyst's actively trying to block the patient's feelings as of the risk of indicating a particular attitude by the way he phrases an interpretation or his tone of voice as he does so. But further Freud warns the therapist against a kind of evasiveness, indicating certain attitudes without saying so, not really standing up for what he believes is going on. Freud's remarks here show his strength and the feel for the truth that he demands of the therapist, as well as his awareness of the kinds of problems the therapist was up against in 1915—not just the gross ones, but the subtle ones. It also highlights the kinds of problems we still face in our work today: the desire to push our patients back into a more compliant state of mind and, even more, the subtle pull of wanting to avoid confronting the reality of the patient's behavior or phantasies in the transference—for example, by a kind of semi-true remark, suggestion, or tone of voice. Such issues would indicate that we are in some way caught up in the patient's problems and that we need to keep the countertransference in check.

Different analysts would approach this section very differently. Some would, I think, base their approach on being prepared to go along with the patient's implied or expressed desires to some extent, or for the time being. Some might justify a less firm approach as an attempt to rectify some lack or basic need in the patient and might see this as an important step forward. But to my mind, Freud's ideas of 1915, so far as they go, and his reasoning in this section are as appropriate today as they were then. Other developments arise from his demand that the analyst avoid urging the patient to repress or renounce her feelings. Of course we could say that this point is basic to psychoanalysis, but the stress on its importance emerges perhaps particularly in Bion's work (1963) on the notion of the analyst's being able to contain the patient's feelings and by interpreting, to mitigate them and then to return them in modified form to the patient, just as the mother needs to contain the infant's feelings and anxieties. Without this kind of containment, sensitivity to the patient and to what is going on could not occur.

I think that this is broadly what Freud means when he advocates that the therapist must "keep firm hold of the transference-love but treat it as something unreal . . . which must assist in bringing all that is most deeply hidden in the patient's erotic life into her consciousness. . . . The patient . . . will then feel safe enough to allow all her preconditions for loving, all the phantasies . . . to come to light" (166). This is surely a picture of the analyst who can contain and the patient who then feels safe enough to bring more of herself into the open.

And yet, to my mind, there is a problem at this point in the paper. Freud speaks of a group of patients in whom the erotization is so great that, he feels, one can get nowhere with them. But then he starts to try to argue with them—to point out the unreasonableness of the patient's attitude, questioning whether she was really in love with the therapist, etc.—and he suggests that with such arguments, and with patience, it is usually possible to overcome the difficult situation.

This seems a strange approach, arguing with the patient in order to reason her out of a pathological attitude sufficiently to go on with the work of analyzing the nature of her loving. It looks like the very near-moralizing attitude Freud has been so firmly abjuring in the earlier part of the paper, as if the acting out of the demands for love and the provocation that goes with it were not in themselves part of the infantile roots of the patient's loving but things that had to be argued against before these infantile roots could be explored. Or is it that Freud worked in this reasoning way because he was not yet sufficiently convinced of the deeply destructive drives being expressed and therefore had to circumvent them?

There is further ambiguity in Freud's discussion of the difference between normal love and transference love. It is not clear whether in the latter case he is thinking only of the erotized type, or of all manifestations of love in the transference. He certainly appears to feel that all love in the transference, being provoked by the analytic situation, is lacking in reality and is intensified; this is different from the idea that the patient brings his or her ordinary life conflicts, inner and outer, into the relationship with the analyst. Or does he mean that we have a model in our minds of normal love and that what we actually see in our patients in analysis is more primitive, unreal, and blind than that model we consciously or unconsciously hold? I think that one aspect of this is that the type of love we see in the transference is, from the patient's point of view, "genuine"—it is his or her way of loving. Its manifestation is exacerbated by the closeness and scrutiny of the analytic situation. In addition, our patients come to us, whatever the symptoms of which they complain, because they have difficulties in relating—therefore in loving. From this viewpoint, transference love is bound to show more pathology and more infantile traits—for example, more narcissism and omnipotence—and therefore to be more unreal than our concept of "normal" loving would suggest.

In any case, from this point of view of technique, the decisive issue he raises here is that the analyst has a particular and deep responsibility; that the analytic situation evokes the patient's love, which is the unavoidable consequence of the treatment; and, therefore, the whole responsibility for handling the situation must lie with the analyst. It is after all the patient's prerogative to try to misuse the situation, according to her personality and pathology, and Freud is clear about the difficulty this raises for the analyst. But once we take seriously the advances in our understanding of the whole idea of transference, it becomes an opportunity to explore what is going on rather than a trouble and a burden. The problem is underscored with Freud's famous statement, "The psycho-analyst knows that he is working with highly explosive forces and that he needs to proceed with as much caution and conscientiousness as a chemist" (170).

I find this a remarkable paper of great relevance today. It clearly starts from anxieties Freud must have been feeling about psychotherapists becoming fascinated with certain female patients and acting out sexually or in other ways with them. But it contains ideas that go far beyond this, into the area of analytic technique, ideas that have become basic to sound analytic thinking and practice. Although, as I have discussed, I feel there are certain points of ambiguity and ares where one now would differ with Freud's thinking, the main issues and indications of struggles for the analytic practitioner have proved to be some of the most important points of growth in psychoanalytic practice over the last decades.

REFERENCES

Bion, W. R. 1963. *Elements of psycho-analysis*. London: Heinemann.
Freud, S. 1910. The future prospects of psycho-analytical psycho-therapy. *S.E.* 11.
———. 1914. Remembering, repeating and working-through. *S.E.* 12.
———. 1920. Beyond the pleasure principle. *S.E.* 18.

Joseph, B. 1985. Transference: The total situation. In *Psychic equilibrium and psychic change*. London: Routledge, 1989.

Klein, M. 1952. The origins of transference. In *Envy and gratitude, and other works*. London: Hogarth.

O'Shaughnessy, E. 1989. Enclaves and excursions. (Unpublished)

Sandler, J. 1976. Countertransference and role responsiveness. *Int. Rev. Psychoanal.* 3:43–47.

Schafer, R. 1991. A clinical critique of the idea of resistance. Paper given to the British Psycho-Analytical Society.

Strachey, J. 1937. The nature of the therapeutic action of psycho-analysis. *Int. J. Psycho-anal.* 15:127–59. Reprinted in *Int. J. Psycho-anal.* 50.

One-Person and Two-Person Perspectives: Freud's "Observations on Transference-Love"

MERTON MAX GILL

This paper is surely one of Freud's most charming. Jones (1955) tells us that Freud liked it best of the technique papers of the nineteen teens. How can one forget such phrases as "the logic of soup, with dumplings for arguments," or remarks like: "Sexual love is undoubtedly one of the chief things in life, and the union of mental and bodily satisfaction in the enjoyment of love is one of its culminating peaks. Apart from a few queer fanatics, all the world knows this and conducts its life accordingly; science alone is too delicate to admit it," or this: "the danger of making a man forget his technique and his medical task for the sake of a fine experience." Surely compassion for the "impossible profession," which must combine intimacy with abstinence, not only for the patient but for the analyst as well, could hardly be better expressed. Another mark of compassion is Freud's recognition that analysts "who are still young-ish and not yet bound by strong ties" may find the handling of an erotized transference especially difficult. As an oldish analyst, it occurs to me that at least as much compassion might be extended to an analyst who is disappointed by the analysand's failure to develop an erotized transference! One may choose not to believe her, but Hilda Doolittle (1956) reports that Freud beat on the head of the couch and said, "The trouble is—I am an old man—you do not think it worth your while to love me" (16).

ONE-PERSON OR TWO-PERSON PSYCHOLOGY

One of the outstanding features of the transference-love essay is its evidence of Freud's dialectical turn of mind: "there is this, but on the other hand, there is this . . . " This dialectical tension in the paper can be understood, I suggest, in terms of the issue of whether analysis is, or should be dealt with in, a one-person or a two-person psychology. The issue has a long history in psychoanalysis, going back to Ferenczi (e.g., 1928). The debate currently has intensified (see, e.g., Mitchell, 1988), and I believe it is becoming progressively clearer (Ghent, 1989; Hoffman, 1991; Sandler, 1991) that the analytic situation is appropriately viewed from both perspectives. If the analysand is seen as a closed system of forces and counterforces, the perspective is one-person. If the analytic situation is seen as a relationship between two people, the perspective is two-person and the analyst is a participant in that situation. A complete vision of the analytic situation involves both perspectives all the time, with the two perspectives alternating between foreground and background. In the one-person perspective, the dynamics of the analysand's neurosis are in the foreground. In the two-person perspective the transference/countertransference is in the foreground. When analysis is proceeding well the two perspectives are shown to be alternate expressions of the same themes. Of course, the one-person perspective of the patient's past or contemporary life outside the treatment includes relationships with other persons. The two-person perspective relates to analyst and analysand in the psychoanalytic situation.

In this paper Freud sometimes takes one perspective and sometimes the other. On the one hand, he takes the "classical" one-person position: the transference is solely the patient's doing; if the patient seeks another analyst, the same thing will happen again, as the analyst is a replaceable cog in the analytic situation; the charms of the analyst have nothing to do with what happens; there is not "a single new feature" arising out of the present situation (this is a regression from his recognition in the Dora case that some real element of the current situation may, however incidentally—his cigar smoking, perhaps—repeat an element from the past); there are arguments against the "genuineness" of this "ostensible" love.

Here is another example of the one-person perspective: Does transference occur only in the analytic situation or extra-analytically as well? Freud argues that the same falling in love will take place not only in some other kind of treatment but also in ordinary life: "being in love in ordinary life, outside analysis, is also more similar to abnormal than to normal mental phenomena" (168).

On the other hand, Freud sometimes takes the two-person perspective: "We have no right to dispute" that the patient's state "has the character of a 'genuine' love"; "the resistance did not, after all, *create* this love"; the analyst "has evoked this love by instituting analytic treatment"; it is the "consequence of a medical situation" (168–69). And again, [transference love] "is provoked by the analytic situation" (168). And yet again: "summoning up a spirit from the underworld by cunning spells [hypnosis!]" (164). These remarks show a two-person perspective. But note that emphasis is primarily on the *situation,* not on the person who set up the situation. Freud similarly attempted to shift personal responsibility from himself to the situation when he said he could not help the Rat Man's having to tell his dreadful story: it was simply a requirement of the treatment! Heinrich Racker (1968) knew better. He said that by putting his name on his office door he was already an accomplice.

The analyst's share of responsibility in a two-person perspective becomes even clearer in Freud's observation about when this demand for love breaks out: "when one is having to try to bring her to admit or remember some particularly distressing and heavily repressed piece of her life-history" (162)—that is, when the analyst is trying to get the patient to submit to him, in the interest of the treatment, of course. Here the emphasis is clearly on the analyst rather than simply on the situation. Again the two-person perspective in the observation that erotic transference in the analytic situation is different from love in ordinary life, even if only quantitatively. "It is greatly intensified by the resistance . . . it is lacking to a high degree in a regard for reality" (168–169). But once again the one-person turn: "these departures from the norm constitute precisely what is essential about being in love" (169).

Although the citation is not from Freud's paper on transference love, I will not resist the temptation to add this wonderful passage from a two-person perspective in which Freud recognizes the patient's "rights" ("Group Psychology and the Analysis of the Ego," 1921):

We shall therefore be prepared for the statement that suggestion (or more correctly suggestibility) is actually an irreducible primitive phenomenon, a fundamental fact in the mental life of man. Such, too, was the opinion of Bernheim, of whose astonishing arts I was a witness in the year 1889. But I can remember even then feeling a muffled hostility to this tyranny of suggestion when a patient who showed himself unamenable was met with a shout: "What are you doing Vous contresuggestionnez!" I said to myself that this was an evident injustice and an act of violence. For the man certainly had a right to counter-suggestions if people were trying to subdue him with suggestions. Later on my resistance took the direction of protesting against the view that suggestion, which explained everything, was itself to be exempt from explanation. . . . suggestion, that is, of the conditions under which influence without adequate logical foundation takes place. (89–90)

In the first paragraph of the same work he writes: "In the individual's mental life someone else is invariably involved, as a model, as a helper, as an opponent; and so from the very first individual psychology, in this extended but entirely justifiable sense of the words, is at the same time social psychology as well" (69). It is important to stress that in this latter citation the two-person perspective goes far beyond the issue of transference love. That perspective is, in innumerable guises, an intrinsic and omnipresent feature of the analytic situation. Of course the overwhelming distinction between crotized love in the analytic situation and transference in other treatments and in extra-analytic life is that in the analytic situation it is analyzed and can "make [a] contribution to the patient's recovery" (161).

To say that the same falling in love will occur in some other kind of treatment or in real life is to minimize the specific realities of the particular two-person analytic situation. Transference love is specific to this *particular* analytic situation. An analysis in which the analyst adopts the "senseless proceeding" (161) of urging the patient to go ahead and fall in love is a different analysis, and even if a falling in love does take place, it is a different falling in love.[1] I may note again, however, that Freud implies that in a correct analytic technique, falling in love occurs spontaneously. Ida Mac-

1. That Freud regarded this "senseless proceeding" to be more prevalent than he had thought at first is suggested by Strachey's remark that in the first edition of this paper "this paragraph (which is in the nature of a parenthesis) was printed in small type" (162n.). Furthermore, whereas in the first edition Freud spoke of the practice as taking place "early" in treatment, thereafter he said it was done "frequently."

alpine (1950) knew better. She compared the analytic situation to the slow induction of hypnosis. Freud had not abandoned hypnosis quite as much as he thought he had! In another sense, however, Freud is correct in wanting the love, if it appears, to be spontaneous—that is, unpredicted and unplanned for. A number of recent discussions of technique (Sandler, 1976; Ehrenberg, 1982, 1984; Fredrickson, 1990; Hoffman, 1992) argue for the inevitability of, indeed the necessity for, a degree of spontaneity on the analyst's part too. Hoffman's paper, in particular, emphasizes his dialectic view, as is apparent in its title, "Expressive Participation and Psychoanalytic Discipline."

Freud moves, then, between one-person and two-person psychologies. But I do not believe that he realizes he is doing so. He, like much contemporary analysis, regards only the one-person perspective as *truly* analytic. The two-person perspective is, as it were, an unfortunate complication resulting from the fact that the analyst, being only human, cannot maintain perfect neutrality. The counterposition is, as I have said, that both perspectives are intrinsic to and always available in the analytic situation; sometimes the one, sometimes the other is in the foreground, as Hoffman (1991) makes clear, depending on the analyst's focus.

A major contemporary version of this one-person/two-person dichotomy is the debate about analysis as intrapsychic or interpersonal. I believe the term *interpersonal* is often misunderstood in this connection by those who object to it because they do not realize that many analysts mean by this term *how what takes place between the two participants is understood in the psychic reality of each participant*. In other words, by "interpersonal" these analysts do *not* mean social psychology in the sense of some "objective" external observer. Heinz Kohut (1971) and Evelyne Schwaber (in press) correctly criticize what they regard as an interpersonal conceptualization of the analytic situation because they take "interpersonal" to mean social psychological in this latter external sense. Freud does not define the term *social psychology* in the citation from "Group Psychology and the Analysis of the Ego," but he must mean it in the sense of intrapsychically experienced.

The intrapsychic experience of their interaction may differ widely for the two participants in the analytic situation. An analyst who believes that he sees truly what took place between himself and the analysand and says that the transference is a "distortion" by the analysand may think that he thus shows true allegiance to psychic reality. But in calling the transference a distortion he denies, paradoxically, that he too constructs matters according to his own psychic reality, not through some special ability to see the true reality made possible presumably by his purification in his own analysis. Many argue, myself (1982) included, that the analyst should apply himself to learning that the analysand's understanding of what takes place between the two participants is plausible, and, indeed, that his own understanding is also only plausible. A "negotiation" (Goldberg, 1988) then can take place between the two until they reach some agreement, which of course may seem incorrect to a third person examining the transaction, because he too sees it in terms of *his* psychic reality.

Here lies an important consideration for systematic research in the analytic situation by observers other than the analyst. For external observers are presumably less influenced by the transference and countertransference of the analysand-analyst couple. But even then, one can speak only of a coherence, not of a correspondence theory of truth. That is, one can know external reality only in terms of the coherence of a set of propositions, not in terms of some unmediated experience of reality that tallies with external reality as such. In advancing the argument that the analyst can discover what tallies with external reality Freud was a positivist. So too is Grünbaum (1984), who does not argue against the alleged necessity for the findings to tally with external reality but rather maintains that the influence of suggestion in the analytic situation makes it impossible to be certain that one has indeed found what corresponds to unmediated external reality. I touch here on the current controversy over the positivist versus social-constructivist perspectives on the analytic situation (Protter, 1985; Stern, 1985; Toulmin, 1986; and especially Hoffman, 1991). The constructivist position is often misunderstood to entail a denial of the importance of material reality—to assert that any construction is as valid as any other; that, as the expression has it, "anything goes." That is *not* true. The argument that we cannot know material reality as such does not mean that we can ignore it. Some constructions make more sense than others, and not solely on the grounds of coherence. The issue is a crucial epistemological one, which I cannot pursue further here.

EROTIC TRANSFERENCE AND RESISTANCE

A less direct admission by Freud of the analyst's share of responsibility for the erotic transference is his recognition that "one will have long since noticed in the patient the signs of an affectionate transference, and one will have been able to feel certain that her docility, her acceptance of the analytic explanations, her remarkable comprehension and the high degree of intelligence she showed were to be attributed to this attitude towards her doctor" (162).

Perhaps at least sometimes an erotic transference need not reach such a peak that it becomes intransigent if its function as a resistance is dealt with earlier. Elsewhere, Freud wrote that one should take care not to let the transference rise to uncontrollable heights. But Freud felt he needed an "unobjectionable positive transference" to further the aims of the analysis. I have discussed (1982) my disagreement with Mark Kanzer (1980), who believes that Freud finally abandoned reliance on the unobjectionable positive transference. I do not think he ever did. There is no question that in the present paper, his view is that he needs it to influence the patient. What he wants is only a *moderation* of the erotic transference" (167). The much-discussed concept of a therapeutic alliance raises the same issue. Of course, we need some cooperation from the patient to continue to work. What those who *seem* to have written against the therapeutic alliance (Kanzer, 1975; Brenner, 1979) mean is only that special unanalyzed manipulations to bring about such an alliance introduce unnecessary suggestion.

Despite Freud's clear recognition in this essay that the erotic transference was serving as a resistance, in another of the technical papers written at about the same time he emphasized that "*transference should be left untouched* until [it] . . . has become a resistance" (1913, 139; emphasis in the original). I believe, on the contrary, that since transference is omnipresent even if in the background, it is always serving as a resistance. This is in keeping with Freud's dictum that "the resistance accompanies the treatment step by step" (1912, 103). Hyman Muslin and I have argued (1978) that an earlier interpretation of the transference resistance might have averted the debacle in the Dora case. Of course, we realize that as far as this case is concerned we are using 20/20 hindsight. We are not overlooking Freud's genius in elaborating the concept of transference in his reflections on the Dora case. I am reminded of Freud's marvelous riposte to Stekel's observation that he could see farther than Freud because he could stand on Freud's shoulders. "A louse on the head of a philosopher does not see farther than the philosopher," said Freud.

Charles Brenner (1969) has also objected to the misleading advice to wait until the transference has become a resistance. Martin Stein (1981) has shown how one can be deceived by a supposedly "unobjectionable positive transference" into believing that an analysis is going well. He has emphasized how this illusion may especially characterize a training analysis in which the candidate feels he must court the analyst's good will. Freud's failure to interpret the signs of a long-since-noted affectionate transference with its alleged "docility" and "remarkable comprehension" may indeed be experienced by the patient as a subtle implicit or, to us another term, indirect suggestion (Oremland, 1991, Gill, 1991) to "go ahead and fall in love," which he so roundly condemns when it is made as an explicit suggestion.

UNOBJECTIONABLE NEGATIVE TRANSFERENCE

At a conference in Bologna, Italy, in June 1991, I had the good fortune to hear Dr. Nella Guidi's proposal of the concept of an "unobjectionable *negative* transference" in parallel to an unobjectionable *positive* transference. The concept seems at once to make good sense. Is it not reasonable at the beginning of an analysis for the analysand to be somewhat wary, skeptical, and cautious? Should we not want the analysand to maintain this attitude throughout, so that when he or she finally does accept an interpretation, it is out of conviction, not submission? Freud attributed the unobjectionable positive transference to earlier experiences that "link the doctor up with one of the imagos of the people by whom he [the patient] was accustomed to be treated with affection" (1913, 139–40). Does not an unobjectionable negative transference arise out of the same source—from enlightened parents who try to see the child's point of view when there is a difference of opinion? It is true that the power and experience of child and parent are likely experienced as even more asymmetrical than are the power and experience of analyst and analysand. Of course, it is common experience that just as a seemingly positive transference can serve as a resistance against negative transference, so too can a seemingly negative transference serve as a resistance to a positive transference.

SEXUALITY

Freud's reductionist insistence on sexuality, never changed throughout his long career, would seem clearly evident in this essay. He compares the jealousy felt by male relatives of a female analysand to how they feel toward her treatment by a gynecologist. In calling his insistence reductionist, I do not mean to belittle the importance of sexuality. Freud was correct when he said in the Dora case that people might object to his talking about intimate sexual matters with a young woman because to talk about sex can be experienced as sexual intimacy. He justifies his action by its necessity for the treatment and by the assurance that he discusses these matters in an impersonal way. He attempted to decontaminate such talk by his manner of talking. *Neutralized* instead of *decontaminated* is the usual metaphor, a metaphor unfortunately taken as a concrete reality in many versions of economic metapsychology. *Relative autonomy* (Hartmann, 1939) is a less objectionable metaphor, but it should never be forgotten that autonomy from drive can never be more than *relative*. In speaking of "drive" I am not subscribing to classical Freudian metapsychology (Gill, 1976). I am implying rather that sexuality may be subordinate to what I will loosely refer to as the self. This last remark calls for an extended discussion which I will not attempt here. I will say, however, that Freud referred to a general overestimation of sex in neurosis. There may be an unfortunate resemblance between such neurotic overestimation of sex and a parallel overestimation in what I have called a reductionist view of sexuality in classical Freudian theory.

It is apposite to note Freud's caution that "the experiment of letting oneself go a little way in tender feelings for the patient is not altogether without danger" (164). We may suddenly go further than we intended. Years later, as Strachey (1958, 158) notes, Freud expressed the same fear to Ferenczi about his experiments (Jones, 1957, 163). Would we feel that Freud's cautionary statement was equally well-advised if he had spoken only of "positive" rather than "tender" feelings?

Freud was indeed speaking from personal experience. Here is an extract from a letter he wrote to Jung in June 1909 regarding Jung's sexual entanglement with his patient Spielrein (McGuire, 1974, letter 145F, 230–31):

> Experiences of this kind, however painful, are necessary and it is difficult to avoid them. Only after going through them do we know life and what it is we have to deal with. As far as I am concerned, I have never completely given way, but I have been very close a number of times and have had a narrow escape . . . but it does not matter. . . . In that way, one's skin thickens as it must. One dominates the countertransference that one gets involved in every time [countertransference is inescapable!], and one learns to transfer one's feelings and place them opportunely. It is a blessing in disguise.

Freud in this paper reveals a possible distaste for the physical aspects of sexuality. When he writes of soup and dumplings, he refers to women who will accept nothing less as of "elemental passionateness," "children of nature who refuse to accept the psychical in place of the material" (166–67). His distinction between psychical and material here is not the same as his usual distinction between psychical and material reality; the latter usage means the differences in how apparently similar external reality may be psychically experienced by different people, whereas the former means only the difference between thinking and talking about sex and actually engaging in a sexual act. Obviously, both the act itself and thinking or talking about it can also be experienced differently by different people.

For another possible devaluation of physical sexuality by Freud, I point to his remark, "It is not a patient's crudely sensual desires which constitute the temptation. These are more likely to repel [!], and it will call for all the doctor's tolerance if he is to regard them as a natural phenomenon" (170). He finds greater temptation in "subtler and aim-inhibited wishes" (the thesis that these are derivatives of bodily desire is clearly implied). But again, contrary views are evident. He writes, as I have already noted, of a "fine experience" and that "the union of mental and bodily satisfaction in the enjoyment of love is one of its [life's] culminating peaks" (169).

CONTROL-MASTERY THEORY

A way in which the one-person/two-person perspectives in this paper can be discussed is by comparison with the "control-mastery" theory advanced by Joseph Weiss and his co-workers (1986). Together with a remarkable attempt to validate their theory by systematic research, they attack the familiar thesis that one must allow instinctual pressure to build up so that it comes to the aid of the analyst in exposing what is repressed. Freud makes this argument in this paper in terms of abstinence: "I shall state it as a fundamental principle that the patient's need and longing should be allowed to persist in her, in order that they may serve as forces impelling her to do work and to make changes" (165). Similarly, Freud wrote in the slightly earlier paper on the dynamics of transference, "He [the patient] seeks to put his passions into action without taking any account of the real situation" (1912, 108).

Weiss et al. argue, on the contrary, that what takes place is that the patient tests the analyst by trying to get him to participate in a neurotic trans-ference/countertransference interaction, to be what Joseph Sandler (1976) calls "role-responsive." If the analyst "passes" the test, they say, the patient feels safe enough to express the allegedly forbidden wishes. But Freud also makes a two-person formulation in this paper on transference love similar to that in control-mastery theory. He speaks of "putting her analyst's severity to the test" (163). He even uses the same word "safe" in this connection as do Weiss et al. He says that if the analyst is "proof against every temptation," the patient "will then feel safe enough to allow all her preconditions for loving . . . to come to light" (166). Again in a two-person perspective he writes: "the resistance is beginning to make use of her love to hinder the continuation of the treatment, to deflect all her interest from the work and to put the analyst in an awkward position" (162–63).

What, then, is the difference between Freud's view and that of Weiss et al.? It is that Freud offers both one-person and two-person formulations whereas Weiss offers only a two-person formulation. Indeed, in one formulation, Freud combines the two. The passage I cited above as a one-person formulation, namely, "that the patient's need and longings should be allowed to persist in her in order that they may serve as forces impelling her to do work," continues in a two-person formulation: "we must beware of appeasing those forces by means of surrogates" (165).

What does Freud regard as the primary perspective? It is the one-person view. Although he somewhat ambiguously regards the test as only *one* of the "motives which further complicate things," he declares himself to be in opposition to Alfred Adler, who, he alleges, regarded these "*accessory* motives . . . as the essential part of the whole process" (163; emphasis added).

A danger in confining oneself to one-person formulations is that they can be understood to mean an automatic repetition. From there, one can easily postulate a mysterious reified force called the "repetition compulsion." What does the patient repeat? Instinctual wishes? That answer could be construed as solely in a one-person perspective. Perhaps the two perspectives can be combined without taking a stand on the controversial issue of the nature of instinctual drive by saying that the patient repeats the patterns of interpersonal relationships he has learned because it is the nature of the human psyche to do so.

I may note that both Freud and Weiss et al. overlook here the possibility that while the patient may in part be relieved to discover the analyst's invulnerability, she may also be confused and frightened by this evidence against her fixed view of what people are like. In short, the patient is in conflict, rather than having a single plan as Weiss et al. seem to think. I also note that their concept of the relationship between therapist and patient in terms of the patient's plan is only a circumscribed aspect of a two-person perspective. As further evidence I cite their belief that the analyst should and can be "neutral," whereas what I mean by a two-person perspective is that the analyst is inevitably a co-participant in the analytic situation. How to define *neutrality* is another complex issue I will not enter here. The primary issue I have chosen to focus on in this chapter is the one-person/two-person dichotomy, but Freud's remarkable essay introduces, even though only in passing, many more crucial points about analytic technique. I mean, for example, emphasis on the centrality of truth in psychoanalysis and the remarks about countertransference. Freud sees the analyst as having to struggle not only against the outside world and against his patient but also "in his own mind against the forces which seek to drag him down from the analytic level" (170)—again an inference that overt sexuality is on a lower level. Freud also gives us an important hint of what he means by freedom: "the extra piece of mental freedom which distinguishes conscious mental activity—in the systematic sense—[he is already thinking in terms of the structural theory] from unconscious" (170).

As he will repeat in the late "Analysis Terminable and Interminable" (1937), the analyst "knows that he is working with highly explosive forces" (170). Freud writes of the "serious danger of this therapeutic method" (170). Why, then, do some of us at least so enjoy this impossible profession—or is that one of the reasons, at least for some of us?

SEX AND LOVE

I have also alluded to the relationship between sex and love. I considered calling this essay "What is this thing called love?" which I will identify for foreign or younger readers as the title of a popular song by Cole Porter. Is Freud's essay about sex or love? The word *love* appears far more often in the text than *sex*. On the one hand, there are the indications I have already noted of Freud's view that love is a derivative of sex. I have also referred to what he says is "essential about being in love"; it is "lacking to a high degree in a regard for reality, . . . less sensible, less concerned about consequences and more blind in its valuation of the loved person" (168–69).

But there are hints of a different view of love in the arguments he suggests can be used to mitigate the erotized transference: "Genuine love, we say, would make her docile and intensify her readiness to solve the problems of her case, simply because the man she was in love with expected it of her" (167). So genuine love includes a consideration of the beloved's wishes. That would seem to be an advance toward a more mature view of love. But can we not do better? Must love include docility? Freud was indeed androcentric in one of his many facets. Where is the unobjectionable negative transference? What about mutuality? Even in the asymmetrical analytic situation? Do we not have to make a sharper distinction between mental versus bodily satisfaction? Does all the world know the gulf between sex and love except a "few queer fanatic" psychoanalysts? Of course Freud knew the difference. Why else "*psycho*sexuality?"

Freud called the patient's love "ostensible." He thus almost says that in the erotic transference sex is masquerading as love. Freud's view of the role of sexuality in the human psyche arose in the framework of a one-person psychology: "The fact of the emergence of the transference in its crudely sexual form, whether affectionate or hostile, in every treatment of a neurosis, *although this is neither desired nor induced by either doctor or patient*, has always seemed to me the most irrefragable proof that the driving force of neurosis lies in sexual life. . . . As far as I am concerned, this argument has remained the decisive one, over and above the more specific findings of analytic work" (1914, 12; emphasis added). On the other hand, there is much talk of "love" in these pages. The title of the paper is "Observations on Transference-Love," not "Transference-Sexuality." Again, these two views of love can be seen as illustrating the differences among one-person, two-person, and combined one-person/two-person perspectives.

To conclude, I emphasize that transference love in Freud's view is only a "sharply circumscribed" aspect of what he says poses the most serious problems in analytic technique: "the management of the transference" (159), to which I believe we are entitled to add, "and the countertransference." That Freud sees transference love as only a circumscribed aspect of transference indicates again, as in his remark cited above, that individual psychology is at the same time social psychology, that his two-person perspective is applicable far more widely than in the specific issue of this paper. Analysis indeed encompasses both one-person and two-person perspectives. It was an erotized transference from which Breuer, the protoanalyst, fled.[2] Freud did not flee:

> One day I had an experience which showed me in the crudest light what I had long suspected. It related to one of my most acquiescent patients, with whom hypnotism had enabled me to bring about the most mar-

2. Since writing this, I have heard a persuasive paper by Marian Tolpin (1992) arguing that what is usually alleged to have happened between Breuer and Anna O. is quite different from what actually happened. I think it is only fair to Breuer to take note of this contention. I am not yet in a position to offer an opinion on the matter.

velous results. . . . As she woke up on one occasion, she threw her arms round my neck. . . . I felt I had now grasped the nature of the mysterious element that was behind hypnotism. In order to exclude it, *or at all events to isolate it,* it was necessary to abandon hypnosis. (1925, 27; emphasis added)

Freud did not flee, but he abandoned hypnosis, and he mistakenly thought, in one of the themes of his work, that he had thereby eliminated himself as a co-participant in the analytic situation. He thought he was "isolating" the mysterious element to the patient. I say "in one of the themes of his work" because although he implies in his account of this experience that it was all the patient's doing, neglecting thereby what the hypnotist does, in other themes of his work, as I have described here, he does implicitly recognize the two-person perspective.

The difference between how Freud responded and how Breuer allegedly did brings the two-person perspective into vivid prominence. So we now have Freud's precious gift to mankind. The work "*man*kind" means the human race, but it also speaks volumes about the relation between the sexes. Freud's essay on transference love was written in 1915. It takes for granted that the analyst is a man and the analysand is a woman. We do not take that for granted so easily now. So, yet again, I can emphasize the theme of this paper. We must see the two-person perspective as well as the one-person perspective as intrinsic and omnipresent in the psychoanalytic situation.

Probably the greatest obstacle to analysts' recognition of their participation in the analytic situation is the assumption that the analyst can choose whether or not to participate. The point is that he participates whether he likes it or not. His participation will be experienced by the patient in all shades of gratification and frustration. The implication for technique is to be aware of the patient's experience of the analyst's participation (Hoffman, 1983) and to deal with it in the analysis of the transference/countertransference interaction. The analyst who believes he can refrain from participation—stay "neutral"—will be handicapped in recognizing how his participation is being experienced by the analysand.

REFERENCES

Brenner, C. 1969. Some comments on technical precepts in psychoanalysis. *J. Amer. Psychoanal. Assn.* 17:333–52.

128 / Merton Max Gill

————. 1979. Working alliance, therapeutic alliance, and transference. In *Psychoanalytic explorations of technique,* ed. H. P. Blum, 137–57. New York: International Universities Press, 1980.

Doolittle, H. 1956. *Tribute to Freud.* New York: New Directions.

Ehrenberg, D. B. 1982. Psychoanalytic engagement. *Contemp. Psychoanal.* 18:535–55.

————. 1984. Psychoanalytic engagement, 2: Affective considerations. *Contemp. Psychoanal.* 20:560–82.

Ferenczi, S. 1928. The elasticity of psychoanalytic technique. In *Final contributions to the problems and methods of psychoanalysis.* New York: Basic, 1955.

Fredrickson, J. 1990. Hate in the countertransference as an empathic position. *Contemp. Psychoanal.* 26:479–96.

Freud, S. 1912. The dynamics of transference. *S.E.* 12.

————. 1913. On beginning the treatment (Further recommendations on the technique of psycho-analysis, I). *S.E.* 12.

————. 1914. On the history of the psychoanalytic movement. *S.E.* 14.

————. 1916–17. *Introductory lectures on psychoanalysis. S.E.* 16.

————. 1921. Group psychology and the analysis of the ego. *S.E.* 18.

————. 1925. An autobiographical study. *S.E.* 20.

————. 1937. Analysis terminable and interminable. *S.E.* 23.

Ghent, E. 1989. Credo: The dialectics of one-person and two-person psychologies. *Contemp. Psychoanal.* 25:169–211.

Gill, M. M. 1976. Metapsychology is not psychology. In *Psychology versus metapsychology,* ed. M. Gill and P. Holzman. New York: International Universities Press.

————. 1982. *Analysis of transference.* Vol. 1: Theory and technique. Madison, Conn.: International Universities Press.

————. 1991. Indirect suggestion: A response to Oremland's *Interpretation and Interaction.* In *Interpretation and interaction: Psychoanalysis or psychotherapy,* ed. J. D. Oremland, 137–63. Hillsdale, N. J.: Analytic Press.

Goldberg, A. 1988. *A fresh look at psychoanalysis.* Hillsdale, N. J.: Analytic Press.

Grünbaum, A. 1984. *The foundations of psychoanalysis.* Berkeley: University of California Press.

Hartmann, H. 1939. *Ego psychology and the problem of adaptation.* New York: International Universities Press.

Hoffman, I. Z. 1983. The patient as interpreter of the analyst's experience. *Contemp. Psychoanal.* 19:389–422.

————. 1991. Discussion: Toward a social-constructivist view of the psychoanalytic situation. *Psychoanal. Dialogues* 1:74–105.

————. 1992. Expressive participation and psychoanalytic discipline. *Contemp. Psychoanal.* 28:1–15.

Jones, E. 1955. *The life and work of Sigmund Freud.* Vol. 2. New York: Basic.

———. 1957. *The Life and Work of Sigmund Freud.* Vol. 3. New York: Basic.

Kanzer, M. 1975. The therapeutic and working alliances. *Int. J. of Psychoanal. Psychotherapy* 4:48–68.

———. 1980. Freud's "human influence" on the Rat Man. In *Freud and his patients,* ed. M. Kanzer and J. Glenn, 232–40. New York: Jason Aronson.

Kohut, H. 1971. *The analysis of the self.* New York: International Universities Press.

Macalpine, I. 1950. The development of the transference. *Psychoanal. Q.* 19:501–39.

McGuire, W., ed. 1974. *The Freud/Jung Letters.* Princeton, N. J.: Princeton University Press.

Mitchell, S. 1988. *Relational concepts in psychoanalysis.* Cambridge, Mass.: Harvard University Press.

Muslin, H., and Gill, M. M. 1978. Transference in the Dora case. *J. Amer. Psychoanal. Assn.* 26:311–28.

Oremland, J. D., ed. 1991. *Interpretation and interaction: Psychoanalysis or psychotherapy.* Hillsdale, N. J.: Analytic Press.

Protter, B. 1985. Symposium. "Psychoanalysis and truth": Toward an emergent psychoanalytic epistemology. *Contemp. Psychoanal.* 21:208–27.

Racker, H. 1968. *Transference and countertransference.* New York: International Universities Press.

Sandler, J. 1976. Countertransference and role-responsiveness. *Int. Rev. of Psycho-Anal.* 3:43–48.

———. 1991. Comments on the psychodynamics of interaction. Paper presented at a panel entitled "Interaction" at the fall meeting of the American Psychoanalytic Association, New York, December 21, 1991.

Schwaber, E. (In Press.) Psychoanalytic theory and its relation to clinical work. *J. Amer. Psychoanal. Assn.*

Stein, M. H. 1981. The unobjectionable part of the transference. *J. Amer. Psychoanal. Assn.* 29:869–92.

Stern, D. B. 1985. Symposium. "Psychoanalysis and truth": Some controversies regarding constructivism and psychoanalysis. *Contemp. Psychoanal.* 21:201–08.

Strachey, J. 1958. Note preceding Freud's "Observations on transference-love." *S.E.* 12.

Tolpin, M. 1992. The unmirrored self. Paper presented at Chicago Regional Psychoanalytic meeting, March 14, 1992.

Toulmin, S. 1986. Self psychology as a "postmodern" science. In Commentaries on Heinz Kohut's *How Does Analysis Cure? Psychoanal. Inquiry* 6:459–78.

Weiss, J.; Sampson, H.; and the Mount Zion Psychotherapy Research Group. 1986. *The psychoanalytic process: Theory, clinical observation, and empirical research.* New York: Guilford.

The Oedipal Tragedy in
the Psychoanalytic Process:
Transference Love

FIDIAS CESIO

The paper on transference love, which, according to Jones (1953, 75), Freud considered one of the best he had written on technique, deals with the foundations of the transference, particularly the transference to the person of the analyst.

Freud gave two definitions of transference: one, in *The Interpretation of Dreams* (1900, 550), refers to the transference stemming from unconscious ideas in preconscious representations; the other, to be found in the epilogue to Dora's case (1905, 7), refers to the transference to the person of the analyst. With regard to the latter, Freud states: "They are new editions or facsimiles of the impulses and phantasies which are aroused and made conscious during the progress of the analysis; but they have this peculiarity, which is characteristic for their species, that they replace some earlier person by the person of the physician. To put it another way: a whole series of psychological experiences are revived, not as belonging to the past, but as applying to the person of the physician at the present moment."

By "transference-love," Freud refers here to the more or less direct sexual manifestations, when the transference overflows the setting and demands direct satisfaction. This, in Freud's metaphor, is "the logic of soup, with dumplings for arguments" (167).[1]

Freud stresses that it is relatively easy to interpret the patient's material—that is, the transferences to the preconscious representations, particularly the words of free association—but he calls our attention to the difficulty inherent in handling the transference to the person of the analyst. "This [transference to the person of the physician] happens . . . to be by far the hardest part of the whole task. It is easy to learn how to interpret dreams, to extract from the patient's associations his unconscious thoughts and memories, and to practice similar explanatory arts: for these the patient himself will always provide the text. Transference [to the person of the physician] is the one thing the presence of which has to be detected almost without assistance and with only the slightest clues to go upon" (1905, 7).

This introduction is intended to underline the resistance accompanying the fundamental sexual transferences which inevitably emerge in an analysis and which, if not adequately resolved, give rise to "transference love," a true drama that brings about the end of the treatment. Freud's most dramatic example, albeit one that is not taken from a psychoanalytic treatment proper, is that of Breuer with Anna O. (Freud, 1920). What should be stressed in this case is Breuer's role as protagonist and the tragic character of the experience, which can be equated with what we know as "negative therapeutic reaction." Breuer, who questioned the sexual etiology of the neuroses, entered into an intense "transference-love" with Anna O., as a result of which he had difficulties with his wife and finally decided to interrupt the treatment. As a consequence of this experience, he abandoned the theory of the sexual etiology of the neuroses and ended his collaboration with Freud. The impact of this experience was such that, according to Freud, it postponed the development of analytic therapy in its first decade.

The Oedipus complex. In this paper, Freud speaks only of the transference love of the female patient for her psychoanalyst. However, observation shows that transference love may also be found in the case of a male patient and a female analyst, as well as in a patient of either sex toward the analyst of the same sex. In other words, transference love develops in accordance with the love possibilities we find in the resolution of the Oedipus complex. For both the girl and the boy, the first love object is the mother, while the other

1. Eickhoff (1987, 103; and see also this volume, above) says that Freud took this metaphor from Heine's poem "Die Wanderratten" [The Roving Rats].

varieties are the result of the vicissitudes of the primary oedipal drama and their resignification through the resolution of the Oedipus complex.

The analyst's capacity. While we can say that what appears on the manifest level as transference love is a feeling that is always latent in the analysis, it finds expression through the secondary oedipal manifestations. In my experience, its direct emergence in a reasonably well-conducted analysis is exceptional, so much so that I have observed it in only one case, at the beginning of my work, when I was not sufficiently experienced. In Freud's example, the case of Anna O., it is the result of a treatment in which the therapist was not ready to analyze the transference. In the epilogue to his account of Dora's case, Freud himself shows us how the treatment failed because he did not discover the transference love that had developed in the course of the analysis, a repetition of the love Dora had felt for Herr K., and he even points out that Dora might have perceived in him traces of attitudes leading to that confusion.

Our observations lead us to conclude that the emergence of transference love is the consequence of the analyst's failure to perceive it while it is incipient and to resolve it by means of interpretation. We assume that the resistance manifested in the transference love of which Breuer was the protagonist and which, according to Freud, postponed the development of psychoanalysis in its first decade is the same as the "crisis of psychoanalysis" that many analysts speak of today. The "spirits of the dead" that the psychoanalyst invokes become manifested in the oedipal, incestuous, tragic transference love and, when not adequately heard and interpreted, end up destroying the treatment.

Outcomes. Freud speaks of the three possible outcomes of transference love: doctor and patient form a "permanent legal union"; "the doctor and the patient part and give up the work they have begun"; and "they . . . enter into a love-relationship which is illicit" (160). These three outcomes are usually found in combination and somewhat masked. For example, the analysis may be interrupted for some reason that eventually reveals the incestuous nature of the resistance behind that decision, as when, some time thereafter, a "love relationship that is illicit is entered into" which may culminate in "a permanent legal union." In the second possibility, the most frequent, the interruption is preceded by violent manifestations that are motivated, as in the cases of Breuer (Anna O.) and Freud (Dora), by unconscious jealousy.

Analytic technique and the emergence of transference love. Let us now consider the characteristics of psychoanalytic technique that lead to the emergence of what ultimately constitutes transference love. In "this phenomenon, which occurs without fail and which is, as we know, one of the foundations of the psycho-analytic theory" the patient "must accept falling in love with her doctor as an inescapable fate" (160–61).

What brings about this result? We shall find the answer in *the setting* in which the psychoanalytic session develops, particularly the rule of abstinence.

The patient must lie on the couch without seeing the analyst, without acting out. All he (or she) can do is associate freely. The analyst is in a similar position—that is, sitting in his armchair, listening to the patient's words, and interpreting. The abstinence in which the analysis develops tacitly includes a prohibition against any direct sexual activity, which thus becomes taboo—that is, incestuous. In externalizing the prohibition, the analyst takes the place of the superego—the parental couple—and the incestuous currents that were repressed now find expression in the patient's unconscious relationship with the analyst, shaping the fundamental transferences, which bring about the transference love.

Abstinence "prohibits" the channeling of incestuous excitement into acting out. When the excitement does not find resolution in interpretation, the only path left to it is unconscious activity, communication between one unconscious and the other, which creates direct identifications between patient and analyst and brings about an oedipal transferential drama between them. This, in its extreme manifestations, acquires the form of "love" we are here considering.

It should be remembered that, when we speak about transference love, the setting has already been altered. Free association—defined by its metaphoric nature—has been replaced by its sexual foundations and by the subsequent demand for direct satisfaction.

These considerations suggest how the pressure toward acting out of transference love may be rectified. What is essential here is to identify and interpret the transference nature of words and acts, their metaphoric, symbolic value, and thus to reconstitute the setting of the analytic situation.

Jealousy. The jealous feelings that are part of the expression of the primitive, narcissistic, incestuous ego accompany transference love. Freud attributes jealousy to the relatives of the patients, but these "relatives" are only the manifest material; jealous feelings are active in the incestuous transference between patient and analyst and play a basic role in the destruction of the analysis. In these ambivalent manifestations we find the tragic nature of the primary, incestuous, oedipal structure, in which love cannot be separated from murder.

Virtual, real, reality, the actual. With the emergence of transference love, the patient, in Freud's words, "gives up her symptoms or pays no attention to them; indeed, she declares that she is well. There is a complete change of scene; it is as though some piece of make-believe had been stopped by the sudden irruption of reality—as when, for instance, a cry of fire is raised during a theatrical performance" (162).

In order to establish the difference between virtuality, the particular type of reality in which transference takes place within the setting of the psychoanalytic session, and the "reality" it acquires when it overflows the setting and becomes acting out, we shall sketch the meanings we attach to the terms *virtual* (or *real*) and *reality* in the psychoanalytic situation.

Even when the fundamental rules are strictly maintained during the session, there are constant alterations that may be regarded as "actual" disturbances, which gain access to consciousness in terms of affects or other manifestations typical of actual neuroses: anxiety, discomfort, tiredness, lethargy, somatic symptoms, etc. These are alterations having to do with the neurovegetative-cellulo-humoral system. While these manifestations are seldom apparent, they have a reality distinguishable from that emerging with the abandonment of the setting, characterized by acting out. The term *virtual*, or *real*, fits this set of circumstances. On the other hand, by *reality* we mean the manifestations that accompany the abandonment of the setting and constitute acting out. We are dealing with "reality" when Freud speaks about the three possible "solutions" for transference love, all of which represent acting out and, as we have said, imply a shift from the "virtual" or "real," in which the analysis takes place within the setting, to "reality."

Although transference is always in part a resistance, resistance is particularly intense in the case of transference love. As Freud states, aspects of love were already present as a resistance, but were manifest in the patient's docile and understanding behavior; however, when love emerges as transference love, and the therapist tries to analyze it thus—bringing its incestuous origin into consciousness—the love that at first gave rise to such positive behavior (docility and understanding) emerges even more strongly as a resistance that ultimately may prove unmanageable.

The analyst's role. A central theme for understanding the emergence of transference love in the psychoanalytic treatment is the analyst's role. The concept of transference includes both patient and analyst, and understanding what one of them is experiencing points to what the other is experiencing. Although on the manifest level the patient's love is in the foreground, the analyst plays a protagonistic role. It is the analyst who conducts the analysis and who, through the unconscious components of his attitudes and interpretations, arouses and shapes the patient's transference responses. In carefully conducted analyses, in which a rigorous technique is used and the transference vicissitudes are interpreted as far as possible through the analysis of free associations before they become acting out, transference love, defined by its concrete nature, never emerges. Instead, in the few cases in which it did emerge and we were able to investigate it, we came to the conclusion that the transference was scarcely and inadequately analyzed, owing to a large extent to the analyst's "passion"—a primary, drive-like affect aroused by this situation. The "feeling" that expresses the incestuous-tragic foundations of the transference then invades the ego and pushes it to acting out. Interpretation-construction is absent or else is used in the service of the analyst's passion. He thus leads the patient into transference love, a psychoanalytic tragedy since, as with the negative therapeutic reaction, the result more often than not is the death of the analysis.

Free-floating attention. In the session, the therapist has images of the patient that are the product of various external perceptions: visual, auditive, olfactory, and tactile. But to the sensory perception we must add those unconscious perceptions impinging on the perceptual surface of the psychic apparatus: words, thoughts, affects. It is the analyst who attributes an external or internal origin to perceptions. The analyst hears the sounds of the patient's free associations—that is, acoustic images are activated in his consciousness which correspond to a language that is his own and which he infers come from the patient. These images, linked to concepts, configurate linguistic signs in which multiple transferences, stemming from the analyst's unconscious, converge, and words with meaning are formed. The sum total of these perceptions and transferences forms an imago in the analyst: the patient as object. On the other hand, the incredibly complex unconscious communication between patient and analyst provides the foundation for basic identifications. When analyzed from the synchronic perspective, these identifications correspond to those that have been described diachronically by Freud (1923) as the first identifications, the direct ones, previous to any object cathexis.

These identifications are the fundamental structures of the psychic apparatus (the original narcissistic ego, the ego of absolute primary narcissism, and of incest) that take part in the constitution of the affects emerging in the session and of the unconscious ideas transferred to the patient's imagos.

It is evident from this description that the analyst operates with his own images and imagos that he attributes to the object of reality, the patient. This projection defines the patient. The more repressed or buried—that is, the more unconscious—these structures, the more intense their reality quality.

Negative countertransference. From these considerations, the role of the analyst in the development of transference love becomes evident. As already stated, through the analytic process and particularly the setting in which it takes place, the imago patient is the recipient of transferences from the analyst's repressed imagos, including the narcissistic-incestuous imagos buried (*untergang*) in the analyst's unconscious (Freud 1924, 73). In this way, the patient's imago acquires incestuous meaning, which is ominous for the analyst's coherent ego. The ego defends itself from this traumatic invasion by endowing it with the quality of reality. A negative transference thus becomes established: the analyst experiences the patient as someone who threatens to introduce him into an incestuous structure. If the analyst is aware of the drama he is experiencing, these transferences will become a stimulus for the analytic work; otherwise, repression will emerge in the form of rejection of the patient, and the oedipal tragedy will culminate with the interruption of the analysis. There may be different outcomes; that is, the analyst's ego may participate in this incestuous enactment in which the oedipal drama, with the violence that characterizes incest, becomes established in the analytic situation.

Countertransference. All of this seems to indicate that the analyst is the protagonist in the development of transference love, which, moreover, he himself defines. These considerations lead us to review the concept of countertransference. According to this concept, in the course of the psychoanalytic process the analyst experiences reactions to the patient's material that are the product of his response to the patient's transferences. When we realize that the analyst is the protagonist, that the patient's transferences are conceived of by him and attributed to the patient, the concept of countertransference loses value; we might just as easily say that the patient's material is a countertransference in that it is a response to the analyst's transferences. It is in fact a play of transferences in which the analyst who discovers them—

ultimately in his self-analysis—is the one who defines them, enunciates them, makes them conscious and attributes them. It is on the basis of this self-analysis (Freud, 1910, 139; Cesio et al., 1988) in which he discovers the transferences that the analyst defines the patient.

The oedipal tragedy and the Oedipus complex. Understanding of the narcissistic, incestuous, tragic structures buried in the id that (as we said when discussing the negative countertransference) become evident through the development of transference love requires us to differentiate the concepts of oedipal tragedy and Oedipus complex.

In *The Ego and the Id* (1923), Freud affirms that there is a primary oedipal structure in the foundations of the psyche, the oedipal protophantasies, which lead to the "first and most important identification. . . . This is apparently not in the first instance the consequence or outcome of an object-cathexis; it is a direct and immediate identification and takes place earlier than any object-cathexis" (31). These primary identifications are the basis of the identifications that a posteriori form the Oedipus complex; they shape the ideal ego, the forerunner of the ego ideal. These protophantasies contain the origin of the Oedipus complex, the incest involving filicide and parricide in the struggle for possession of the mother-wife, just as Freud describes it in his account of an original mythical time. In the psychoanalytic process, current evidence of that mythical time can be seen in condensed form in incest. It stages the struggle for the sexual possession of the mother-wife. Its clinical manifestation is the negative therapeutic reaction, and transference love is one of the forms it takes.

Thus, we could say that there are two oedipal structures: one is that of incest with its narcissistic, passionate, tragic nature, the *oedipal tragedy,* while the other results from working through the former with the parents of personal history: the *Oedipus complex,* described by Freud in *The Ego and the Id* as characterized by tenderness and ambivalence. As for their manifestation, the latter seeks the inhibited sexual aim and its symptoms are those of the psychoneuroses.

Negative therapeutic reaction. In some analyses, after a few years of treatment and as they evolve in an atmosphere of intense sexual positive transference, when the achievements fulfill our expectations, we are faced with demands on the part of the patient that exceed our capacity to meet them within the analytic setting, as this would constitute a transgression. At the same time, and inseparably from the dominant passion, jealous feelings emerge, masked as love demands, and may become so violent that they jeopardize the treatment, thus forming what we know as negative therapeutic reaction (Cesio, 1960; Obstfeld, 1977). The tragic oedipal nature of this reaction leads us to infer the presence in its foundations of the affect known as transference love, which overflows the limits of the setting with its peremptory nature. What is now manifested in transference love is what was repressed or buried in the unconscious. It returns to life in the form of this narcissistic expression. The "wonderful baby"–phallus, reappears in the constitution of the wonderful patient-analyst couple. These are the "loves that kill," passions that end up destroying what is so intensely desired. These are loves that seek absolute possession of the object to the point of destroying it and bringing about self-destruction.

Tragedy and resistance. To sum up, transference love emerges as a narcissistic-incestuous manifestation that is tragically expressed and that, in extreme cases, is brought near to consciousness by the progress of the analysis, with the negative outcome we have described. We should add, with Freud, that the negative nature of this love is reinforced by the use resistance makes of it.

Narcissistic ego and coherent ego. The analysis of transference love, as already pointed out, reveals the double structure of the mental apparatus. In transference love, incestuous love, we find on one hand manifestations of the narcissistic, tragic ego that forms its foundations and on the other hand those of the coherent ego: the perceptual, moral, ethical ego that represses the feeling belonging to the narcissistic ego. If these feelings gained access to consciousness, they would either be violently rejected or, disguised as a genital ego, accepted. Thus, two extreme expressions of resistance are defined: the patient, the analyst, or both regard this love as authentic but impossible and this makes them feel they have to interrupt the analysis and part ways or else seek satisfaction, also putting an end to the analysis. Freud says that the analyst's or the patient's rejection of these feelings, even for ethical reasons, as well as the acceptance of the feelings are all products of resistance and that the analyst can deal with them only by using the resources of analytic technique.

Considerations of analytic technique. When transference love emerges, one solution might be that the analyst realize that he has no right to accept the patient's fond feelings and that he "put before the woman who is in love with him the demands of social morality and the necessity for renunciation, and . . . succeed in making her give up her desires, and, having surmounted the animal side of herself, go on with the work of analysis" (163). What Freud calls here the animal side corresponds to the drive like, incestuous manifestations that characterize the original narcissistic ego, for which incestuous strivings are "natural," while ethical demands address the coherent ego. Freud goes on to say that these are false solutions to be replaced by "considerations of analytic technique." This stems from the idea that solutions based on prohibitions are futile since the prohibition itself is, after all, an incestuous manifestation. (Incest always involves murder and castration, later expressed by the prohibitions of the superego.) However, enunciating the setting and establishing abstinence, its fundamental rule, amount to acting out, which nevertheless is indispensable for the progress of the analysis in that it brings incestuous organization to the foreground by establishing it in the transference. In the very act of enunciating the setting as a "prohibition" of direct sexual activity, the analyst is the protagonist of incest but, as Freud says, he is so with due "considerations of analytic technique," that is, as a technical device that brings into transference the foundations themselves, the source of neurotic developments, thus making psychoanalytic treatment possible.

Abstinence. Freud says that "declaring that one returns the patient's fond feelings but at the same time avoiding any physical implementation of this fondness until one is able to guide the relationship into calmer channels and raise it to a higher level" is also futile. He adds that "psycho-analytic treatment is founded on truthfulness. In this fact lies a great part of its educative effect and its ethical value." The paragraph ends as follows: "In my opinion, therefore, we ought not to give up the neutrality toward the patient, which we have acquired through keeping the counter-transference in check" (164–65). Later he concludes, "It is quite out of the question for the analyst to give way. . . . She [the patient] has to learn from him to overcome the pleasure principle" (170).

When reflecting on the limits Freud sets for the analyst's participation in the patient's transference love, we find that, as he states, they are justified by technical principles. Freud says that it is not a question of making demands of social morality by asking the patient to give up her desires, since these must be present as the driving force of the process, but, as we have already pointed out, he does not analyze the enforcement of the setting, which, as he says, is a deprivation—that is, implies prohibitions.

This is a technical device that brings into the present of the analytic situation the sexual needs and the deprivations underlying the genesis of neuroses, since, in principle, neurosis is founded on frustrated loves that are renewed and seek satisfaction in the treatment. Those now become manifest in transference love and, in principle, are checked by means of the rule of abstinence. The setting-abstinence thus repeats the original frustration. A neurotic is a person who has not developed sufficient ethical principles, hence the need to enforce a setting that takes their place by demanding that the patient "[surmount] the animal side of herself." On the other hand, as Freud points out, the analyst also suffers, to a greater or lesser degree, from "frustrated loves" similar to the patient's—although their intensity is supposedly different—which he keeps in check by means of the setting. The enforcement of the setting compensates for the ethical failures inherent in neurosis, turning "need and longing" into "forces impelling [the patient] to do work and to make changes."

Gradiva. As Freud points out, when the analyst responds directly, in reality, to the patient's need for love, he only gives her surrogates, since transference itself, in so far as it is imaginary,[2] results from the failure to find an object capable of adequately satisfying the need, and the analyst, or rather his image, only allows for wish-fulfillment; he is only the image of a dream whose fulfillment leads to a bitter awakening most of the time. In Freud's charming analysis of the Gradiva (1907, 7) we find an example of transference love. In its development we find the imaginary (wish-fulfillment) in Hanold's hallucinations, the "real" in the affects being excited, and, finally, "reality"—that is, Hanold and Zoe enter into a love relationship. Through a process in which he combines fantasy, hallucinations, and reality, Hanold experiences his infantile love in the present. This is the transference love that emerges as the outcome of an analysis. As in Hanold's case, transference fantasies with their connotation of "real" become so actual that they finally acquire the value of "reality." Its infantile, narcissistic nature shows that this is neurotic love which soon will lay bare its incestuous roots, bringing about a fate similar to the original one, that is, the "tragedy"—the interruption of the analysis—and the repression, or burial, that now becomes manifest in the departure of the object that "woke up" and made its way to the surface.

Incest. The incestuous, narcissistic roots of transference love determines its ominous, taboo nature and also its tragic, violent outcome, marked by the

2. We are not taking into account here the "real" quality in the transference. We want only to clarify the difference between "reality" and "imaginary" transference.

"murder," an inseparable component of incest. As we have already said, the analyst is the protagonist, with his incestuous transferences, in which the patient takes the place of his primordial objects. The patient's transferences thus merge with the analyst's, and the acting out of these transferences is particularly due to the analyst's transference, which is therefore the strongest resistance.

The analyst's aim. Freud emphasizes that, if the analyst satisfied the patient's love demands, "the patient would achieve *her* aim, but he would never achieve *his*" (165). We find this statement questionable and feel that it is the other way round. Experience shows that it is usually the analyst who in these cases achieves his neurotic aim, for, if he remains within the setting, this outcome is precluded. The patient's "aim" is to find relief for her neurotic suffering. The sexual transference that emerges in the course of the analysis disturbs her aim, which nevertheless remains latent. The analyst, in his neurotic response, takes the patient's sexual response to be her aim. Patients are usually grateful when they feel that the analyst understands that their "aim," the one that moves them to make the tremendous effort of being in analysis, is precisely that, to be analyzed.

The real and the actual. We might say that considerations about the need for abstinence are based on the idea and observation that, when the love that emerges in the analytical situation becomes "reality," the analyst as such is destroyed. We should remember that the analyst's drama is that the technique, the setting, elicits incestuous sexual transferences and, at the same time, frustrates them. These transferences are neither a mere imaginary play of representations nor "reality," but are what we call "virtual," or "real." By *imaginary* we mean the play of representations; by *reality,* dramatic acting out with things of the world; by *real,* that which implies the expression of the foundations, the affects, all that gives rise to "actual" manifestations: those that have not been re-signified.

Thus, analysis moves along a razor's edge and can easily fall into one or the other extreme, that is, either the "imaginary" or acting out, or into both, since, when it remains in the "imaginary," the "real" unconsciously grows until it finally overflows into acting out, that is, "reality." In Dora's case, Freud stresses that it was easy for him to analyze the dreams (the imaginary) but he could not analyze the transference to his own person (actual, real) which led to acting out, that is, to the interruption of the analysis.

In our view, the analytic space is "real" in that, although it is not reality in the sense of acting out, it includes, together with verbal and other images, affective manifestations, to which we attribute a somatic-neurovegetative, cellulo-humoral, involuntary-muscular figuration. Through his participation, the analyst perceives these alterations and infers those corresponding to the patient. When these actual experiences overflow the limits of the setting and massively invade the coherent ego, they finally reveal their incestuous sexual nature and configurate transference love.

Succinct definitions of the concepts we use will help clarify the differences. By *real* we mean the drama that takes place within the setting of the session, reaching consciousness in terms of affects ranging from anxiety to the tenderest of sentiments. This is an original experience, a more or less direct presentation of the unconscious. As such it is also *actual* in the sense that we apply this term to the anxiety neuroses. The word *act* denotes the verbal construction that describes the actual drama based on the analysis of the free associations; it leads to the reconstructions that place the act into history.

Falling in love. What is the difference between the love characterizing transference love and love outside the analysis? Freud stresses the repetitive nature of the infantile reactions we find in both kinds of love in order to show that one difference between them is that the "love" that emerges in the analysis is used by the resistance. From this we may infer that, for Freud, normal falling in love is not a resistance. However, we wonder whether falling in love is not always a resistance to the expression of genital love, since it is characterized by its drive-like nature and seems to be reactive to castration anxiety, which it denies, whereas genital love is the result of the transmutations of castration anxiety through the elaboration of the Oedipus complex with the parents of one's personal history.

"Normal" love and transference love. In spite of the similarities between normal love and transference love, Freud finds that the latter "is characterized by certain features which ensure it a special position. In the first place, it is provoked by the analytic situation; secondly, it is greatly intensified by the resistance, which dominates the situation; and thirdly, it is lacking to a high degree in a regard for reality" (168–69). We believe that the first of these characteristics is what unquestionably defines it as transference love, since we consider it as such when it is supported by abstinence in its "real" limits within the setting of the session. After all, the manifestations we find in the analytic setting differ from situations taking place outside of it in that the analyst regards them as the material and the resistance for the discovery of

the unconscious. As soon as he stops being the analyst, that is, when he abandons the setting, transference love becomes a manifestation of love comparable to those situations occurring outside the analytic setting. It is obvious, then, that it depends on the analyst's capacity to maintain the setting whether or not the love provoked by the psychoanalytic situation will reach the extreme intensity that turns it into transference love.

As to the statement that "it is greatly intensified by the resistance," we do not feel that this is a distinctive feature, for, as we have already said, the falling in love that takes place outside the psychoanalytic situation is also "greatly intensified" by the resistance to genital love.

The third point is also questionable, for "lacking to a high degree in regard to reality" characterizes all kinds of falling in love; "love is blind," says a popular proverb.

Synchrony and diachrony. Insofar as it is an actual incestuous oedipal drama, transference love has a drive-like manifestation, in the nature of the presentations of the unconscious dominated by repetition compulsion. From this point of view, it is original and has no history, like actual neurosis (Cesio et al., 1988; Marucco, 1982, 31). By means of the interpretation-construction, we introduce it into a temporal, diachronic dimension and then see it as the repetition of an infantile love.

When we analyze the images and experiences that make up the material of a session, we notice that we can discover in them all the imaginable structures, and that they are all "actual" and synchronic, some more obviously than others. Their discovery depends on the resistances to discovery being unmasked; the last to be discovered, and the more important ones, are those more intensely resisted. We may conclude that we are working with a synchronic conception that is in harmony with the atemporality of the unconscious, which in this way gains access to consciousness. Resistance becomes manifest in the establishment of a temporal order; what is more intensely resisted is discovered last, what is discovered last is expressed in experiential terms and threatens to find its way to acting out, as happens with transference love. According to the intensity of the resistance, a temporal scale is established and at the same time a causal sequence: what is first gives rise to what follows. Thus, we place the ego of the Oedipus complex—primary, incestuous, narcissistic—at the origin, and we call it original ego, the foundations of the subsequent ego structures. This series of structures that may be described in a temporal order appears synchronically in the transference.

Among them, transference love shows the repressed or buried oedipal structure most directly.

Interpretation-construction. Freud suggests the technical approach to the analysis of transference love when he places "considerations of analytic technique" above all other approaches. Dora's case is a good example. Freud offers a masterful analysis of the transferences, from the unconscious ideas to the words in the narration of dreams and free association; but he points out in the epilogue that he could not analyze the transferences to his own person, the person of the analyst. He then tells us that Dora's words contained the key for the discovery of the experiential oedipal drama, of the "act" taking place between them, in which he played a *protagonistic* role. He then suggests that the solution would have been to interpret-construct the "act" of which he was the protagonist, which could have been formulated as follows: "It is from Herr K. that you have made a transference onto me. Have you noticed anything that leads you to suspect me of evil intentions similar (whether openly or in some sublimated form) to Herr K.'s? Or have you been struck by anything about me or got to know anything about me which has caught your fancy, as happened previously with Herr K.?" Dora's associations concerning her passion for Herr K., which had allowed Freud to discover the history of her libidinal organization, also revealed the latent, actual love scene that was taking place with Freud. Her descriptions of scenes with Herr K. were metaphors for the actual scenes with Freud. Finally, Freud's remarks show that the absence of this interpretation-construction (Cesio et al., 1988) brought about the end of the treatment, the oedipal "tragedy," a common outcome in these cases.

The hypothesis is that, when the interpretation-construction is made at the right moment, transference love finds its way into consciousness, and a careful analysis of it resolves the transferences by binding its unconscious, emotional components. Thus, the actual drama is endowed with the nature of a repetition of other experiences, particularly infantile ones, with which it is then introduced into time, that is, it becomes history. The realization that these memories are a re-living, only now with the analyst, makes it possible to free the libido from these primary, incestuous fixations that made it tragic, impossible, and to channel it, through the meanings it gradually acquires, toward a secondary oedipal structure (Cesio, 1986).

The oedipal tragedy. Transference love arouses the strongest resistance and, at the same time, is the strongest resistance. Its discovery and working-through by bringing it into consciousness leads the analyst to incest and fills him with horror vis-à-vis the threatening tragedy. The analyst's situation is comparable to that of Oedipus, who, in the course of his investigation-analysis, discovers that he himself is the protagonist of the incest murder of Laius and the sexual union with Jocasta; the outcome is tragedy. We believe that this horror stops the analyst's investigation and leads him to the alternative "solution," that is, to acting out in which the tragedy that was supposed to be avoided ultimately reappears.

REFERENCES

Bergmann, M. S. 1982. Platonic love, transference love and love in real life. *J. Amer. Psychoanal. Assn.* 30:87–111.

Cesio, F. 1960. El letargo: Contribución al estudio de la reacción terapéutica negativa. I y II *Rev. de Psicoanálisis* 18:10–26, 289–98.

———. 1986. Tragedia y muerte de Edipo. *Rev. de Psicoanálisis* 43:239–51.

———. 1987. Tragedia edípica. Sepultamiento. Acto. Transferencia y repetición. *Rev. de Psicoanálisis* 44.

Cesio, F.; D'Alessandro, N.; Elenitza, J.; Hodara, S.; Isod, C.; and Wagner, A. 1986. La "palabra" en la obra de Freud. *Rev. de Psicoanálisis* 39:897–922.

Cesio, F.; M. Davila, M.; Guidi, H.; and Isod, C. M. 1988. Las intervenciones del analista. I. La interpretación: Interpretación propiamente dicha y construcción. *Rev. de Psicoanálisis* 45:1217–40.

Eickhoff, F. 1987. A short annotation to S. Freud's "Observations on transference-love." *Rev. Psycho-Anal.* 14:103.

Freud, S. 1900. *The Interpretation of Dreams. S.E.* 5.

———. 1905. *Fragment of an analysis of a case of hysteria.* Epilogue. *S.E.* 7.

———. 1907. Delusions and dreams in Jensen's "Gradiva". *S.E.* 9.

———. 1910. Future prospects of psychoanalytic therapy. *S.E.* 11.

———. 1920. An autobiographical study. *S.E.* 20.

———. 1923. *The ego and the id. S.E.* 19.

———. 1924. The dissolution of the Oedipus complex. *S.E.* 19.

Jones, E. 1953. *Sigmund Freud: Life and Work.* Vol. 1. London: Hogarth.

Marucco, N. 1982. Transferencia idealizada y transferencia erótica. *Rev. de Psicoanálisis* 39.

Obstfeld, E. 1977. Más alla del "Amor de transferencia." *Rev. de Psicoanálisis* 34.

A Cry of Fire:
Some Considerations
on Transference Love

JORGE CANESTRI

A SIGNIFICANT SEMANTIC FIELD

If the reader of this paper—of which the author, as we know, was justly proud—were to contextualize it in relation to certain letters Freud wrote to Jung and Pastor Pfister several years earlier, he would witness the unfolding of a unique semantic field.

Within the text itself can be found the expression I have used in the title of the present chapter. Freud says that there is a change in the analytic scene "as when, for instance, a cry of fire is raised during a theatrical performance" (162). Moreover, the psychoanalyst works with "highly explosive forces" (170), and in his practice, as in medical practice, fire is essential, because "those [diseases] which fire cannot cure are to be reckoned wholly incurable" (171; quoting Hippocrates).

In a letter to Pfister dated 9 February 1909, Freud states that the results of both pastoral work and psychoanalysis are based on the implementation of erotic transference. The letter ends in a stylistic crescendo that unleashes "sparks" and invokes a "fire" to ignite new flaming "brands."

There can be no doubt that Freud was fully aware of his semantic choices. One month after the Pfister missive (9 March 1909), he writes to Jung at length in answer to a letter received two days earlier:

To be open to slander and to be burnt by the love with which we operate, these are the dangers we meet in our work, but most certainly, we will not abandon our profession because of them. Navigare necesse est, vivere non necesse. Besides: "Living side by side with the devil, why should you fear a tiny flame?" This is more or less what grandfather used to say. This quotation comes to my mind because in describing this experience of your life, you fell into a decidedly theological style. A similar thing happened to me while writing to Pfister: I used the entire range of fire similes: flame, conflagration, pyre, etc. I couldn't help it; my respect for theology had fixed my attention on the quotation (!): "It doesn't matter! The Jew is burning on the pyre."

I shall forgo reference to Freud's quotations (from Goethe and Lessing), even though they are not without interest, in order to recall that these letters between the two analysts concerned the well-known Jung-Spielrein episode. As we shall see in a reexamination of transference love, this case was anything but irrelevant and certainly does not deserve to be dismissed as mere slander, as, indeed, it does not appear to have been.

As can be noted, the semantic field configured in "Observations on Transference-Love" is identical with that of the letters. It is interesting to emphasize that Freud believed he "couldn't help" the fire metaphor; when he writes about the erotic transference, he also runs the entire gamut of fire analogies, even though respect for theology is not involved. In my opinion, this is an indication of a necessity imposed by the subject itself: the meaning, the value, the destiny of the passions that exist in psychic life and in analytic practice.

A PARAPHRASE WITH SPECIAL ATTENTION TO TEXTUAL AND CONCEPTUAL PROBLEMS

In order to trace a small map that will enable us to single out the core of Freudian reasoning and at the same time review the questions that are left open, I shall paraphrase a few passages from the text with special attention to some terminological and conceptual difficulties. I have numbered the different themes so as to facilitate the subsequent discussion.[1]

1. Among the most significant difficulties, those related to the management of transference, Freud selects a particular type of situation: the patient falls in love with her analyst. (It is important to note that the field of investigation has been arbitrarily limited: the patient is female, the analyst male.) This fact is important for its real aspects as well as for its theoretical validity.

2. The first technical indication in the paper, directed to the analyst, is a "warning" (*Warnung*), an admonition: the analyst must know how to control any tendency toward countertransference. There are two motivations here, apart from the deontological one; both are theoretically relevant and should be kept in mind: (a) the amorous phenomenon appears because it "is induced by the analytic situation" (160–61); the German term is slightly stronger: *erzwungen* (122), forced; (b) therefore the patient's love has nothing to do with a particular quality of the love-object (in this case, the analyst). The object is indifferent; the culprit is the situation.

3. But what is the specific quality of the situation we are examining? Freud's description is thought-provoking and has given rise to more than one comment. I give the entire quotation: "There is a complete change of scene; it is as though some piece of make-believe [*Spiel*, 124] had been stopped by the sudden irruption of reality [*Wirklichkeit*, 124]—as when, for instance, a cry of fire is raised during a theatrical performance" (162). The imaginary/real discriminant is meaningful and implies technical and conceptual differences. The example of fire, as has already been noted, is part of a semantic field concerning passions.

4. While still not pronouncing on the nature of this intrusive love, Freud allows no doubt that it is at the service of resistance. One must bear in mind that the definition of resistance used here is the one elaborated in *The Interpretation of Dreams:* anything that interferes with the continuation of analytic work is seen as an expression of resistance. This explanatory model corresponds to the old idea that resistance increases in the vicinity of the pathogenic nucleus as well as to his complementary and more recent notion of avoiding a painful recollection and substituting repetition (Freud, 1914a).

Even this model will give way to subsequent divergences in psychoanalytic thought.

---

1. References to English terms are taken from the *S.E.* References to German terms are taken from the *G.S.* (Freud 1925).

5. The patient does not "produce" her love *de novo*. For a long time, the analyst has been able to recognize in her the signs of "an affectionate transference" (162); in German, *eine zärtlichen Übertragung* (124), a tender transference. This attitude was functional to the cure, but now everything is turned upside down. The transference love is used against the treatment and serves to put the analyst "in an awkward position" (163), *peinliche Verlegenheit* [124]: a painful embarrassment, which will be difficult to overcome. In other words, the patient is trying to checkmate the analyst. This complex mixture of passion and resistance, of passion that becomes resistance, and of resistance that masquerades as passion causes Freud to wonder: What can be done?

6. The answer to this question is one of the highlights of the paper. To Freud it is clear that "universally accepted standards of morality" (deontology) are not of great use, and therefore he attempts "to trace the moral prescription back to its source" (163). His sources are technical considerations related to psychoanalytic practice itself. In this way, ethics are closely linked to the science in which moral principles find their "ratio."

But to what theoretical and technical considerations does Freud appeal? There is a passage in the text that leaves us in no doubt: "Analytic technique requires of the physician that he should deny to the patient who is craving for love the satisfaction she demands. The treatment must be carried out in abstinence" (164–65). The implications here induce me to make a few terminological distinctions. The German term corresponding to "deny" is *versagen* (127). In this case the translation is correct since it deal precisely with denying—that is, refusing—a patient's request. The problem implied is relational inasmuch as one says "no" to somebody and refuses his or her demands. Normally Strachey translates the noun *Versagung* as frustration, and this dyad, frustration-gratification, can cause several deviations in meaning (see the excellent article by Laplanche and Pontalis, 1967). Abstinence (*Entbehrung:* privation, renunciation) is the driving power of treatment, and Freud promptly puts forward what is known as the principle of abstinence, one of the fundamental principles (*Grundsatz*). We shall see that this stylistic recourse to the basic principles at the foundations of analytic construction appears twice in the text, both times with considerable force.

But why is abstinence the driving power of treatment? Because the analyst could not offer the patient anything but surrogates and therefore, besides cheating her, he would saturate those needs and desires that are the impelling force of work and therefore of change.

7. The first fundamental principle is a result of the structural tie between ethics and technique. The second basic principle of treatment is identified by Freud as the love of truth. To force back the spirits from the underworld after having invoked them, says Freud, would be anti-analytic. Furthermore, "the passions are little affected by sublime speeches." And no compromise solution is possible because "psycho-analytic treatment is founded on truthfulness. . . . It is dangerous to depart from this foundation. . . . Since we demand strict truthfulness from our patients, we jeopardize our whole authority if we let ourselves be caught out by them in a departure from the truth" (164).

As can be seen, the concept of foundation reappears in full force. On the part of the analyst, a departure from truth is any attitude that does not take into account the desire for truth, which bears and is the foundation of all psychoanalytic work. Apart from being unethical, departure from truth is not therapeutic, because the only authority the analyst could invoke—that is, one based neither on a mirage nor on the power of suggestion—would fail. If the analyst betrays the desire and respect for truth that give meaning to analytic work, he would fall short of his role and his function. On this point Freud is inflexible: any sort of bargaining is anti-analytic, every compromise is betrayal (Freud uses precisely this term). These two principles, the former, which binds the analyst's refusal (*Versagung*) to the necessity of not satisfying the patient's desire (abstinence), and the latter, which promotes the quest for truth as fundamental to psychoanalytic treatment, are the cornerstones of psychoanalytic ethics.

8. What technical indications result from these observations? More simply, what can be done? In relation to his patient, the analyst must not abandon the neutrality acquired through the control of countertransference. As we know, countertransference is a concept that seldom appears in Freudian theory; many of the related technical indications are the result of post-Freudian thought, and I make only brief reference to them.

Let us linger for a moment on neutrality, a concept that is not very popular among analysts of some contemporary schools. It is worthwhile to note first that in this paper Freud speaks not of neutrality but of indifference. Actually, the relevant clause: "In my opinion, therefore, we ought not to give up the neutrality towards the patient" (164) in the original German reads: *"Ich meine also, man darf die Indifferenz . . ."* (127). The term *indifference*, seemingly harsher than *neutrality*, is not synonymous with lack of consideration for the suffering of others, or lack of empathy, a term that Kohut (after T. Reik) contributed to the technical lexicon. The advantage of this word lies in the theoretical bond established by the vocabulary defining the fundamental principles that regulate the patient's talking (free association) and the analyst's listening (evenly suspended attention). The analyst's indifference, therefore, corresponds to an attitude of equal availability, a uniformly spread attention, distributed without distinction over all the "material" presented by the patient. This bond has been underlined by Laplanche (1987).

9. Transference love, therefore, must be neither gratified nor suppressed. The course to be followed by analysis is one for which "there is no model in real life" (166). Transference love has to be experienced and the analytic content extracted from the situation; that is, the related fantasies, the principal characteristics of sexual desire, the infantile object-choice must be brought to light. This is the only method that will enable us to modulate and gradually transform amorous passion.

The analyst is assisted in this effort by his awareness that the patient's feeling of security depends upon the analyst's capacity to preserve his analytic function.

But, on the basis of all these facts, can we safely affirm that transference love, consisting of multiple passions that are explicated during treatment, is neither real nor genuine? Certainly not. On this point there is no doubt. It is correct to stress the use that resistance makes of love, but resistance does not *create* love. It *uses* it. The affirmation that the love proclaimed and demanded by the patient is a reedition of past loves is a weak argument; Freud rightly asks himself what love is not a reproduction of infantile situations or infantile object-choice. Transference love, then, is genuine love.

10. There exists, however, a type of patient, or rather a class of patient (Freud says of women), with whom treatment of "the erotic transference for the purposes of analytic work" is unsuccessful (166). Freud's causal argumentation is weak and constitutes one of the inconsistencies of his paper. In fact, what could "the elemental passionateness" of these women be? We shall see that the attempt to answer this question has developed into a rich and fertile field for post-Freudian thought.

SOME CONSIDERATIONS ON METHOD

Until now, the text paraphrasis has permitted us to examine more closely, as if with a magnifying glass, the technical questions posed by Freud. We have rapidly inferred that many theoretical problems—or, if you prefer, meta-psychological dilemmas—have been raised. At this point it becomes necessary to focus on a wider field in order to illustrate how this problem of transference love has been treated by the various psychoanalytic schools.

The first observation that can be made after scanning the voluminous bibliography on transference in general is the striking agreement among authors of diametrically opposed schools (for example, ego psychologists, and Lacanians): all consider the theory of transference a precise and fundamental discriminant among the various analytic theories. R. Greenson apodictically maintains that "every aberration in psychoanalysis can be demonstrated in the deviant way that transference phenomena are regarded" (1967, 151). This observation reminds us that transference love is a particular modality of transference. Although the paper we are examining is obviously limited to this modality, it should be no less obvious that we have to bear in mind all the theoretical variants on the conceptualization of transference elaborated by the different psychoanalytic schools; clearly that cannot be examined here.

To this indispensable methodological requirement can be added still another. All theories, including psychoanalytic ones, have their own internal consistency and coherence. It is not good practice to isolate an element of a theory or model without considering the place it occupies within the complex system as a whole and the determining link it establishes with other elements of the system. One example will suffice: D. W. Winnicott published "Primitive Emotional Development" in 1945 and "On Transference" in 1956. The clinical varieties of transference described in the latter paper are intimately linked to the ideas put forward in the 1945 paper. If the thesis on primitive development were refuted, perhaps the modes of transference analyzed by Winnicott would not disappear as a clinical event, but his considerations on the analyst's "attitudes" would find no theoretical support.

It would be pointless to deny that the theories on transference elaborated since 1915, the year Freud's paper was published, have enlarged and significantly modified the Freudian concept, whichever psychoanalytic school is referred to. It is equally true that Freud himself considerably broadened his entire theory when formulating the new drive dualism (1920) and the theoretical considerations on the splitting of the ego, without, however, further elaborating a corresponding transference theory.

Furthermore, transference is a concept of psychoanalytic practice, of what J. Sandler et al. (1969) have called the "clinical moment" of psychoanalysis.

As these authors have aptly noted, it is not always easy to relate it to meta-psychology.

Freud "arrives late" at the conceptualization of destructive drives and the consideration of their impact in analysis, and, by his own clear and explicit decision, he never arrives at all at the treatment of psychotic pathologies. As we shall see, this is not without consequences.

A RE-EXAMINATION OF THE PROBLEMS

I shall now attempt to summarize briefly some of the problems delineated in the preceding paraphrases.

1. Freud limited his observations to analytic work between a male analyst and a female patient. There is no reason to argue that transference love belongs exclusively to such relationships. Greenson (1967) maintained that transference love, in his experience, did not present itself in an evident manner where the analytic relationship was man-to-man unless the patient was a self-declared homosexual. There should be a corresponding absence of transference love between a female patient and a female analyst, except, again, in the case of manifest homosexuality. None of these conditions describes today's clinical scenario. It does not appear true that transference love is nonexistent between male patients and female analysts; it does not even seem true that transference love cannot manifest itself in analysis when both participants are of the same sex without there being homosexual implications.

Instead, it is important to consider that: (a) the bibliography on transference love between male patients and female analysts is rare, if not nonexistent; (b) it is possible that transference in these cases has unique characteristics that must be investigated (Lester, 1985); (c) the development of both types of transference (paternal and maternal) in male and female patients toward male and female analysts, stated by Fenichel (1945), is incontrovertible but, at the same time, insufficient to describe the great variety of object-relations that can be found in clinical observation; (d) the "real" characteristics of the analyst, in this case gender, and their incidence in analytic experience must be studied with greater attention.

Some interesting reflections have recently been published on this topic: E. P. Lester (1985), M. Goldberger and D. Evans (1985), E. Torres de Beà (1987), and E. S. Person (1988).

2. I have quoted the Freudian tenet that the amorous phenomenon appears because it is "induced [or provoked] by the analytic situation." If we consider it from the viewpoint of Freud's ethical preoccupations and his admonition to future analysts, this statement is easy to interpret. If, on the other hand, "induced" or "provoked" has causal significance—and Freud's oscillations support this interpretation—it becomes necessary to define these terms clearly. To put it synthetically, this entails deciding whether the amorous phenomenon is an effect of the analytic situation in itself (causal meaning) or emanates from the patient's internal object world and is merely highlighted in analysis. Clearly, taking one stand or another concerns not only transference love but the entire transference phenomenon. There is no doubt that Freud believed transference to be a permanent psychological phenomenon independent of psychoanalytic therapy and evident in many circumstances of everyday life.

Nevertheless, Macalpine (1950) has stressed that patients have a "readiness" for transference which transforms itself consequent to the analytic situation into "transference reactions." D. Lagache's (1951) thinking is oriented in the same direction and illustrates the role played by the abstinence principle in "stimulating" the patient's regression and "transference reactions." In commenting on the danger implicit in the concept of "producing" transference—that is, inducing transference by power of suggestion (which is not necessarily the result of an explicit active seduction on the part of the analyst but can be the consequence of far more unconscious manipulations)—Laplanche (1987) hypothesizes that analytic treatment, because of some of its characteristics and rules "entails a sort of structural reproduction of the conditions of sexual awakening" (161). He therefore agrees with Lagache about the defensive aspect of certain Freudian formulations on transference and considers transference to be a product of the analytic situation, although his theoretical arguments are different from those of Lagache and Macalpine.

Still, from this point of view, it would seem impossible to explain fully the presence of intensely erotized psychotic or parapsychotic transference that appears in analysis, sometimes from the very first session. We shall say more about this under point 10.

Freud's admonition also serves to highlight the fact that the particular quality of the analyst love-object is largely irrelevant, in consonance with what Freud had already explained about the role of narcissism (1914) in the composition of the libido. Actually, the fact that he could speak of transference and no longer of transferences is an indication that he understood the libidinal nature of transference. It is worthwhile to quote his explicit clarification in "On Narcissism: An Introduction":

He [the neurotic] then seeks a way back to narcissism from his prodigal expenditure of libido upon objects, by choosing a sexual ideal after the narcissistic type which possesses the excellences to which he cannot attain. This is the cure by love, which he generally prefers to cure by analysis. Indeed, he cannot believe in any other mechanism of cure; he usually brings expectations of this sort with him to treatment and directs them toward the person of the physician. The patient's incapacity for love resulting from his extensive repressions, naturally stands in the way of a therapeutic plan of this kind. (101)

It follows that the incapacity to love and the expectation of being loved, which the patient brings with him as a therapeutic project, are resolved by "loving" in what we call transference love. This substitution between ego and object (from lover to beloved and vice versa) has been well illustrated by Lacan (1991).

We must wait for "Group Psychology and the Analysis of the Ego" (Freud, 1921) for a complete picture of the problematics implied: the object put in the place of the ego ideal or of the ego, the idealization of the object, the role of the ideal-ego, that of the analyst qua idealized object. In two papers, Greenacre (1966a, 1966b) explores this aspect of "over-idealization" of the analyst and the analysis that can shape a particular type of transference.

This rapid glance at the role of narcissism in transference love does not do justice to the complexity and variety of the phenomena involved but is merely an attempt to trace the path followed by Freud in investigating the love phenomenon so as to dispel from psychoanalysis any suspicion of suggestion.

3. The Freudian phrase that likens the analytic situation to "a piece of make-believe" proves once again that certain ambiguities and oscillations are present in the concept of transference. On the one hand, the invasion of passion in the analytic situation is compared with the invasion of reality; on the other hand, the theatrical terminology—"change of scene," "piece of make-believe," "theatrical performance"—suggests an "as if."

The problem raised has inevitably allowed for different modulations in the answers. Mannoni (1982) deplores the inadequate lexicon at our disposal to deal with the unique nature of the reality of transference. Words like "real," "illusory," "imaginary," and "fictional" seem insufficient to describe the specific aspects of analytic experience. He concludes that if one must of necessity speak about "imaginary" and "real," then transference love is surely on the side of reality; it is in consonance with the character of genuineness that Freud had already attributed to it. Even so, Mannoni persists in using Freud's "theatrical" lexicon, including a reference to Fechner's famous "other scene" (*ein anderer Schauplatz*, a phrase quoted several times by Freud), and thereby tilts toward a description of transference as "imaginary."

From a point of view diametrically opposed to Mannoni's, one encounters a similar difficulty. If, for example, we analyze ego psychology's concept of a "working alliance" with particular attention to transference love, we meet the same type of obstacle. The papers of Zetzel (1956) and Stone (1961) provide antecedents to the concept of "working alliance" as defined by Greenson (1965). In speaking of transference love, Greenson says that when transference reactions are ego-syntonic, the first step is "to make the transference reaction ego-alien. The task is to get the reasonable ego of the patient to realize that his transference feelings are unrealistic, are based on a fantasy, and have some ulterior motivation" (233). But did Freud not say that sublime speeches (that is, those addressed to the reasonable ego) are useless in the face of passion?

The possible objections to this theoretico-technical proposal are many: Does a reasonable ego exist, bearing in mind that the resistance at work (as defined by Freud in this paper) is precisely the ego, which prevents facing the pathogenic nucleus? Why should transference love be defined as unrealistic when Freud qualified it as genuine? Doesn't this technical formula leave the criterion of reality in the hands of the analyst, called to judge now which passions of his patient are real and which are not, and again, by what authority? Didn't Freud specify that every love is based on a fantasy and has an ulterior motivation?

This is not the occasion to further investigate these objections, which go far beyond the treatment of transference-love; my intention is rather to point out how even following the theoretical orientation proposed by Greenson one still risks the "as if" and manipulation.

Perhaps Freud's own answer is more consistent. "There is no model in real life" to describe the analytic experience, with its load of passions. And therefore there can be no satisfactory analogy to the analytic work in which transference love must be *experienced* in order to extract from the situation what is specifically analytic: the fantasies, characteristics of sexual desire, the infantile object-choices, as stated in point 9.

4. A substantial concordance exists among all the psychoanalytic schools on the resistance mobilized by transference love. There is probably a greater divergence about the significance of repetition of the past that substitutes for a memory. Even though there is considerable agreement that the actual modes of object-choice reproduce internal "clichés," there is no such conformity of opinion about repetition. It was Lacan (1973) who theorized transference as being not the shadow of preceding experience, of ancient deceits or trickeries of love, but instead an encounter between the patient's desires and those of the analyst. According to Lacan the concept of repetition deserves recognition in its own right because of its link with the compulsion to repeat (*Wiederholungszwang*) and the death instinct. Incidentally, if we bear in mind what has been discussed in point 3, the idea of an encounter between the analyst's desires and those of the patient confronts us with still another model of the production of transference and transference love (and love in general): this time a model of trickery.

5. The importance assumed during treatment by "affectionate transference" as well as by positive sublimated transference, present and functional in certain periods, varies noticeably according to different theories and their corresponding techniques. It is obvious that this type of transference will assume a primary, positive role among those who uphold the therapeutic alliance, prerequisite to psychoanalytic process, but will be much less meaningful in those schools that center on deep interpretations and early interpretations of negative transference, such as the Kleinian school

6. and 7. The Freudian enunciation of the structural tie between ethics and technique in analytic experience needs no further comment. However, the centrality of truth in analytic work may raise some questions about the concept of truth itself. It appears to be strictly dependent on the conclusions that must derive from clinical experience and not on some transcendental idea of truth, pre-existent to the analytic experience.

This reasoning stems from the clinical tenet that the refusal (*Versagung*) to satisfy the patient's request—that is, the imposition of privation (abstinence)—favors the nonfulfillment of the wishes that keep the search in motion. This is the technical norm. The analyst's desire for truth, together with his exercise of denial, permits the emergence of the patient's genuine desire and its analysis.

It is known that Lacan (1973) insisted on this aspect of the analytic work. The main point of the Lacanian argument stresses the risk of specularization and of suggestion implicit in certain conceptions of transference. If, as Freud has illustrated in this work, the analyst, when confronted with the expression of his patient's love, would find it difficult to boast of such an imaginary "conquest"—since the object of this love is absolutely indifferent—the analytic operation should promote the search for the other (internal) object, the one that confers on any (real) object whatsoever a value it does not possess.

At this level, then, the Lacanian theory on transference pivots on the function of fantasy (*fantasme*) and, more specifically, on the function of the object of the fantasy. Many psychoanalytic schools could recognize their own theories in the model thus formulated.[2]

8. Having defined the significance of the point of conjunction between ethics and technique in psychoanalysis, it is evident that, apart from the specific technical difficulties of transference love, Freud perceives further problems relative to its effect on countertransference. Breuer's experience with Anna O. served as a warning, and other personal observations can be traced in Freud's correspondence with Jung. Given, therefore, that control of countertransference is a natural consequence of the ethico-technical equation, we may now wonder whether Freud did not in some way underestimate the importance of passions in analysis. It is worth recalling that he himself (1926, appendix C) declared that we know very little about the psychology of the emotional processes. In developing and continuing a line of thought known to us since 1973, André Green (1990) insists on Freud's insufficient theoretical and clinical answers to the problem of passions and "madness" in analysis and on the fact that both must be accepted and shared through analysis. Although Freud certainly does not advise exorcising the demons, it is perhaps true that when they become too cumbersome he is ready to declare that a dialogue with them is not possible. Thus the demons become unanalyzable psychosis or "elemental passionateness."

9. The evolution of psychoanalytic thought on the type of patient described by Freud as sensitive only to "the logic of soup, with dumplings for arguments," to whom he attributes an "elemental passionateness," has brought about a differentiation in transference love. According to Gitelson (1952) and Rappaport (1959), it was Blitzsten (1944) who first spoke about erotized

2. As is well known, the singularity of the Lacanian construction lies in the postulation of the radical difference and the specific character of the object of fantasy (*fantasme*)— object "petit *a*"—inasmuch as this object cannot be specularized. There is a long series of correspondences with—and differences from—the concept of the partial object, but it is not within the scope of this paper to investigate this subject.

transference as a form of transference that deviates from the more normal erotic transference, though he never wrote about it. They mention this in connection with their own investigation of countertransference and the analyst's participation in producing a type of transference characterized by an excess of the erotic component right from the start (Rappaport's "ready-made transference"). We find here a weakness in the transference accompanied by an exaggerated tenacity, a great resistance to any modulation or transformation, a strong dependency, a remarkable intolerance for "frustration"—that is, an inability to tolerate the analyst's refusal (*Versagung*) to satisfy the amorous request—a corresponding resistance to analytic work, and a significant destructiveness that become explicit in the request for love.

Both Gitelson and Rappaport have insisted on the diagnostic and prognostic importance of the patient's first dream in analysis if the analyst appears in person. This can be a clear sign of the excessive proximity of the "original relationship" to the present situation. Further investigation would be necessary to determine what role the analyst could play in the genesis of this sort of transference. This difference between erotic transference and erotized transference has imposed itself on the vocabulary and the conceptualization of transference love. Implicitly or explicitly, two forms of transference love have been identified: the first is neurotic in nature, the second psychotic. The logical consequence of these views is the wider hypothesis proposed by Etchegoyen (1986) regarding the existence of several "clinical forms" of erotized transference: strictly psychotic (delusional and manic), perverse, psychopathic, symptomatic expression of borderline states, and so on. [3]

However, this theme could benefit from a more general consideration, as has already been suggested. We must remember that the limitation in the analyzability of patients who present an "elemental passionateness," as proclaimed by Freud, is the result of the Freudian exclusion of psychotic pathology from the analytic experience. Moreover, it is only well after writing the paper we are examining that Freud recognizes the importance of destructiveness in psychotic pathology.

We have already mentioned the Spielrein-Jung "case." With a precedent of "amorous madness" on her side and a grave lapse of psychoanalytic ethics on Jung's, Spielrein (1912) brought to Freud not only the truth about her own madness in transference but also, in a certain way, a pioneer work on the importance of destructiveness. Freud was able to appreciate it, even though it

---

3. I shall not investigate this aspect in the present paper. See Etchegoyen, 1986.

was unthinkable for him, as can be deduced from the letter he wrote to Jung on 21 March 1912.

We admit, then, that the erotized transference in its various forms appears during analysis. But as an answer to the Freudian declaration on the non-analyzability of a certain type of patient, we respond that this becomes possible to the extent that we include within the clinical situation and analytic reflection that which Freud had excluded from clinical work: psychoses and psychotic levels. Inevitably, the clinical consideration of serious psychic pathology leads the analysts investigating these problems to construct hypotheses on primitive development. The history of theoretical and technical differences in treating forms of erotized transference will then correspond to the wider history of theoretical differences regarding the very first moments of psychic life. But this is not the moment for such investigation.

Suffice it to say that from the moment in which the clinical work includes psychotic pathology, psychoanalytic literature begins to abound in considerations on the peculiarity of transference, and the very concept of transference (and in particular of transference love) becomes much wider and is transformed.

Perhaps the greatest changes have occurred in the Kleinian tradition. The historical antecedents of Klein's work can be traced back to the work of Abraham (1908) and Ferenczi (1909). But starting in the 1940s, it was Melanie Klein herself who began to treat transference as an unconscious fantasy, a "global situation," stressing the importance of negative transference and partial objects in transference (Klein, 1952). It is her pupils who will test the consistency of Klein's ideas in the "classic" analysis of psychotic patients. And it is to them—H. Segal, H. Rosenfeld, W. R. Bion (to name only a few)—that we owe a good part of what has today become our working knowledge in the analysis of psychotics.[4]The acceptance of psychotic pathology in clinical work as well as theoretical psychoanalysis has been extremely fruitful not only for the Kleinian school. Mahler et al. (1975, 1976) and Searles (1965) represent another pole of theorization, but they are not the only ones.[5]

4. See, for example, H. Rosenfeld (1963, 1964, 1987) on the specific subject of transference love in psychosis.
5. For a panorama of the multifarious ideas of transference and the changes this concept is undergoing following the inclusion of grave pathologies in clinical analysis along with the consequent reflections on primitive development, see the papers on transference presented at the Nineteenth International Psychoanalytic Congress of

According to these authors, however, the notations on erotized trans-ference of a predominantly psychotic nature are only secondary. Of primary importance is the deepening of our knowledge about these pathologies and, consequently, about their manifestations, even on a level of early, persistent, and resistant erotization of the transference (such as to submit the analyst as well as the analysis to a difficult trial). As the pathology considered broadens, so too will the modalities of transference love. Such, for example, is the case of borderline pathology (see Kernberg, 1975).

To sum up, perhaps one should enquire whether the assimilation of erotized transference to psychotic or borderline pathology, taken for granted in a great part of the literature, corresponds to truth.

In fact, not all of the analysts who have investigated this subject agree that such an identification is legitimate. See, for example, H. Blum (1973) and S. J. Coen (1981), who extend erotized transference or the sexualization of transference to all types of patients. Both hypothesize situations of seduction and early trauma in the patient's life. Gaddini (1977, 1982) considers erotiza-tion a potent and elementary defense to which the patient resorts in different ways during different phases of the analytic process.

From another theoretical point of view, even André Green (1990) main-tains that passions and madness must be dissociated from the psychosis of transference. In his opinion, all transference contains passions and madness. (Transference psychosis has its own specific characteristics, and erotized transference undoubtedly plays a significant role in it.) Some of Green's concepts—for instance, the idea of "passivization" and that of fusional dan-ger (return to the "madness" shared between mother and infant)—can be useful in treating erotized transference (1973, 1990). Along the same lines one can recall Bion's ideas about the "psychotic part" of the personality and Winnicott's conception of inaugural fusion in the mother-infant relationship.

To conclude, it can be said that transference love remains a central point in psychoanalysis. We have seen how the fire of this very special passion caused Breuer to flee, Jung to be seared, and Freud to undertake a profound specula-tion. Nowadays, we acknowledge that in some cases the problem continues to be extremely difficult to resolve with analytic instruments. Sometimes,

---

Geneva, published in volume 37 of the *International Journal of Psycho-analysis*. Two of these papers, by Spitz (1956) and Winnicott (1956), investigate the hypothetical relation between manifestations of transference and the earliest aspects of the mother-child relationship, opening the way for new insights into certain transference prob-lems.

with a certain degree of awareness on the part of the analyst, the treatment is interrupted. At other times, he may not be able to respond to the situation with an accurate control of his countertransference. Any one of us with sufficient years of analytic experience may have taken for a second analysis a patient whose first analysis had ended in a sexual acting out with the analyst. Clinical experience with these patients reveals how iatrogenic of pathology the analysis that finishes in sexual acting out, how devastating its effects, and to what extent the patient's possibilities for benefiting from a new analysis are compromised. Yet, to my knowledge, there is practically no literature on this theme. Beyond the Freudian call to ethical values and to a love for truth, I feel that these re-analyses could represent a most valuable field for research in order to shed more light on transference love in those cases where the patient and his first analyst had both remained entrapped and were unable to resolve the experience analytically by "a cry of fire."

REFERENCES

Abraham, K. 1908. The psycho-sexual differences between hysteria and dementia praecox. In *Selected papers on psychoanalysis*. London: Hogarth, 1973.
Bion, W. R. 1956. Development of schizophrenic thought. *Int. J. Psycho-Anal.* 37:344–46.
Blum, H. 1973. The concept of the erotized transference. *J. Amer. Psychoanal. Assn.* 21:61–76.
Coen, S. J. 1981. Sexualization as a predominant mode of defense. *J. Amer. Psychoanal. Assn.* 29:893–920.
Etchegoyen, R. H. 1986. *Los fundamentos de la técnica psicoanalítica*. Buenos Aires: Amorrortu Ed.
Fenichel, O. 1945. *The psychoanalytic theory of neurosis*. New York: W. W. Norton.
Ferenczi, S. 1909. Introjection and transference. In *Sex in psychoanalysis*. New York: Basic, 1950.
Freud, S. 1914a. Remembering, repeating, and working-through (Further recommendations on the technique of psycho-analysis, II). *S.E.* 12.
———. 1914b. On narcissism: An introduction. *S.E.* 14.
———. 1915. Bemerkungen über die Übertragungsliebe. *Gesammelte Schriften* 6. Internationale Psychoanalytischer Verlag. Vienna: 1925.
———. 1920. Beyond the pleasure principle. *S.E.* 18.
———. 1921. Group psychology and the analysis of the ego. *S.E.* 18.
———. 1926. Inhibitions, symptoms and anxiety. *S.E.* 20.

————. (1940 [1938]). Splitting of the ego in the process of defence. *S.E.* 23.

Freud, S., and Jung, C. G. 1974. *Briefwechsel.* Frankfurt am Main: S. Fischer Verlag.

Freud, S., and Pfister, O. 1963. *Briefe, 1909–1939.* Frankfurt am Main: S. Fischer Verlag.

Gaddini, E. 1977. Note su alcuni fenomeni del processo analitico. In *Scritti, 1953–1985.* Milano: Raffaelo Cortina Ed., 1989.

————. 1982. Acting out in the psychoanalytic session. *Int. J. Psycho-Anal.* 63:57–64.

Gitelson, M. 1952. The emotional position of the analyst in the psychoanalytic situation. *Int. J. Psycho-Anal.* 33:1–10.

Goldberger, M., and Evans, D. 1985. On transference manifestations in male patients with female analysts. *Int. J. Psycho-Anal.* 66:295–309.

Green, A. 1973. *Le discours vivant: La conception psychanalytique de l'affect.* Paris: P.U.F.

————. 1990. *La folie privée: Psychanalyse des caslimites.* Chap. 4, Passions et destins des passions. Sur les rapports entre folie et psychose. Paris: NRF Gallimard.

Greenacre, P. 1966a. Problems on training analysis. *Psychoanal. Q.* 35:540–67.

————. 1966b. Problems of overidealization of the analyst and of analysis: Their manifestations in the transference and countertransference relationship. In *Psychoanalytic study of the child* 21:193–212.

Greenson, R. R. 1965. The working alliance and the transference neurosis *Psychoanal. Q.* 34:155–81.

————. 1967. *The technique and practice of psychoanalysis.* Vol. 1. New York: International Universities Press.

Kernberg, O. 1975. *Borderline conditions and pathological narcissism.* New York: Jason Aronson.

Klein, M. 1952. The origins of transference. *Int. J. Psycho-Anal.* 33:433–38.

Lacan, J. 1973. *Le séminaire. Livre XI, Les quatre concepts fondamentaux de la psychanalyse, 1964.* Paris: Seuil.

————. 1991. *Le séminaire. Livre VIII, Le transfert, 1960–1961.* Paris: Seuil.

Lagache, D. 1951. Le problème du transfert. In *Le transfert et autres travaux psychanalytiques.* Paris: P.U.F., 1980.

Laplanche, J. 1987. *Problématiques V, Le baquet: Transcendance du transfert.* Paris: P.U.F.

Laplanche, J., and Pontalis, J.-B. 1967. *Vocabulaire de la psychanalyse.* Paris: P.U.F.

Lester, E. P. 1985. The female analyst and the erotized transference. *Int. J. Psycho-Anal.* 66:283–93.

Macalpine, I. 1950. The development of the transference. *Psychoanal. Q.* 19:501–39.

Mahler, M. 1979. *Selected papers.* New York: Jason Aronson.

Mahler, M., et al. 1975. *The psychological birth of the human infant.* New York: Basic.

Mannoni, O. 1982. L'amour du transfert et le réel. *Etudes Freudiennes* 19/20:7–14.

Person, E. S. 1988. *Dreams of love and fateful encounters. The power of romantic passion.* Chap. 10, Transference love and romantic love, 241–64. New York: W. W. Norton.

Rappaport, E. A. 1959. The first dream in an erotized transference. *Int. J. Psycho-Anal.* 40:240–45.

Rosenfeld, H. 1965. Notes on the psychopathology and psychoanalytic treatment of schizophrenia. Chap. 9 in *Psychotic states.* New York: International Universities Press. 1966.

———. 1964. An investigation into the need of neurotic and psychotic patients to act out during analysis. Chap. 12 in *Psychotic states.* New York. International Universities Press.

———. 1987. *Impasse and interpretation.* London: Tavistock.

Sandler, J., et al. 1969. Notes on some theoretical and clinical aspects of transference. *Int. J. Psycho-Anal.* 50:633–45.

Searles, H. F. 1965. *Collected papers on schizophrenia and related subjects.* New York: International Universities Press.

Segal, H. 1986. *The work of Hanna Segal: A Kleinian approach to clinical practice.* New York: Jason Aronson.

Spielrein, S. 1912. Die Destruktion als Ursache des Werdens. *Jb. Psychoan. Psychopath. Forsch.* 4:465–503.

Spitz, R. A. 1956. Transference: The analytical setting and its prototype. *Int. J. Psycho-Anal.* 37:380–85.

Stone, L. 1961. *The psychoanalytic situation.* New York: International Universities Press.

Torres de Beà, E. 1987. A contribution to the papers on transference by Eva Lester and Marianne Goldberger and Dorothy Evans. *Int. J. Psycho-Anal.* 68:63–67.

Winnicott, D. W. 1945. Primitive emotional development. *Int. J. Psycho-Anal.* 26:137–43.

———. 1956. On transference. *Int. J. Psycho-Anal.* 37:386–88.

Zetzel, E. 1956. Current concepts on transference. *Int. J. Psycho-Anal.* 37:369–76.

Amae and Transference Love

TAKEO DOI

Since this paper attempts to discuss Freud's "Observations on Transference-Love" from the viewpoint of *amae*, I shall first have to explain what *amae* is.[1] In brief, *amae*, a Japanese word, signifying "indulgent dependency," primarily describes what an infant feels when it seeks its mother. Interestingly, it can also be applied to an adult when that person is supposed to entertain a similar feeling of being emotionally close to another. In other words, there is a continuum between children and adults as far as *amae* is concerned. In the case of an adult one may or may not acknowledge one's *amae* on reflection, depending on circumstances.

It is important to remember in this regard that the feeling of *amae* in itself is nonverbal. It can be conveyed only nonverbally and should be acknowledged thus. Therefore it is not a manifest emotion, but rather a silent emotion.

1. Wisdom (1987a, 1987b) has commented on the utility of *amae* for illuminating some aspects of object relations theory. For a more thorough exposition of *amae* as a universal nonsexualized drive for close dependent affiliation, see Doi, 1964, 1973, 1989, and 1992. For a recent comprehensive cross-cultural summary of developmental and psychoanalytic contributions to the theory of indulgent dependency, see Johnson, 1992.

(Perhaps that is why many languages manage without a word like *amae*.) However, in frustrated states it may turn into a desire, thus entering into the formation of many emotions, such as love, envy, jealousy, resentment, or hatred. I do not want to give the impression that this is common knowledge among the Japanese, for whom *amae* is a household word. But many thoughtful Japanese find it easy to recognize the workings of *amae* in various emotions. Furthermore, it is my contention that where such a concept is lacking, one would nonetheless intuit something similar in order to make out how the mind works.

Freud begins his paper "Observations on Transference-Love" with a reminder that the only really serious difficulties in conducting psychoanalysis lie in the management of the transference. He cites as a typical example the case of a woman who falls in love with her analyst. What should the analyst do in such a case? To reciprocate her love is out of the question, since that would mean giving up the very purpose for which the two persons came to know each other. But if the woman insists in her demand for love? To reproach her for her passion, Freud warns, would solve nothing. Should one then compromise by at least returning her fond feelings without further involvement? Freud does not approve of this either, saying that it goes against the spirit of psychoanalysis, which is founded upon truthfulness. Moreover, there is no guarantee that one can stop at fond feelings. He also calls our attention to the fact that the erotic transference becomes the medium by which the resistance to therapy manifests itself. He concludes as follows:

> It is, therefore, just as disastrous for the analysis if the patient's craving for love is gratified as if it is suppressed. The course the analyst must pursue is neither of these; it is one for which there is no model in real life. He must take care not to steer away from the transference-love, or to repulse it or to make it distasteful to the patient; but he must just as resolutely withhold any response to it. He must keep firm hold of the transference-love, but treat it as something unreal, as a situation which has to be gone through in the treatment and traced back to its unconscious origins and which must assist in bringing all that is most deeply hidden in the patient's erotic life into her consciousness and therefore under her control. (166)

Reading this passage, one would think that it contains Freud's final word on the subject. But that was not the case; he goes on at some length. For a while he seems to be taken up with proving how the patient's manifest love cannot be genuine since it serves as resistance and is also made up of repetitions of earlier reactions, including infantile ones. Then, suddenly, so it appears to me, he reverses the argument, saying that this is not the whole story. True, the resistance makes use of the patient's love, but it did not, after all, create such love. Freud asks whether there is any love worthy of that name that does not have an infantile prototype. Thus he declares that we have no right to dispute the genuineness of the transference love, though it may be less free than love under ordinary circumstances. Having thus established the genuineness of the transference love, Freud comes back to the fact that nonetheless it is provoked by the analytic situation. It is evident, then, that the analyst is no more justified in taking advantage of the patient in such a state than in other medical situations. Besides, it is in the nature of the illness for which the patient seeks analytic help that her vulnerability in the sphere of love is so exposed. It therefore behooves the analyst to help her overcome a crisis in her life. With this admonition Freud concludes the paper.

I hope I have not done injustice to the complexity of the subject. At any rate, I am impressed by Freud's masterly exposition whenever I read this paper. His opening statement is that "the only really serious difficulties" in conducting psychoanalytic therapy "lie in the management of the transference" (159). Does he then show us in the paper some safe way to deal with it? No; if anything, he confirms the difficulties. Certainly he is enlightening and even inspiring at times. I don't know if he would mind my using the word *inspiring*. Perhaps he would not, though he would object to *inspirational*, because he knows very well that what he is arguing about borders on the moral sphere, but he would not want it to be known that he is giving a lesson in morals. However, at one point, toward the end of the paper, he actually makes the following recommendation: "For the doctor, *ethical motives unite with the technical ones* to restrain him from giving the patient his love" (169; emphasis added). Also before this sentence, in the middle of the paper, when he advocates abstinence for the patient because "the patient's need and longing . . . may serve as forces impelling her to do work and to make changes" (165), we cannot help but read the double meaning that the message is also addressed to the psychoanalyst. In fact later he adds the following forthright statement: "The more plainly the analyst lets it be seen that he is proof against every temptation, the more readily will he be able to extract from the situation its analytic content" (166). No doubt the point that Freud keeps belaboring is very important, and I hope that my comments from the viewpoint of *amae* will not minimize the difficulties.

There are three points I would like to discuss here. First is the phenomenology of the transference love, "the case in which a woman patient shows by unmistakable indications, or openly declares, that she has fallen in love, as any other mortal woman might, with the doctor who is analysing her" (159). I wonder if Freud fully realized that such a one-sided confession of love on the part of the woman patient was more likely due to the basic rule of psychoanalysis, which stipulates that one ought to tell whatever comes to one's mind without reservation, than otherwise. True, Freud says later that the confession "is provoked by the analytic situation" (168), but did he really mean that it was so provoked with good reason? For it is certain that the analytic situation fosters a childlike mentality. Then, will not the transference love approximate the case of a small child saying "I love you" over and over again to its mother? It may be of interest in this regard that Japanese children don't say "I love you" to their mothers, not necessarily because there is no expression equivalent to this in Japanese, but rather, I believe, because they know how to communicate with each other in nonverbal *amae*. Along this line of thought one may say, therefore, that the "I love you" of the children in Western societies does stand for *amae*. Isn't it possible, then, to assume by extrapolation that behind the transference love of Western adults as well hides the psychology of *amae?* I believe this to be a quite plausible proposition.

This reasoning leads to my second point, the question of how to cope with the transference love. I think Freud's view on this matter can be summed up as follows: The patient's demand for love should not be responded to, yet it deserves to be respected since one cannot dispute the genuineness of her love. Suppose that the kernel of the transference love is *amae*, as I indicated above. Would that change Freud's injunction with regard to the management of the transference? I don't think so. I may say, however, that to understand the transference love as an expression of *amae* would probably make it less tempting or less threatening to the analyst. What about the patient? Can that understanding be conveyed to the patient? I say it can and, as a matter of fact, should be. But the difficulty lies in the fact that this understanding cannot be given to the patient in the form of an interpretation. For if one did give an interpretation using the term *amae,* it would sound terribly condescending or even reproachful, because, as I said at the beginning of this paper, *amae* should be acknowledged only nonverbally. Still, it is possible that the patient herself will come up with the interpretation, if she happens to be a native speaker of Japanese, that it was only *amae* which drove her to behave as she did. Or she might say substantially the same thing without using the word *amae.* At any rate, in such a case the analyst cannot but agree with her, which undoubtedly will fortify her in her new insight. But what if the concept of *amae* is not known to the analyst or the patient, as in Western clinical situations? All the same, I think, something quite like an insight into *amae* on the part of the patient and its acknowledgment on the part of the analyst will take place in a successful analysis. To prove this, let me quote certain clinical vignettes from recent works by an American analyst, Dr. Evelyne Albrecht Schwaber. The paragraph quoted below is from one of her most recent papers (1990).

A patient was talking one session without much affective colour, of different things—some memories of his mother, depriving, seductive. I was quiet; he went on. Then he said, with a sharp affective immediacy, "I have this feeling I want you to hold me." "Just now?" I asked. "Yes." Thinking of what he'd been saying about his mother, I then asked, "Did she ever hold you?" "Not really," he replied, and he spoke, poignantly, of how, when he was little, he would go into her bed and just watch her breathing while she was asleep; at times he'd put his arm around her. . . . "What made you feel this now, to me?" I wondered. "An emptiness," he answered, but without elaboration, and his associations went back to mother and to his girlfriend. The next session he spoke of an intense longing he'd felt the previous day, for a warm greeting from his girlfriend—a painful yearning for physical contact; he even felt it at a meeting with female co-workers, just wishing he could hug them. He talked of how terribly hurt he'd been by this girlfriend's apparent rebuffs; when he came home she seemed tired and preoccupied, while he wanted a more loving response. I wondered what might have happened that intensified this sense of hurt—since the session, perhaps? He replied, "Something bothered me here; when I said I wanted you to hold me, you shifted to my mother. I felt you were uncomfortable. It was useful talking of my mother as I did, but you shifted right to her. You've often pointed out how I do that; now you did it." "Oh," I said, "so you left the session still looking for a hug—not met." He agreed. (235)

I think it is quite clear that this patient's transference love, though it had a strong erotic component, was really a manifestation of *amae*. This Dr. Schwaber implicitly understood when she said at the end, "So you left the session still looking for a hug—not met." The concluding sentence of the paragraph—"He agreed."—is very significant in this respect. It means he understood that she understood what he really meant to say. And that in itself was good enough, because what he was really hoping for was not a hug itself but to be understood in the depth of his mind.

This paper also reports another case, a woman patient, who almost came to articulate her wish for *amae*. In the transference she would become angry again and again at something Dr. Schwaber said or did not say. Dr. Schwaber tried to make sense of her experience after each such incident, but to no avail, since it did not prevent her from creating angry scenes anew. One day an idea occurred to Dr. Schwaber, and I quote the passage describing it.

> Then I realized there was an element I had not addressed. The patient's way of relating was to recount an experience she'd had without any hint apparent to me that she was seeking a particular response and to become furious with me afterwards when I failed to comment about the concern which she only then made explicit. I shared my observation of this sequence with her, asking her why she made her feelings clearer to me only afterwards. And she answered: "I want you to understand me without my having to spell it out. If you really care about me, you would know; if I have to ask, it feels like begging. Even if you then understand, it is no longer the same." (234)

Dr. Schwaber notes following this passage that after she acknowledged this patient's confession of a hitherto hidden wish, the patient made considerable progress, enacting no more angry scenes. I am sure I could cite more examples from other analysts, but I believe that these two are sufficiently illustrative, so let me proceed to my last point.

It concerns a remark by Freud in the previously quoted passage. After he states that the patient's craving for love should be neither gratified nor suppressed and that the course the analyst must pursue is altogether different, he adds: "It is one for which there is no model in real life" (166). If by this sentence he simply meant that nobody ever attempted what he did in ways of dealing with transference love, I have no objection. But if he literally meant that no model existed in real life that matched his recommended course, I would have to disagree. I think the reason for my disagreement must be obvious, because I am almost (but not really) equating transference love with *amae*. The silent acknowledgment or denial of *amae* often happens in real life, not only in childrearing, but in adult life as well. In fact, I should say that *amae* is an important ingredient in any interpersonal relationship. Thus I cannot help wondering if part of the reason Freud could not conceive of any real-life model for his recommended course might have been the unavailability of the concept of *amae* or something similar to him, at least at the time of his writing the paper under discussion.

Now my final warning. Even if the argument of this paper proves to be sound, one should not jump to easy interpretation in terms of *amae*. *Amae* is not something open for everybody to see. One has to dig deeply in order to discover it anew in each case. Therefore, the difficulties in the management of the transference as Freud saw them will continue to baffle us for a long time, whether one likes it or not.

REFERENCES

Doi, T. 1964. Psychoanalytic therapy and "Western man": A Japanese view. *International Journal of Social Psychiatry* 1:13–18.

———. 1973. *The anatomy of dependence*. Tokyo: Kodansha International.

———. 1989. The concept of *amae* and its psychoanalytic implications. *Int. Rev. Psychoanal.* 16:349–54.

———. 1992. On the concept of *amae*. *Infant Mental Health Journal* 13:7–11.

Johnson, F. A. 1992. *Dependency and Japanese socialization: Psychoanalytic and anthropological investigations into amae*. New York: New York University Press.

Schwaber, E. A. 1990. Interpretation and the therapeutic action of psychoanalysis. *Int. J. Psycho-anal.* 71:229–40.

Wisdom, J. O. 1987a. The concept of *amae*. *Int. Rev. Psychoanal.* 14:263–64.

———. 1987b. Book review: *The anatomy of self*. *Int. Rev. Psychoanal.* 14:278–79.

Acting versus Remembering in Transference Love and Infantile Love

DANIEL N. STERN

Freud alerts us right away that there are two reasons for this paper and that one is more pressing than the other. The more urgent is the "practical aspect"— how to handle transference love technically. Second, and only "partly" responsible for occasioning the paper, is the "theoretical interest" raised by transference love. Today the second reason is perhaps the more pressing one. Psychoanalysis has come a long way in incorporating and elaborating the technical recommendations Freud gives in this paper. It has made less progress in working out some of the issues of "theoretical interest"—in particular, the interrelations between transference love and normal love, between remembering and acting, and between early experience and transferential behavior in the analytic situation. It is these issues that I will address. However, I want first to say something about the primary reason, since it provides the historical and intellectual context for the theoretical aspects.

First and foremost, Freud is addressing other practicing psychoanalysts. There is a history here that cannot be avoided. From the very beginning of psychoanalysis in Freud's collaboration with Breuer, the issue of transference love and countertransference was not unknown to him. However, he was slow to address it. This potentially explosive problem became even more real

172

in the years leading up to the writing of this paper when his (at the time) logical heir, Jung, fell in love with and began a relationship with one of his patients. And not long after, Ferenczi, Freud's friend and colleague, did the same with one of *his* patients. The implications for the psychoanalytic movement were not trivial. The necessity for such a paper was apparent and was discussed by Freud in his correspondence. The paper was considered overdue (Haynal, 1989). This work is a strong plea and warning, in terms of clinical and theoretical rationales, to avoid the dangers of countertransference when faced with transference love. Public and medical opinion were also a targeted audience. The political goal of making psychoanalysis accepted was a constant reality for Freud. Given the potential risks and damages to psychoanalysis posed by transference love and its countertransference, the weight of this "political" consideration was amplified. It is reflected in the way Freud ends the work—drawing a close parallel between the recommended technique for dealing with transference love and justifiably strong medical practices. I mention this historical context because one can readily imagine that it may influence the propositions stated or at least provide one reading of them.

The first issue I want to take up is the key notion of acting (out) versus remembering. This will be considered in relation to the issues of past versus present, and transference love versus normal love. Freud introduces the acting-remembering distinction in this paper by way of developmental considerations. He places the origin of transference love squarely in infancy. He speaks in terms of "infantile roots" and "infantile prototypes." This placement of the source in infancy is in line with Freud's already established ontogenetic theories (1905) and simply adds one more piece of adult experience to be seen from his developmental perspective.

Love in infancy, however, is not simply the point of origin of transference love; it provides the exact model for it: transference love is "entirely composed of repetitions and copies of earlier reactions," it contains "not a single new feature," it "reproduce[s] infantile prototypes" and "repeats infantile reactions." It consists of "new editions of old traits." And the analyst as the object of transference love is only a "surrogate." The relationship between past (infantile) love and the present (transference) love is one of marked isomorphism or fidelity.

Why is Freud so insistent on this fidelity? When considering most clinical phenomena that are rooted in the past, Freud is very careful to nuance this issue of fidelity and to point out that the remembered phenomenon that emerges in the analytic situation is not a faithful replica of the lived or even previously remembered earlier phenomena. Rather, the present version is a transformation ("distortion") created during the repeated steps of construction-reconstruction of the original events that occur developmentally—plus the final transformative step that permits the (re)construction to emerge in the analytic situation. Memories have made a long journey from past to present, and fidelity has disappeared as the most important issue and been replaced by continuity/coherence. So why does Freud emphasize here the fidelity aspect of transference love?

The answer lies in Freud's conceptualization of acting out, which is key to his view of transference love. He saw acting out and remembering as opposite and antithetical paths for bringing the past into the present. Acting out occurs in the motor sphere of action, remembering in the "psychical sphere" of mentalization and verbalization. Accordingly, acting out does not undergo the same transforming process of serial (re)constructions that a memory inevitably does. As a motor phenomenon—encapsulated from psychic mutations—it remains faithful to its origins. Freud would never have said that a memory or dream as reported in a session was an "exact replica" of the originally lived experience, "with no new features." Quite the opposite, he states that "dreams are distorted and mutilated by memory" (1900). Even "normal love" is a very transformed phenomenon, far from a replica. "In the normal attitude [of love] there remain only a few traces unmistakably betraying the maternal prototype behind the chosen object" (1910). So the strict fidelity model is applicable to acting out but not to remembering in general, and not to "normal love."

Freud is very clear that "if the patient's advances were returned . . . she would have succeeded . . . in acting out, in repeating in real life, what she ought only to have remembered, to have reproduced as psychical material and to have kept within the sphere of psychical events" (166). So we have two states in which the phenomena of transference love can exist: a state of motor expression (acted out) in which the action is faithful in form and content to its origins, and a state of psychical expression (as appropriately contained by Freud's recommendation) in which roughly the same infidelity expected of dreams or screen memories would be expected to prevail.

The reason I stress this distinction is that throughout much of the paper Freud fails to distinguish whether he is talking about transference love as acted out or as psychically expressed. In his comments on the relationship of infantile loves to transference love (the fidelity issue), it is as if, when writing about transference love in general, he really had transference love acted out in mind. There are several possible reasons for this somewhat confusing situation. First, it is reasonable to speculate that Freud's major concern with the technical and political aspects of this paper took the upper hand over the theoretical aspects. And indeed, acting out in the transference and countertransference was the real target of the paper. If transference love is seen as (just) acting out, the injunctions (recommendations) against countertransference are that much stronger and easier to justify.

Deeper levels and readings of this apparent confusion exist. Freud suggests that so far as love is concerned there is no real distinction between the acted out and non–acted out states. Love is always acted out. In several places, he emphasizes the "immediacy" of the feelings and desires in transference love. Indeed, clinically one gets the impression that transference love is often on the fence between the "state" of being acted out and the state of being a "psychical event"—always pushing in the direction of being acted out. Further, it is not always so easy to decide in which of the two states a given expression exists. Even with purely verbal expressions, this distinction is not necessarily so clear. For instance, the statement never made before, "I love you!" can be seen as a declaration of fact existing in the psychical sphere, or it can be seen (and taken) as a type of act (in speech-act theory) which, in its being said, is performative of an action of loving—performative in the sense that speech-acts such as "I christen this ship the USS *Missouri*" or "I declare the XVIIth Winter Olympiad open" perform specific acts that can only be executed in words (Searle, 1969). These are acts in the guise of psychical expressions.

We now have several of the major issues of "theoretical interest" before us. Does love exist in a non–acted (out) state? Where is the dividing line between motoric and psychical expressions in loving? Does each have a different developmental course and different energic features, and how different?

Before returning to these issues, and while keeping them in mind, we can now turn attention to the developmental history of love—on which transference love will be closely based.

What has Freud in mind when he writes about the infantile prehistory of transference love? In this paper, Freud focuses mainly on "sexual love." There are several reasons for this. First, there is the immediate reason that the form of acting out of the transference-countertransference made possible by sexual love represented the pressing danger to patients, analysts, and the psychoanalytic movement. Second, there was Freud's greater interest in the forms of love made possible by the work and achievements of the oedipal phase. And finally, as several authors (e.g., Cooper, 1991) have noted, Freud tended to treat love as a basic given, as an "elemental phenomenon," something "unquestionable, a core emotional state." In this regard, while he did explore psychological differences in object choice, intensity, sublimation, and so on, he did not seek too far to unpack the central feeling state. This remains largely true in spite of his identifying the affectionate versus the sexual contributions of sexual love and mentioning some of the contributions from the different psychosexual stages. The job of dissecting love or, alternatively, of composing the nature of love developmentally from point zero was not something that Freud felt it necessary to do (and understandably). Nonetheless, in this paper, he leaves the door open for others to do just that. In fact, he urges us to make such an exploration, since everything that appears in the transference love will have existed in previous infantile loves. Knowing the nature of such early loves becomes important. And Freud gives us a wide-ranging list to work with:

• "all her preconditions for loving" (In Freud's paper on the psychology of love [1910] he speaks of the "conditions of love"—for example, "love for a harlot" or the "need for an injured third party." I assume that by "preconditions" he means the earlier versions that will evolve into the "conditions of love.")

• "all the phantasies springing from her sexual desires"

• "all the detailed characteristics of her state of being in love," and

• "the patient's infantile 'object' choices."

Let us then look at infantile love, taking into account some of the more recent knowledge and perspectives gained from infant observations, but holding in mind that this developmental interest will be justified by what it tells us about transference love and the theoretical issues raised.

Expressions of love begin strikingly early. The most basic physical language of affectionate love is both performed and learned by the fourth or fifth month of life. A comparison of infants' and aspects of adults' motor love behavior illustrates this point. The overt behaviors by which one recognizes adult lovers in the phase of falling in love consist mainly of gazing into each other's eyes without talking; maintaining very close proximity, faces inches away and parts of the body always touching; alteration in vocal patterns; movements in synchrony; performing special gestures such as kissing, hugging, touching, and holding the other's face and hands. We see the same set of behaviors performed in infancy with the mother or other primary caregiver.

Beginning around two and a half months, when infants begin to engage in mutual gaze, they (and their mother) may spend tens of seconds, even a minute or more, locked in silent mutual gaze. Infants do not do this when looking at other objects. Prolonged mutual gaze without speaking is a very rare event in adult human life. If two adults look into each other's eyes without talking for more than five seconds or so, they are likely to fight or make love. The use of mutual regard between parents and infants and between lovers constitutes a separate register.

Similarly, parents and infants, like adult lovers, use a separate register of proxemics. In each culture, the distance that two adults must maintain from each other is narrowly fixed. Only intimates, lovers, and babies are allowed to breach this distance. In fact, mothers and infants spend much of their intimate time together working at very close distances that violate the cultural norm, just as lovers do.

Speech, too, occupies its own special register. When parents talk to infants, and sometimes when lovers talk to each other, they violate the norms of speech. They emphasize the music over the lyrics, they use "baby talk," they rely on a wider range of nonverbal vocalizations, and they alter established word pronunciations. Similarly, a distinct register of varied facial expressiveness is brought into play. Lovers and parent-infant dyads make parallel alterations, violations, and exaggerations of facial as well as vocal expression patterns with each other.

Lovers tend to move synchronously together in choreographed patterns of simultaneous approach-approach, and simultaneous withdrawal-withdrawal. Parents and infants show the same patterning of their joint movements. It is largely these patterns that alert us within seconds of the lover status.

There are also the special gestures and actions seen in lovers that infants develop very early. Kissing is usually learned before the second year and hugging long before. At the same time children like to caress and cradle in their hands the face of a parent. When lying against or on a parent, children before the age of two years frequently make pelvic thrusts as part of what appears to be a wave of affection. Exquisite expressions of coquetry are seen well before the onset of the oedipal phase.[1]

All these variations in a special register are not simply the forms or configurations of affectionate love. Passion—in the sense of the temporal flow of excitation, of dramatic crescendos and climaxes and decrescendo of

1. See Stern, 1977, for a fuller description of the parent-infant nonverbal love language, and Person, 1988, for descriptions of the parallel behaviors in adult lovers.

activation—is involved. The temporal play of the elements in these special registers is very much in the service of creating "thrills." We are not speaking here of only tranquil, beatific love. Sensuality and "non-specific excitation" are not being equated here. However, the excitation envelopes that will one day be filled with sensual (sexual) content-contours are being established.

Not only is the point of origin for this physical language of love very early and preverbal, but the language itself is one of action. These various love-behaviors are shaped differently in time, intensity, frequency, and eliciting conditions in each family. In other words, the most basic physical language of love—the way affection is physically manifested—is also a candidate for wide individual variability, just as is the person of the object choice. Preferences, ranges of tolerance, permissible and impermissible intensities and durations of certain acts—all are part of the "chemistry" of love that may parade under the guise of "object choice." Is not this basic language part of "all the detailed characteristics of her state of being in love" and a type of "precondition" for loving?

These considerations raise another question. Do infants in the first year of life fall in love with their parents, or do they somehow slip quietly into the more stable state of being in love? Or are they not in love at all? Does one need the sensual current—be it repressed, sublimated, or not yet developed—to fall in love? The question is important to the extent that the experience of falling in love, with all its intensity and immediacy, is or is not an infantile experience. After all, the more violent and immediate parts of transference love that Freud describes are best attributed to the phase of falling in love. Do they have an infantile antecedent? My reading of infants is that they do fall in love and do so several times over as development progressively gives them a new set of capacities with which to fall in love all over again or "deeper." The form is largely established. New contents will be poured into it.

Let us now move from overt behaviors to intrapsychic experiences, since love is largely a psychic state. Beginning toward the end of the first year, infants develop the capacity for intersubjectivity. By this is meant the ability to sense that one has subjective experiences that are separate and different from those of others. Initially, these experiences cover a limited but important number of states of mind, such as focus of attention, intentions, and affects (see Stern, 1985). Some developmentalists say the infant then has discovered what philosophers call a "theory of separate minds." Once this leap to inter-subjectivity has been made, the possibility of psychic intimacy, as well as physical intimacy, is realizable. States of mind can now be shared, and if they are not shared the infant has developed means to bring the two minds into alignment. The inner worlds that are subjectively sharable are being discovered, which will lead one day to the ability to think or say "I know that you know that I know . . . " or "I feel that you feel that I feel . . . "—that is, to the path that falling-in-lovers take and retake in their mutual discovery process. Intersubjectivity and its resultant psychic intimacy, once possible, become a wished-for state, an attraction, a pull of greater or lesser importance for each individual. It is a potent feature of love.

In this paper, Freud traces back to infancy "all [the] preconditions for loving." Psychic intimacy—or intersubjective sharing—is a cardinal precondition. Furthermore, it is one that the analytic situation puts into high relief. The analyst's empathic understanding assures that. The patient's past history of intersubjective experiences then becomes crucial. Which of all the possible and actual subjective experiences will a parent deem sharable, and at what intensity? What must be withheld? and so on. The intersubjective precondition for loving begins early in life and has wide individual variability that will be reflected in the characteristics of the transference love. Once again, the locus of origin for reconstruction is nonverbal and preoedipal. The nature of the intersubjective relationship sought may similarly define the "conditions of love"—for example, love for someone who is intersubjectively unavailable, opaque, or transparent.

Toward the end of the second year of life there is a third new capacity which in the child can evolve into a precondition as well as means of falling in love: the sharing of meanings. After the onset of speech (actually as part of the process of speech acquisition) the parent and infant must negotiate meanings. In this process it is never clear whether the word exists "out there" and is given by the parent to the child, whether the child discovers it, or whether it is only found or taken when the infant already has a concept or feeling to attach it to—that is, it is simultaneously given and discovered. This process occurs in a transitional space à la Winnicott. There is the thrill and wonder of world-making. But this is exactly what adult lovers must do. They mutually define the meanings for themselves of many common words as well as of code-words and concepts. And in doing so they arrive at shared meanings about the things that will make up their daily lives (see Person, 1988). This is very similar to what patient and analyst must mutually negotiate in putting names and meanings to previously unnamed or unknown or repressed experiences that emerge in the treatment. The style of negotiating meanings—that is, the extent of all experiences that require a mutually agreed-upon meaning—or the tolerance for mutual fuzziness in meanings can become "conditions of love." Again, a characteristic of falling in love and being in love has a very early origin.

Another of the defining experiences of love is the exclusive focus on one specific person and a preoccupation with that person's existence. This too is presaged in infancy. During the first year of life there is a gradual narrowing of feelings of intimacy, security, and attachment to one single caregiver. This focalizing process is clearly evident by nine to twelve months of age. Furthermore, infants show a form of preoccupation with the presence and potential absence of the main attachment figure (as do lovers with the beloved). The experience, then, of narrowing to a specific, single object is also a process-experience of early infancy. The same can be said of the experiences of partial boundary permeability involved in the processes of imitation and identification that are so manifest during the early years of life.

To summarize, the experiences of falling in love and being in love have a rich early developmental history. Exploring this terrain further we find that the infantile "roots" and "prototypes" encompass far more than the object choice in the strict sense. They include at least the particularities of the physical language of love; the range and depth of intersubjective sharing; the way in which meaning is mutually created and the intensity of the need to negotiate shared meaning; the degree of singularity occupied by the chosen object; and the temporal and intensity dynamics of the falling-in-love process.

For our purposes here, it is important to note that most of these "preconditions" and prototypes are registered in memory as motor memories, as procedural knowledge (as against symbolic knowledge), as sensory-motor schemas (as against conceptual schemas), as episodic events (as against semantic events). Accordingly, they cannot be readily or directly transformed into the currency of the psychic domain of ideas.

Given this early history of love, we can take up the state of events in transference love again. The question can be approached with several smaller questions. Is the way the patient in the throes of transference love looks at the analyst (a split-second too long; a touch too gently; or the opposite of these, in a motor act of inhibition) or the way she changes and softens the quality of her voice to be considered acting out? These are motor expressions of mental states that may be and usually are unconscious. Technically speaking, they are generally tolerated—with restraint—to let the process build. While this may be wise from the technical point of view, theoretically it is nonetheless acting out, but in an "acceptable" range.

In a similar vein, a patient's desire for and establishment of intersubjective sharing with the analyst (which, granted, furthers the analytic work and the working alliance) may nonetheless be mainly in the service of (re)creating "conditions" for loving. Furthermore this (re)creation is done with speech-acts contextualized paralinguistically, that is, the content (ideas, memories, and so forth) is secondary to the pragmatic action-function of acting in concert with the analyst to achieve and maintain a certain kind of psychic intimacy. The same can be said about the negotiation of meanings—almost any meanings. In those situations action is parading as "psychical" material, and to the extent (considerable) that a speech-act is an action, it is acting out.

There seems, then, to be a spectrum of actings out from "weak" to "strong." The nature of falling in love or being in love (whether in or out of treatment) assures a rich production of actings out—otherwise one simply is not in love.

It could be argued that one can be in love without ever revealing it to the other. This is the stuff of romantic novels, real life, and phases of the transference love. But even in these situations the "acting" is not and cannot be totally redirected into psychical activity. Its motor expression is countered with agonistic motor expressions and with active motor inhibitions. A part of the expression thus always remains in the domain of motor action until one is no longer in love. In fact, the motor actions of antagonism and inhibition amplify the feeling state. They can be part of its exquisiteness.

Psychoanalysis has come to accept somewhat less abstinence on the part of the therapist in the handling of transference love than Freud recommended in 1915. Many have argued the necessity and desirability of a certain amount of countertransferential love to optimize the therapeutic outcome. And there has been an explosion in the acceptance and therapeutic use of the counter-transference. The technical question, then, turns around what is "too strong" a dose of acting out. On theoretical grounds, however, acting out is acting out. It concerns modality of expression. The "strength" of the actions doesn't alter their theoretical status.

In this light, it is not so clear that a theoretical boundary line exists between transference and acting out in the situation of transference love. And the boundary line even as "technically" determined is very relative. It seems, in fact, that technically "going too far" in the direction of transferential-countertransferential acting out is largely determined by the prevailing social mores that determine what is acceptable and at what point(s) matters have changed irreversibly, so that a prior interpersonal state can no longer be reinstituted. Such a boundary point is only a "technical" landmark in a secondary and trivial way. It works "technically" because we share the same socio-cultural-legal constraints, not for theoretical reasons inherent to the psychoanalytic situation or process.

These considerations, among others, have prompted Laplanche and Pontalis (1988) to conclude:

> [while] Freud . . . describes even transference onto the analyst as a modality of acting out, he fails either to differentiate clearly or to show the interconnections between repetition phenomena in the transference on the one hand and manifestations of acting out on the other. . . . One of the outstanding tasks of psychoanalysis is to ground the distinction between transference and acting out on criteria other than purely technical ones. (5–6)

There is a more general question. Why has Freud, and psychoanalysis since, considered acting (motor expression) antithetical to remembering or thinking, so that, translated into technique, it becomes the analyst's task "to divert into the work of recollection any impulse which the patient wants to discharge in action" (Freud, 1914).

While clinical experience has abundantly demonstrated that acting out as a form of resistance can short-circuit thinking and remembering, separation and opposition between the two are not normally the case. Psychoanalysis has overstated the general argument for this division into acting and remembering by not distinguishing the different kinds of actions of which Freud was well aware. A fuller exploration of the relationship between thinking-remembering and the different classes of actions is in order.

In the Project (1895), Freud defined "specific actions" (for instance, sexual orgasm) which achieve their specific aim with a specific object and accomplish optimal discharge and satisfaction. For this separate class of actions it is intuitively appealing to think that the "psychical field" is bypassed. It is also theoretically reasonable that this bypassing occurs because these actions are so genetically programmed that neither thinking nor recollections are needed to assure or guide their reappearance. Genes replace memory. Acting and mentalization are not even in opposition. There is no possible competition and no real transmutability from the action sphere to the psychic sphere.

There is a second group of actions that are more "symbolic" and are transmutable back and forth between the "psychical" domain and the domain of action. Certainly conversion, as a symptom, falls into such a category. It is initially the transmutation of an idea into a bodily form of expression, after which this motor expression can, with therapy, be "retransmuted . . . into the mental field" (Freud, 1894). And indeed, Freud takes the same position in this article concerning acting out and remembering. If acting out can be prevented with appropriate technique, the repressed original event (infantile love) can be redirected into remembrances and accordingly handled in the psychoanalysis. In fact, Freud writes as if the technical problems of transference love concern mostly this class of actions. As our review of the early ontogenetic history of loving suggests, this is not the case. We must refer to yet a third class of actions.

This third class consists of acts and their motor memories, where transmutability into and out of the "mental field" is less certain or clear. This category would include most preverbal experience and much nonverbal experience that is part of the fabric of psychodynamically relevant life events. And it includes much of what has been described above concerning the earliest "conditions" and prototypes for loving. For these motor phenomena the relationship to reminiscences is quite different. Here, the widest, straightest (and sometimes only) path to remembrances lies in the performance of the motor action. Accordingly, the technical recommendations must be different. The analysis must permit the enactment of these action patterns. At first this sounds contrary to Freud's principal recommendations. However, as it turns out, this does not create great technical problems or wreck havoc with the general thrust of Freud's argument because most of these motor memories reside in overt behaviors that fall into the "acceptable" range of acting (out) discussed above (for example, how the patient looks at the analyst and then looks away, a particular gesture or position sequence while lying down on the couch, and so on). So, while there is no technical problem, there is a theoretical one: namely, that action is used as a legitimate and desired route into the psychical domain.[2]

More recently, we have come to consider most of the memories retrieved and used in psychoanalysis as autobiographical or episodic—memories of a specific subjective experience contextualized in a specific time and physical surround (Tulving, 1972). These memories consist of all the attributes of the lived event: the feelings, motives, thoughts, perceptions, sensations, and motor actions. From this point of view, action is one participating attribute of

2. The economic assumptions about the amount of energy dischargeable by motor action compared to psychic acts does not greatly help with these problems. Stating that motor action drains or depletes the system for psychic processes is just another way of putting the basic supposition of antithesis between the motor and psychic spheres.

a larger memory unit—the lived subjective event. Each attribute (including actions) is connected by associative networks to all the others, and any one of them when reexperienced can serve as the retrieval cue to recall the entire lived event with all its original attributes. Specific movements, as well as a smell, a color, a thought, and so on, can evoke a remembrance. And an acted-upon wish can trigger other memories via the route of motor memory.

The division, then, into acting versus remembering need not be the case—except when the action is in the service of resistance (or is serving as a symptom). We have moved from a general statement to a much less inclusive one. Freud clearly states that transference love always involves resistance. Is it the deployment of resistance, then, and not the nature of psychic function-ing that has pitted acting against remembering? If this is so, the battleground has shifted from the effects of acting out on memory to the effects of resis-tance on memory. A fuller set of criteria is required to distinguish acting out as a special subset of resistance. Or to put it differently, is the relationship between acting and thinking/remembering different during resistance than at other times?

Freud has left us with a series of crucial questions that intrigued him in 1915 and that continue to stimulate psychoanalysts today. What is the basic difference between repeating (or remembering) in the transference and re-peating via acting out? Where is the line between action and actualization? Where does motor memory stand in relation to other forms of memory—technically and theoretically? How many of the "conditions" and "charac-teristics" of loving are present in infancy? And if they all are, how are they packaged in memory? Does resistance (or symptom formation) make action the enemy of thought, or is the psychic system constructed that way? Is love, by its very nature, always enacted as well as psychically experienced? And perhaps above all in this work of Freud's, exactly where and how do theory and technique part company—and why?

REFERENCES

Cooper, A. M. 1991. Love in clinical psychoanalysis: Masochism, voyeurism and tender love. Paper presented at the Italian Philosophical Institute, Naples, Novem-ber 1991.
Freud, S. 1894. The neuro-psychoses of defense. *S.E.* 3.
———. 1895. Project for a scientific psychology. *S.E.* 1.

————. 1900. *The interpretation of dreams. S.E.* 4–5.

————. 1905. Three essays on the theory of sexuality. *S.E.* 7.

————. 1910. A special type of object choice made by men. *S.E.* 11.

————. 1914. Remembering, repeating and working-through (Further recommendations on the technique of psycho-analysis). *S.E.* 12.

Haynal, A. 1989 [1988]. *Controversies in psychoanalytical method: From Freud and Ferenczi to Michael Balint.* New York: New York University Press.

Laplanche, J., and Pontalis, J. B. 1988. *The language of psychoanalysis.* London: Karnac Books and the Institute of Psychoanalysis.

Person, E. S. 1988. *Dreams of love and fateful encounters: The power of romantic passion.* New York: W. W. Norton.

Searle, J. R. 1969. *Speech acts: An essay in the philosophy of language.* New York: Cambridge University Press.

Stern, D. N. 1977. *The first relationship: Infant and mother.* Cambridge, Mass.: Harvard University Press.

————. 1985. *The interpersonal world of the infant.* New York: Basic.

Tulving, E. 1972. Episodic and semantic memory. In *Organization of memory,* ed. E. Tulving and W. Donaldson. New York: Academic.

Contributors

JORGE CANESTRI is a training and supervising analyst at the Argentine Psychoanalytic Association and a member of the Italian Psychoanalytical Society.

FIDIAS CESIO is a training and supervising analyst at the Institute of Psychoanalysis and has been director of this institute and scientific secretary of the Argentine Psychoanalytic Association.

TAKEO DOI is a training and supervising analyst at the Japan Psychoanalytic Association. He is a consultant at St. Luke's International Hospital in Tokyo.

FRIEDRICH-WILHELM EICKHOFF is a training and supervising analyst at the German Psychoanalytic Association and co-editor of the *Jahrbuch der Psychoanalyse*.

PETER FONAGY is Freud Memorial Professor of Psychoanalysis in the University of London and co-director of the psychoanalysis unit, University College London. He is also treasurer and associate chairperson of the publications committee of the International Psychoanalytical Association, and research coordinator at the Anna Freud Centre.

MERTON MAX GILL is emeritus professor of psychiatry at the University of Illinois at Chicago, and a supervising analyst at the Institute for Psychoanalysis in Chicago and at the Chicago Center for Psychoanalysis.

AIBAN HAGELIN, in addition to being a training and supervising analyst of the Argentine Psychoanalytic Association, is the former associate secretary of Latin America to the IPA Executive Council. He is also an associate chairperson of the publications committee of the IPA.

MAX HERNÁNDEZ is a training and supervising analyst. He has held, among other posts, the presidency of the Peruvian Psychoanalytic Society and the vice-presidency of the IPA.

BETTY JOSEPH is a training and supervising analyst of the British Psychoanalytical Society.

ETHEL SPECTOR PERSON is a training and supervising analyst at the Columbia University Center for Psychoanalytic Training and Research and a professor of clinical psychiatry at Columbia University. She is chairperson of the publications committee of the IPA.

ROY SCHAFER is a training and supervising analyst at the Columbia University Center for Psychoanalytic Training and Research.

DANIEL N. STERN is a member of the faculty at the Columbia University Center for Psychoanalytic Training and Research. He is a professor of psychology at the University of Geneva and adjunct professor of psychiatry at the Cornell University Medical Center.

ROBERT S. WALLERSTEIN is a past president of both the American Psychoanalytical Association and the International Psychoanalytical Association. He is a training and supervising analyst at the San Francisco Psychoanalytic Institute.

Index

Abstinence, 39–40, 41, 133, 139–40, 149; Ferenczi on, 51; and freedom of thought, 46–50; versus neutrality, 68; second-degree, 45
"Abstinence of the Psychoanalyst, The" (Novey), 68–69
Acting out, 83, 106–8, 162, 174–75, 180, 181–82
Actions, classes of, 182–84
Actual, the, 134, 141–42
Aesthetic experience, 39
Affectionate transference, 157
Aggression, 87
Alpha elements, versus beta elements, 45
Amae, 12; acknowledgment of, 168–70; and children, 168; definition of, 165–66; real-life model for, 170-71
Ambivalence, 61
"Analysis Terminable and Interminable" (S. Freud), 125
Analyst: aim of, 141; capacity of, 132; idealization of, 155; participation of, 127; role of, 135
Analytic situation, 39, 148, 154, 155–56
Analytic technique, 112, 133, 138–39, 149

Anna O., therapy of, 1–3, 34–35, 62–63, 126, 131
Appeasement, versus interpretation, 37–42
Arguing with patient, 81–82, 111

Beta elements, versus alpha elements, 45
Bibring-Lehner, Grete, 52
Bion, W. R., 45, 110-11, 161
Bleuler, Eugen, 61
Blitzsten, Lionel, 51–52, 65, 158–59
Blum, H., 52, 65–66, 161
Borderline pathology, 53, 161
Borge, Jorge Luis, 101
Brenner, Charles, 120
Breuer, Josef, 1–3, 34–35, 62–63, 126, 131

Canestri, Jorge, 11–12
Cesio, Fidel, 10-11
Characterological countertransference, 85, 88
Chasseguet-Smirgel, J., 49
Children: and amae, 168; infantile love, 105–6, 173, 176–80
Coen, S. J., 161
Coherence theory of truth, 119

Coherent ego, 138
"Comment on Anti-Semitism, A" (S.
    Freud), 40
Communication, enactment as, 83
Constructivism, 119
Containment of patient's feelings,
    110-11
Continuum concept, 66
Control-mastery theory, 123-25
Conversion, 182-83
Correspondence theory of truth, 119
Countertransference, 40, 66-67, 84-
    89, 108-9, 136-37; characterologi-
    cal, 85, 88; negative, 136; therapeu-
    tic use of, 181

Death instincts, 106
"Delusions and Dreams in Jensen's
    'Gradiva'" (S. Freud), 35-36
Depressive position, 92
Desublimation, repressive, 42
Developmental help, 53
Diachrony, and synchrony, 143-44
Dichotomous thinking, 76-77
Direct transference, 53
Doi, Takeo, 12
Doolittle, Hilda, 115
Dora case, 36, 120, 130, 132, 144
Drive, 64, 65-66
"Dynamics of Transference, The" (S.
    Freud), 59-60, 69-70, 99

Ego, 64, 138
"Ego and the Id, The" (S. Freud), 137
Eickhoff, Friedrich-Wilhelm, 5-6, 67
Eissler, K. R., 41
Emotional experience, 82
Enactment. See Acting out
Erotic transference, 159; versus ero-
    tized transference, 65-66; expect-
    able, 66; and falling in love, 3-4;

management of, 80-84; and resis-
    tance, 119-21; versus unobjection-
    able positive transference, 69-70
Erotized transference, 38-39, 51-53,
    65-66, 158-59, 161
Etchegoyen, R. H., 46, 159
Expectable erotic transference, 66
"Expressive Participation and Psycho-
    analytic Discipline" (Hoffman), 118

Falling in love, 3-4, 103, 117, 142,
    178
Falzeder, E., 51
Fantasy, 158
Female patients, hysterical, 63-64
Female sexuality, 99-100
Ferenczi, S., 50-51
Fire, semantic field of, 146-47
Fonagy, P., 53
"Fragment of an Analysis of a Case of
    Hysteria" (S. Freud), 36
Freedom of thought, and abstinence,
    46-50
Free-floating attention, 135-36
Freud, Anna, 50
Freud, Sigmund: "Analysis Terminable
    and Interminable," 125; charac-
    terological countertransference in,
    85, 88; "Comment on Anti-
    Semitism, A," 40; "Delusions and
    Dreams in Jensen's 'Gradiva'," 35-
    36; "Dynamics of Transference,
    The," 59-60, 69-70, 99; "Ego and
    the Id, The," 137; "Fragment of an
    Analysis of a Case of Hysteria," 36;
    "Further Recommendations" series,
    96-97; "Group Psychology and the
    Analysis of the Ego," 116-17, 155;
    Interpretation of Dreams, The, 35,
    42, 130; Introductory Lectures on
    Psycho-Analysis, 48-49; "Lines of

Advance in Psycho-Analytic Theory," 41–42; "On Narcissism: An Introduction," 155; patriarchal
orientation of, 89–91; "Remembering, Repeating and Working
Through," 36–37; technical writings
of, 57. See also "Observations on
Transference-Love"
"Further Recommendations" series
(S. Freud), 96–97

Gaddini, E., 161
Gaze, mutual, 177
Gender, role of, 49, 86, 91, 153
Gill, Merton, 10
Gitelson, M., 52–53, 158–59
Goldberg, Lea, 49
Gombrich, Ernst, 37
"Gradiva" (Jensen), 35–36, 140
Gratification, versus interpretation, 37–
42
Green, André, 158, 161
Greenacre, P., 155
Greenson, R., 70, 152, 156
"Group Psychology and the Analysis of
the Ego" (S. Freud), 116–17, 155
Grünbaum, A., 119

Haynal, A., 51
Heine, Heinrich, "Roving Rats, The,"
42–44
Hermeneutic view of psychoanalysis, 93
Hernández, Max, 9
Hoffman, I. Z., "Expressive Participa-
tion and Psychoanalytic Discipline,"
118
Hypnosis, 126–27
Hysterical patients, 63–64, 67

Illusion, 37
Imaginary, the, 141, 148

Incest, 139, 140-41
Indifference, versus neutrality, 150-51
Indirect suggestion, 121
Infantile love, 105–6, 173, 176–80
Internal world of patients, transference
from, 109–10
Interpersonal analysis, versus intrapsy-
chic analysis, 118–19
Interpretation, 37–42, 48
Interpretation-construction, 144
Interpretation of Dreams, The (S.
Freud), 35, 42, 130
Intersubjectivity, 178–79, 181
Intrapsychic analysis, versus interper-
sonal analysis, 118–19
Introductory Lectures on Psycho-
Analysis (S. Freud), 48–49

Jealousy, 133–34
Jensen, Wilhelm, "Gradiva," 35–36, 140
Jokes, 41
Jones, E., 62 63, 114
Joseph, Betty, 9–10, 83
Jung, C. G., 50–51, 122, 147, 159–60

Kanzer, Mark, 120
Klein, Melanie, 109, 160
Kleinian analysts, 92, 160
Kohut, Heinz, 39, 118

Lacan, J., 155, 157–58
Lagache, D., 154
Laplanche, J., 154, 182
Libido, 154–55
"Lines of Advance in Psycho-Analytic
Theory" (S. Freud), 41–42
Loch, W., 45, 51
Loewald, H., 37, 39, 78
Love: and neurosis, 97–98; normal
versus transference love, 111–12,
142–43; physical language of, 177–

Love (*continued*)
78; preconditions for, 179; real
versus transference love, 4, 77; sadomasochistic, 105–6; sexual, 175–76;
singularity of object of, 180. *See
also* Falling in love; Infantile love;
Transference love
Lovers, motor behavior of, 176–77
Love transference, versus transference
love, 42–46

Macalpine, Ida, 117–18, 154
Madness, and passions, 158, 161
Make-believe, analytic situation as,
155–56
Management of transference, 80-84,
166
Mannoni, O., 155–56
Marcuse, Herbert, 42
Material reality, versus psychical real-
ity, 122–23
Maternal transference, versus paternal
transference, 88–89
Meanings: shared, 179–80; trans-
ference meaning, 98–99
Memories. *See* Remembering
Motor expression, versus psychical ex-
pression, 174–75
Motor memories of acts, 183–84
Muslin, Hyman, 120
Mutative transference interpretation, 48
Mutual gaze, 177

Narcissism, 104, 138, 154–55
Narration, 91–94
Negative countertransference, 136
Negative therapeutic reaction, 137–38
Negative transference, 59–60, 69–70,
100-101; unobjectionable, 121
Negotiation in analysis, 119

Neurosis, 140, 159; and love, 97–98;
and normality, 59; transference neu-
rosis, 36–37, 66
Neutrality, 40, 50, 68, 150-51
Newness, concept of, 78–79
Neyraut, M., 53
Normality, and neurosis, 59
Novey, R., "Abstinence of the Psycho-
analyst, The," 68–69
Nunberg, H., 52

"Observations on Transference-Love"
(S. Freud), 17–29; datedness of, 58–
59; demolition of conventional
boundaries in, 76–79; historical con-
text of, 50-51, 172–73; naivete of,
58–59; paraphrase of, 147–51
Oedipal tragedy, 137, 144–45
Oedipus complex, 100, 131–32, 137
One-person psychology, versus two-
person psychology, 115–19, 124,
126, 127
"On Narcissism: An Introduction" (S.
Freud), 155
O'Shaughnessy, E., 108

Palos, Elma, 51
Paranoid-schizoid position, 92
Passion, 149, 177–78
Passions, and madness, 158, 161
Paternal transference, versus maternal
transference, 88–89
Pathological personality, 103–4
Pathologies: borderline, 53, 161; psy-
chotic, 46, 159–61
Patriarchal orientation of Freud, 89–91
Person, E. S., 49
Perspectivism, 91–94
Pfister, Pastor, 146
Phenomenology of transference love,
168

Physical language of love, 177–78
Physical sexuality, devaluation of, 122–23
Pontalis, J. B., 182
Positive transference, 59–60, 100-101; unobjectionable, 69–72, 120
Positivism, 91–94, 119
Preconditions for loving, 179
Projective identification, 108
Protophantasies, 137
Proxemics, 177
Pseudoparameters, 41
Psychical expression, versus motor expression, 174–75
Psychical reality, versus material reality, 122–23
Psychoanalytic schools, 152
Psychotic pathology, 46, 159–61, 161

Racker, Heinrich, 116
Rappaport, Ernest, 51–52, 64–65, 158 59
Real, the, 134, 141–42, 148
Reality, 122–23, 134
Regressive transference neurosis, 66
Reich, Annie, 85
Relative autonomy, concept of, 122
Remembering, 101, 106–7, 173–74, 183–84
"Remembering, Repeating and Working Through" (S. Freud), 36–37
Repetition, 124, 157
Repressive desublimation, 42
Resistance, 39, 41, 80, 104, 134, 148, 184; and erotic transference, 119–21; and passion, 149; and tragedy, 138
"Roving Rats, The" (Heine), 42–44

Sadomasochistic loving, 105–6
Sandler, J., 152–53
Schafer, Roy, 7–9

Schwaber, Evelyne Albrecht, 118, 169–70
Second-degree abstinence, 45
Segal, Hanna, 46
Sexual acting out, 162
Sexuality, 99–100, 121–23, 125–27
Sexual love, 175–76
Sicker than-neurotic patients, 65
"So-Called Good Hysteric, The" (Zetzel), 67
Social psychology, 118
Specific actions, 182
Speech-acts, 175, 181
Speech register, 177
Spielrein, Sabina, 50-51, 122, 159–60
Spontaneity in analysis, 118
Stein, Martin, 120; "Unobjectionable Part of the Transference, The," 70-72
Stern, Daniel, 12–14
Sternberger, Dolf, 44
Strachey, J., 48, 109, 149
Structure, shift from topography to, 82
Sublimation, 48
Suggestion, indirect, 121
Surrogates, 41
Symbolic actions, 182–83
Synchrony, and diachrony, 143–44
Szasz, Thomas, 2

Testing of analyst by patient, 123–24
Therapeutic alliance, 70, 120
Therapeutic reaction, negative, 137–38
Topography, shift to structure from, 82
Tragedy: oedipal, 137, 144–45; and resistance, 138
Transference, definitions of, 130
Transference love: coping with, 168; discovery of, 34–37; emergence of, 133; fidelity aspect of, 173–74; genuineness of, 151, 167; versus love transference, 42–46; versus normal

Transference love (*continued*)
love, 111–12, 142–43; as opposition, 80; outcomes of, 132; phenomenology of, 168; versus real love, 4,
77; special status of, 46–50
Transference meaning, 98–99
Transference neurosis, 36–37, 66
Transference reactions, 154
Truth in psychoanalysis, 40, 119, 150,
157
Two-person psychology, versus one-
person psychology, 115–19, 124,
126, 127

"Unobjectionable Part of the Transference, The" (Stein), 70-72
Unobjectionable transference: negative,
121; positive, 69–72, 120

Virtual, the, 134

Wallerstein, Robert, 6–7
Weiss, Joseph, 123–25
Winnicott, D. W., 37, 152, 161
Working alliance, 70, 156

Zetzel, E. R., 70; "So-Called Good
Hysteric, The," 67